ALL TO THE GOOD

ALL
TO THE GOOD

W. Lionel Fraser

HEINEMANN

LONDON   MELBOURNE   TORONTO

William Heinemann Ltd

LONDON   MELBOURNE   TORONTO

CAPE TOWN   AUCKLAND

THE HAGUE

First published 1963

Printed in Great Britain
by Bookprint Limited
Kingswood, Surrey

Illustrations

In gratitude to my wife
and
to the memory of my mother

Introduction

THIS BOOK EMBRACES some of the personal experiences of my life, as well as reminiscences and opinions, interwoven with the workings and evolution of a City banking house over the last fifty years or so. None of it is written in too serious a vein. It is in no way technical, nor do I conceive it as my function to describe in detail the various national economic crises which have occurred during my life, nor the remedies applied. I am a long way from being qualified to do this and prefer to leave it to the economists and other experts. Neither will it be a 'social' diary, material for which has, in any case, been almost entirely lacking in my life.

A publisher once told me: 'There is *one* good book in everybody.' This may or may not be right: I doubt it. But I can say that, for myself as I grow older, there is very little I like so much as just writing. Whilst working on this book, I have been able to revive memories of people and to re-live situations, mostly of a pleasurable nature, which would otherwise have gone from my recollection for ever. So, I unashamedly admit that I have enjoyed letting my thoughts roam on paper. Of course that does not mean I do not have some reservations in this first attempt at a book, but I have consoled myself in the realization that Picasso would probably have been deterred from ever painting a picture if he had first stopped to compare himself with Rembrandt. Not that I regard myself as a writer in the rare category of Picasso as a painter, far from it, but my point is that one can make a start and not be inhibited.

I confess also that I have hesitated before revealing some of my inner feelings and other private matters, but I have been brought to realize that without them the story would be incomplete. One of my desires has been to show the remarkable way in which The City of London has during my lifetime emerged from being a stronghold of tradition and conservatism, albeit of immense importance, into a vital and dominant force, more flexible and open-minded, whilst retaining its reputation for integrity and honest dealing. If I am right, what better conditions could there be for young people in which to start a career? Boundless opportunities offer for interesting and rewarding lives.

As I have never kept records, correspondence, nor diaries of my own, I have had to rely in the main on my recollections, but memory plays such strange tricks that it is likely I can be faulted in certain instances. If so, I pray forgiveness.

On a further personal note, writing this book has made me realize more and more how exceptionally fortunate and blessed I have been in so many ways with my human contacts: with my family and those with whom I worked for so many years, partners and staff at 41 Threadneedle Street, and with a host of friends and associates all over the world. I have no axes to grind – only deep gratitude for everything and particularly for a life of constant unfoldment and interest.

None of my business colleagues has had a preview of this book, nor taken any part in its writing. I say this to underline that they have no responsibility whatsoever for the views and opinions expressed. These are entirely my own and I alone stand or fall by them. Some are of necessity pointed; none, I hope, will be regarded as unkind or unfair.

A writer of a book owes thanks to many. Apart from my wife, Cynthia, and my two sons, Nicholas and Robert, who have been intimately associated with me in this effort, and all three of whom have contributed an endless number of most helpful improvements as the manuscript was being written, I am under a debt to my secretaries, Miss Chrysta Corridon and Mrs Jean Mackintosh. They have not only submitted to the drudgery of constant re-typing of my drafts but have made numerous suggestions of value. I would have been lost without their support.

I am also indebted to Writer's & Speaker's Research for some useful investigation, as well as to the Editors of *The Times*, *The Sunday Times* and *The Daily Telegraph* for kindly giving me permission to make reference to certain articles or letters contributed by me in the past.

Chapter 1

AFTER NEARLY FIFTY-TWO YEARS of work in The City of London, I find I have reached the stage when I can do the things I *want* to do, rather than those I *have* to do. That is an achievement, even if fortuitous, but if I think about it more closely, what does it mean? Only that in reality, whilst I seem to have as much to do as ever, there is time to reflect and to ruminate. Hence this book. In it I shall look back over the years, in gratitude for them and for the good fortune which took me into The City of London for my livelihood, but in deeper respect to, and appreciation of, my parents. By their sacrifices for my sister, my brothers and myself they showed us the path to careers and opportunities far removed from their own way of life, and enabled us to follow professions not shared by any of our forbears.

My father was in domestic service, as was my mother until her marriage. My paternal grandfather was a watchmaker and jeweller with his own little business in Kilmarnock, Scotland. The only inheritance I received from my father was a gold lever watch, made by my grandfather's hand, in which he inscribed his name 'William Fraser'. The true Scots would say that my 50% Scottish blood was ample inheritance. Fraser is anyhow a fine Scottish name to bear. Both my paternal grandfather and grandmother died within a few weeks of one another and the family of six young children were distributed to various friends and relatives all over the world, including the U.S.A., whither the youngest was sent as a baby in arms. It was my father's lot to be dispatched to Oxford to an uncle who did not prove to be the happiest patron. Very early in his boyhood my father was sent off to be a pageboy. He was, however, lucky enough to be employed by a family which travelled a good deal. They had an extensive library and during their absences my father was given access to it and so was able to acquire more knowledge and learning than others of his standing.

My mother was one of a Norfolk family of eight. Her parents were of humble stock and at the age of eleven my mother started work as a maid. As time went by, my father and mother met whilst in the same employ and they were married in the ancient parish church of Old Buckenham, in the county of Norfolk in 1893.

Between 1894 and 1902 they had four children, a daughter, myself and two younger sons, in that order. My sister Edith early learnt how to fend for herself, eventually graduating to a responsible position in the banking firm, Helbert, Wagg & Co. Ltd, of which I became Chairman. But for her sex, she would surely have merited even higher status than she actually attained. My brother Douglas, just commissioned to the Territorials, 3rd London Regiment, was killed in action on the Somme in March 1916 immediately after reaching the firing line. He was only nineteen years of age. My father and mother felt his death deeply. It caused them intense grief and my mother never forgave the Germans. Douglas was reported 'missing, believed killed', but we never were able to get confirmed news of him. His arrival in the front line trenches coincided with the big German attack, during which he vanished and we heard no more. The months which followed were agonizing for my mother, waiting and praying, like so many other parents, for any indication that her son was living. My brother was a tall, attractive, handsome fellow, with considerable intelligence, and even at nineteen had made a mark for himself in the City banking house of Lazard Brothers in which he was employed. He gave hope of a brilliant career.

My younger brother, Harold, who was just old enough to serve with the Artists' Rifles for a short time at the end of the 1914 war, started his business life with Higginson & Co. the merchant bankers, and then after serving with the Deutsche Bank in Hamburg, he joined the British Overseas Bank, and later the Anglo-Polish Bank in Warsaw. Years ago he became associated with the Australian Mercantile Land & Finance Co. and is now a Director of this firm, as well as of other companies. I believe it was pure coincidence that my two brothers followed me into the banking world.

My father was a man of strong character and he was a good father and husband. Of necessity he played a lesser part in our lives than my mother. Physically he bore a striking resemblance to Disraeli. His plum job was his last, that of butler to Mr Gordon Selfridge, a post which he held from the time when the Selfridge Emporium was opened in Oxford Street in 1909 until his death in 1923. I think the Selfridges would be the first to admit the debt they owed my father for his help in so many ways in their integration into London society and in the lavish entertaining which they undertook. By his intimate backstairs experience of social life in England, my father knew how to steer clear of some of the gaffes to which so frequently the unwary newcomer can fall victim, and which cause so much merriment and so many sarcastic jibes in English life; perhaps less so nowadays than fifty years ago, although the *nouveaux riches* will always be regarded as fair game. But they must learn somehow, and be prepared to pay for it.

Mr Selfridge brought something revolutionary, something original to London shopkeeping. It was a sense of service, and keenness to please: the shop assistants were trained to welcome their customers. He installed rest rooms, general information offices and gave the store a special background where one could walk and look without being questioned, or approached to make a purchase. Actually to buy anything seemed a secondary consideration, yet one did. This introduction of American ideas into London caught the imagination of the British public and from its inception the store never lacked for success. Mr Selfridge, in top hat and frock coat, was constantly seen in the store, alert and observant, an inspiration to all his staff. I believe he died in a tiny flat in Putney sustained only by a small pension – a tragic end to a brilliant career. My father was very proud of working for such a leading figure as Mr Selfridge and was thoroughly loyal to him. Incidentally his mother and wife were two of the sweetest women I have ever met.

We children were all born in No. 6 Holland Place Chambers, a three-roomed flat off Church Street, Kensington, near my father's work in Palace Green. His pay was £65 per annum. Although this was good by the standard of the day for male servants, the struggle my mother had to bring us up respectably can well be imagined. A heavy burden fell on her and although one or two maiden aunts, also in domestic service, often helped us, my mother's life during those early years was very hard indeed.

She was a tall woman, with beautiful hazel eyes, the softest of soft complexions and a distinguished, dignified bearing. In her childhood there was no compulsory education; her schooling was extremely brief and her actual education slender. However, like so many others, she and my father had managed a degree of self-education, to the immense advantage of us children. I remember how helpful she was to us with our homework, and what excellent letters she always composed. And her handwriting was that of an educated woman. She was equipped with natural wisdom and intelligence, farsightedness and persistence, and nothing could turn aside her ambition for her children. She devoted herself to our interests and slaved to ensure that we should have better opportunities than she and my father had had. I always wonder how my mother kept us well fed and clothed on the insignificant sum of money available to her. The secret was no doubt her ability 'to manage' – nothing was ever wasted. If by chance any food was left over at a meal, it was brought forward next time. Every bit had to be consumed. She threw nothing away. She was economical and precise in all her purchases – she *had* to be. She stood over the butcher or the grocer to make sure she got the right weight and the best value. Yet she was a popular customer because she always paid her bills promptly. She inculcated this into us all – so successfully that I have always had a horror of outstanding accounts and it makes me unhappy ever to owe a penny. (Many a small shopkeeper has gone broke because of the length of debts by customers who can well afford to pay, yet who do not see how improper it is to withhold settlement, which in reality is merely thoughtlessness!) Even towards the end of my mother's life when her financial position was easier, she would take a bus rather than a taxi, unless time pressed unduly. When we remonstrated with her, she used to say 'You can't change me now, so please don't try,' and that was that. 'Look after the pence and the pounds will look after themselves' was a saying the truth of which she firmly believed in and frequently quoted.

She was a natural cook and most adept seamstress, and attended to the needs of the whole family without any outside assistance. She made most of our work-a-day clothes out of bits of material given to her, or by adjusting cast-offs discarded by my father's 'gentry', working far into the night at her noisy old sewing machine. Some of the results were not always exactly to our liking, notably a Norfolk jacket she knocked up for me out of a heavy reddish-brown cape, so much in vogue in those days. I thought it made me altogether too conspicuous, and being cut on the cross, the seams were in odd places. The belt was almost a jigsaw puzzle. When fourteen, with much ceremony and careful choosing, I bought my first suit at Hope Brothers for twenty shillings out of money which I had saved. I can see it now, rather nondescript, so as not to be noticed if it lasted a long while. For a period my mother had proudly dressed me up on Sundays in an Eton jacket suit, a hand-me-down discarded by my father's employers. For myself, I was part ashamed and part self-conscious to be thus bedecked in case the other boys at Sunday School should ridicule me, as they inevitably did.

More than anything else, it was my mother's loving but firm influence which directed the family, with my father always playing a loyal supporting role. Her strict adherence to her own high moral sense might today be considered Victorian and rigid, even puritanical, but she set her children standards which were protection against temptations.

Our flat was very cramped. All three of us boys were squeezed into the same bed. The family washed in turn under the kitchen tap and once a week we had a bath in the kitchen in a tin tub in front of the fire. Fifty or sixty years ago bathrooms were non-existent for the lower classes. We were never allowed to roam the streets, but in our play-time were sent off into Kensington Gardens, which we knew almost tree by tree. Opposite us there was a long passage between high walls, flanked on one side by the Barracks, linking Church Street with Kensington Palace Gardens. We used to race one another along this passage, shouting loudly to produce a resounding echo. What memories the Gardens bring back to me; rolling over and over down the grass bank in the Broad Walk when the keeper's back was turned: the Round Pond on which we never had a boat to sail for lack of funds: collecting the conkers: flying tiny kites which always got stuck in the trees, and later participating in the game of diabolo, which was one of the crazes for a short time in those days. Once a big boy met me when I was alone there, and threatened to dig a hole and bury me if I did not give him a ha'penny. As I hadn't one I took to my heels and arrived home in a breathless panic. My mother came with me the next day to try and find the bully, but we never saw him again. Woe betide him if my mother had caught him!

At the beginning of the twentieth century Kensington was a thoroughly genteel neighbourhood, and duly conscious of being the 'Royal' Borough of Kensington. Not that there has been much change since. The tone was high, the thinking was right-wing and the Vicar of the Parish Church, St Mary Abbots, who had at least seven curates, was one of the centre-pieces of social life. I remember when I was a boy it was Canon Pennefather (accent on the second syllable!) – a distinguished, haughty person, very dignified, with a melodious voice, perfect for the intonation of prayers. He filled his church every Sunday and I was very impressed by the fact that the then Lord Chief Justice of England, Lord Alverstone, sang in the choir – certainly on a voluntary basis and, as I see now, because he enjoyed singing, but I could not fathom it then. Church dress for the nobs was always top hat and tail-coat – it was a veritable fashion parade, which, after Church, was continued into Hyde Park along Rotten Row, where all the grand people would congregate, chat and gossip about one another. Kensington Gardens were always full of beautiful aristocratic babies pushed in superb perambulators by that most snobbish but dependable class of women, the nannies, now rapidly and sadly disappearing. The splendid buxom English nannie was the envy of good and rich families all over the world.

My father and mother were a happily married couple and their example to us in this respect could not have been bettered. Owing to my father's form of employment, they were often separated except for occasional periods when with my mother we were housed where my father worked. It was therefore inevitable that we knew more of our mother than of our father, but this was not due to any lack of interest in us on his part. Unlike my mother, he was not a person with an urge, and was perfectly content to spend his few leisure hours with his family. We rarely went out with my father and there was not that degree of paternal intimacy which characterizes most families, nor the exchange of views or seeking of advice which is usual in normal family life. Yet my father was in many ways a remarkable man. He had integrity, and like so many Scotsmen, contrary to general belief, was generous to a fault.

My Mother

He was near the top of his profession and was, I heard, once offered a job as footman in Buckingham Palace. He was abstemious, and smoked only an occasional pipe. Despite his menial duties, he retained perfect dignity, with a complete lack of obsequiousness. Watching him occasionally with some of his employers, who so often had little taste or feeling, I could not help thinking that he was vastly superior in his bearing to them with their money and position. And this was in no spirit of hero-worship. I remember being amused by the attitude of those for whom my father worked, towards us, his children. Later, when we were growing up, and could begin perhaps to hold our own, I think we may have embarrassed them. They hardly knew how to treat us and tended to be either patronizing or condescending. Nevertheless, generally speaking, we were wont to regard them with awe and interest, keeping ourselves at a distance as much as we could. On the whole, most of my father's employers were well disposed towards us and, as I have said, showed this by generous gifts of old clothes and other things which stood the family in good stead. Occasionally, we would be called in, if we were handy, to help with the washing up. We enjoyed this, as we were invariably compensated by some tit-bit or other and sometimes a sixpence or so if the work lasted for a while. His fellow domestics, footmen, housekeepers and so on were very kind to us.

Those were the days of big establishments; my father had at least four footmen of varying importance and ages and the senior servants ate their meals away from the servants' hall. Sometimes, especially when my father worked for a family named Spitzel and we lived in their house at No. 2 Inverness Terrace, Bayswater, we were permitted to peep in at the dining-room, all laid for a party, and goggled at the display of silver and glass, the candlesticks and the flowers. My father looked so majestic in his butler's uniform of tail-coat and white tie. At Inverness Terrace there was what to us seemed a staggering thing, a private theatre inside the house! It was called 'the bijou theatre' and we were thrilled to witness an occasional performance, all tremendously exciting, though I never recall the appearance of any spectacular actor or actress. Strangely enough, I am not aware of any feelings of resentment or jealousy, which might well have been there when contemplating the distinction between the classes – the haves and the have-nots. In those days the difference was

B

most marked, but my parents were such dutiful God-fearing citizens that none of these thoughts ever occurred to us, or if they ever did, I am sure they were swept out of our heads by a pooh-pooh from my mother. They accepted, and we accepted, the state of life to which it had pleased God to call us – not complacently at all, but finding ourselves in it, there was nothing to be done but to work and improve our lot as we knew best. It never entered our heads to rail against those who employed my father, even if he were usually underpaid and overworked – sweated labour in fact; we just got on with our lives. And I am certain my father voted Conservative, if he voted at all.

On this subject I do recall something which did affect me and which was perhaps typical of the early 1900s. One of our maiden aunts who was older than my mother, but would never admit to it, was a lady's maid in a big house in Roehampton, long since torn down, and now the site of council flats. Her employer was a Mrs Brown, whose husband – a very rich man – made boot polish. Mrs Brown did all the right things and went to all the right places – Cannes, Montreux and so on in their proper seasons. Aunt Emma used to say of her 'My word, she is a tartar', but the remuneration of 10/- a week was attractive and the household was comfortable.

One day Aunt Emma who had been staying with another sister in the country for a brief respite, showed my mother a letter she had received from Mrs Brown asking her to be back on such and such a date. There was nothing special in that, and Aunt Emma took the whole thing for granted. But I was shocked by the method of address. The envelope was addressed 'Barnard' with the street. Just 'Barnard' – not 'Miss Barnard' and the letter itself was even more degrading. At the top it again said 'Barnard' – not even 'Dear Barnard', and was signed 'Mrs Brown'. No 'Yours truly' or 'Yours sincerely' – worse than addressing a dog, I thought. Happily this would hardly be possible these days, unless an employer desired to provoke an immediate resignation!

My father was at the beck and call of his employers morning, noon and night. Domestic service at the beginning of the century may be said to have been one of the last relics of the feudal system. It almost amounted to slavery – being at the end of a bell at all sorts of irregular hours. How conditions have changed! All the same I do not wonder sometimes at the present marked unwillingness to enter domestic service, even though the tables have now been turned.

My father made one valiant attempt to obtain release from the drudgery and confinement of domestic service although finally he became resigned to the bonds which encircled him. His chance came when he heard of a small general shop to be let in a village called Gamlingay, near Cambridge, so we were taken off down there full of hope. He signified his freedom from domestic service by growing a moustache. To our surprise it turned out to be fiery red! Alas! his training ill equipped him for the work, particularly the financial side, and after two years he was forced to give up. It was a bitter blow to my father's pride. Like so many apparent setbacks, it proved however to be a blessing in disguise for the family in the long run, especially for our education. After our life in town, we did not take kindly to village routine or to the village school. We felt shut off from the world. My father gained his freedom from domestic service but we had lost ours, as we saw it. We occupied a small semi-detached cottage with a huge garden which was a constant challenge, and never really a successful producer. We children were too young for the jaunt to make much impact on us. We were in the country for the first time in our lives and I even had a dog, a mongrel fox-terrier called Jack which I loved dearly but which we had to drown before our return to the confines of a flat in London, much to my distress and sorrow. My father was out of work for a long period before he could get back to his former type of employment. That was the blackest, most doleful period of our childhood days, but my father's effort was heroic. Finally, very despondent, he was compelled to take a job in Hampshire and we hardly saw him for a long time.

I used to help a bit by doing a newspaper round and any other errands for which I could earn the odd coin. Out of the proceeds I was given a halfpenny per week for myself and I would dart off each Saturday morning to buy with it four ounces of sweets called 'American Gums', for even in those days I had a sweet tooth. I had discovered they lasted the longest and were the cheapest. Once or twice, with some other boys, I blackened my face and put on a mask on Guy Fawkes' Day, soliciting 'a penny for the guy', but I did not enjoy it much. All the same, it has made me sympathetic towards the lads who pester us in the streets around the beginning of November each year. I even **tried** to join St Mary Abbots Church choir, but my complete lack of musical tone was at once detected by the choirmaster and to my sorrow I was turned down. He asked me to sing a note from his tuning fork. As if I could! That would have meant two shillings a week. At Gamlingay my mother, always wishing to extend our interests, had me given violin lessons, but that was a hopeless failure.

When I was ten I contracted diphtheria which in those days was serious. I remember being transported in an ambulance to Segrave Road Isolation Hospital, off the Fulham Road, where had it not been for the unpleasantness of the illness, I should have enjoyed luxury for the first time in my life. All seemed to be going well when I had a relapse and was put on the danger list. This meant I could have visitors and I can even now picture my mother anxiously coming towards me in special overalls, with a hood, out of which I could just detect her anxious eyes peering at me. Apparently my life was in the balance for some days. When however I eventually recovered, I found I had been put in a men's ward, and until I left was thoroughly spoilt. One of my excitements was wearing a blue hospital suit, with long trousers for the first time. This illness was supposed to leave me with a weak heart, and although it took me but a few months to recover my strength, it was made a reason for me not to play games. Luckily that was no particular hardship to me for I was not a little boy who adored chasing a ball! Indeed, I was extremely unathletic.

As part of my convalescence it was arranged that I should go and stay with my great aunt and uncle – Aunt Jane and Uncle Thomas whom I had never seen. This was a real adventure. She was the sister of my maternal grandmother and had married a publican who owned the Crown Hotel near the station at Haslemere, Surrey. They gave me a warm welcome. Aunt Jane was sedate and proper, but Uncle Thomas had a rollicking, jolly approach to life. He was very stout, with a huge great beard, and not a tooth in his head. 'I wouldn't bother with them false things,' he would say. He did not need them, for his gums were so hard that he could eat the toughest meat and would amaze us by using them to crack nuts. There was a married daughter, Cousin Florrie, known to me as Co Flo. She had an enormous nose – the longest and biggest I ever saw; Mr Punch wasn't in it. I dreaded her kissing me, which she did on every possible occasion, and in spite of my skilful manœuvring, try how I would, that huge, icy nose would press into my face. It was the only cloud in an otherwise joyful period. One of my thrills was being allowed into the bar, and now and again when there was a rush I was permitted to draw a pint of beer for a customer – a skilled job I soon discovered.

Since those days I have had very little experience of public houses. Only a short while ago I was chided by a friend because I do not frequent them and was told that I could never know what the man-in-the-street was really thinking unless I did. That may be true, but I doubt it, and anyhow standing at bars has never amused me. For one thing I am too impatient to waste my time in this way. I am inclined to want to go on to the next thing and I consider lamentable the number of hours which men spend gossiping away to one another. Life is too urgent for me, but perhaps it is that I am unsociable. Trying to recall those days in the Crown Hotel at Haslemere, I do not think much has changed. Men sat there arguing over a pint of beer, benign and cordial, only going home when my Uncle Thomas's ringing voice cried out: 'Time, gentlemen, time, please.' I can hear it now.

Co Flo's husband, an ex-sergeant in the cavalry, straight-backed and rosy, was an inspector in the RSPCA and was responsible for a very big area. As I got stronger, Uncle Bert as he was to me, would take me all over the countryside looking at animals and seeing that all was well with them. In this way, over the months, I got to know the Haslemere, Hindhead, Petersfield district very well – always on foot. It was tiring but fun. Sometimes Uncle Bert got bad cases which he had to report. This made me feel sad, but important. My biggest thrill came when he let me accompany him to the Magistrate's Court at Petersfield to hear a case concerning a lame horse. I thought Uncle Bert was so fair and restrained as he gave his evidence in the witness box.

During my visit to Haslemere I had my first love affair which I believe is not unusual at the age of ten. There was a coalman, Jack, bearded and dirty, who lived next to our pub, and I fell heavily for one of his daughters. I asked her to wait for me until I was old enough to marry her, promising her a ring as soon as I could afford it. She replied on a crumpled scrap of paper that she did not understand and asked for a full explanation. I never wrote again. It taught me caution in later life!

My mother took us down to Old Buckenham in Norfolk to her mother for a brief holiday each year and we would save up for this at school by means of what was known as the Children's Country Holiday Fund. My grandmother – a dear old Norfolk woman, with a wrinkled face brown from working so much in the fields – was always proud to receive her daughter and her London grandchildren, and made much of us. We were thrilled by being taken to St Pancras in a four-wheeler with all our luggage on top, and this was matched only by the excitement of the horse and trap which met us at Attleborough Station and joggled and rattled us blissfully over the all too short journey to Old Buckenham three and a half miles away, to be hugged and kissed by grandmother. For me the only unpleasant aspect was being looked at questioningly by the ticket inspector as we went on to the platform at St Pancras Station, and my sweet mother assuring him that although I was tall, I was still young enough to have the benefit of a 'half ticket'. My grandmother's cottage was near a farm, and we were in demand at harvest time for one thing or another. We were often armed with sticks to kill the rabbits as they darted terrified out of the corn when the cutter went by. They always eluded me but I was as glad about that as they were. It was all deeply absorbing to us town birds, and the mysterious farm pursuits and open air life distracted us from the overcrowding our presence caused in my grandmother's tiny cottage. I can see it now, sitting back in a little lane with a grass border and beautifully thatched roof which seemed to dwarf the cottage with its tiny windows. Inside were many photographs and knick-knacks. There was no washing accommodation of course and the lavatory was in the back garden.

We always accompanied our grandmother on Sundays to Old Buckenham Baptist Chapel. To this day I can remember the words of the hymn so often sung: 'Count your blessings, count them one by one, and it will surprise you what the Lord hath done.' Simple, but profound and true, I thought then, and still think now.

As children we did not lack for occasional treats and pleasures. A favourite aunt used to take us to see a pantomime each year at the King's Theatre, Hammersmith. I remember Dan Leno, the famous comedian, took part on one occasion and we screamed with delight at some of his antics. But there were no such things for us as children's parties, though usually each Christmas we were included in the servants' party in the houses where my father was serving as butler. To my dismay we were always expected to do a recitation, or sing a song. Being utterly incapable of the latter, I would mug up a rhyme of sorts, which I would blurt out to an unusually appreciative audience, pleased to get the ordeal over. I remember that after I had started German I learnt 'Die Lorelei' off by heart and decided to recite it to my father's colleagues and guests at the next Christmas party. I was hurt that this effort, made in dead earnest, fell absolutely flat on my listeners. Not one of them understood a single word, except, I remember, a pert little German-Swiss lady's maid, who pretended to be very impressed. Anyhow thereafter she never failed to address me in German, which of course I was quite unable to understand!

A little later I was to have another country excursion which left its impression on me. We had a maiden aunt, Aunt May, who was a lady's maid in Kensington Palace Gardens. Her employers had a country house, Bramble Hill, in the New Forest, about seven miles from Lyndhurst. Aunt May was being courted by a handsome young carpenter who lived at Emery Down, a picturesque little village a mile or so from Lyndhurst, and as a very special treat I was invited down to stay with the young man's family. His father was a local gardener who had never been further than Southampton, eight miles away, and his mother was a washerwoman. She perspired daily over her washtub, beating the sheets with a cricket stump and doing all the smalls by hand. They were splendid people for whom I had a great affection. They regarded me with some awe, coming from London Town, and I had nothing but admiration for their knowing so much about vegetables and flowers. This was my first introduction to the New Forest, although I had already read Marryat's *Children of the New Forest*. I roamed over it freely and found the unspoilt beauty, the mystery and the vastness of the area had been in no way exaggerated in the book.

On a borrowed bicycle I used, as often as possible, to visit my Aunt May, at her place of work, as she only had one half-day off a week. It was, however, a mixed pleasure for me. The route took me past the gypsy encampment near Rufus Stone at Stony Cross put there to com-memorate the spot where William Rufus was killed by an arrow when hunting on 2 August 1100. The stone has been a tourist attraction of the Forest for very many years. The trip was invariably somewhat frighten-ing to me as a young boy from London, for as I passed, looking straight ahead of me and pedalling madly, the gypsies came running on to the road towards me from all directions, probably with no harm in their thoughts, but to beg for a copper. They seemed very menacing, and always made my heart beat faster until I had shaken them off.

Later when Aunt May had married her carpenter Adonis and settled down in Lyndhurst, where he established his own business, we were destined to spend many wonderful holidays with her, and our new Uncle Jim. Later Uncle Jim took up one of the most lucrative of small businesses. He was always a hard worker, but found increased prosperity as the village undertaker.

Chapter 2

OUR EARLY EDUCATION until the regrettable visit to Gamlingay had been at St Mary Abbots, then a Higher Grade Church School, off High Street, Kensington. If I remember rightly the fees were a penny a week per pupil, until the school was eventually taken over by the London County Council when it was free. After Gamlingay we had made many moves, and we had to go to whatever school would accept us. In consequence my education had been of a rather sketchy nature. It lacked continuity.

At one time we lived in Fulham Road over a fish shop where we were rent free and got fish at half price, a barter agreement which involved my mother's looking after, and cooking for, the fishmonger's daughter who was manageress down below. As this lady got up at dawn each morning to go to the fish market at Billingsgate, she would stay in bed all day on Sunday, during which we had to be exceptionally quiet. My mother was constantly remonstrating with us. Although this whole arrangement was arduous for my mother, we liked it there and were helped and encouraged by the manageress, especially in our studies. We flitted from flat to flat, wherever was the cheapest, for nobody wanted young children and my mother had much trouble in getting us lodgings. In one horrible place near Earl's Court we were burgled and many of our poor belongings were stolen; of course we had no insurance. The week's rent was taken too and my mother looked upon it as an act of Providence when the next day she detected a gold ten-shilling piece shining in the mud in the street.

It was good fortune which took us back to our old block of flats in Holland Place Chambers, still three rooms only, thus enabling us to return to our beloved *Alma Mater*, St Mary Abbots School. It was like going back home. The education was of a higher order than our other schools, with a first-class teaching staff. The Headmaster was a Mr Peck and his principal assistant was Mr Benjamin Jones. The latter became almost a member of the family and visited us often. He was a bachelor, very Welsh, with a delicious sense of humour, and a unique capacity to coach. He was a typical schoolmaster, with pince-nez, thin and neat, and he loved escaping to his native Conway. Our curriculum was the usual: reading, writing and arithmetic basically, with English, history and geography thrown in. Arithmetic, especially mental arithmetic, came easily to me. Grammar was my *bête noire*, and I hated parsing. Curiously enough it was only late in life that I began to understand and apply some of the finer points of English grammar. Ben Jones took me in hand and really taught me how to swot at my work. So much so that I gained quite a number of prizes each year in the school. They were presented at our annual school prize-giving in Kensington Town Hall, either by the Mayor of Kensington or the Vicar of St Mary Abbots Church.

At the age of thirteen, encouraged by our friend Ben Jones, I sat for three different entrance scholarships and being fortunate enough to gain all three, I had a choice. One would have entitled me to free education at the Chelsea Polytechnic, one gave me entry to Latymer Upper School and the third, which I decided upon, was called a Campden Charity Scholarship. This was particularly attractive because it brought the holder £20 a year for four years towards his fees, with freedom to choose his own school. Much to Ben Jones's delight, and ours as well, I believe I managed to top the list for the Campden Scholarship which was open to all schools situated in Kensington, and deep is my gratitude to this dear old gentleman who gave me so much of his spare time in those two valuable and formative years of my life, between the ages of eleven and thirteen.

My mother and I had dreams of a classical education, leading me on possibly to Oxford or Cambridge, but after most carefully weighing up the outlook, we finally had to discard these hopes for financial reasons. In the end I decided to go to Pitman's School in order to equip myself to earn my living as quickly as possible in business. It was not long before I was steeped in the study of commercial subjects, book-keeping, French,

German, Spanish, shorthand and typewriting, and I devoted myself to them ten hours or more a day for three years, at which time it became obvious that the financial strain on the family was near breaking point. So at the age of sixteen I gave up my fourth year of the Campden Scholarship and went out to work. My father had got a rise from Mr Selfridge, earning £100 per annum, but my two young brothers were growing up rapidly and my sister, who had been working in the Bought Ledger Department at Harrods, was earning comparatively little.

My two brothers each gained what was known as an L.C.C. Junior County Scholarship and became day scholars at King's College School in the Strand where they had the usual classical, semi-public-school education. By this time there was less worry about money. I was keeping myself, and indeed contributing something to my mother's thrifty purse.

Pitman's School in Southampton Row near Russell Square was a long way from Church Street, Kensington, and for me an expensive journey. Every farthing had to be counted. After some investigation I found that if I walked across Kensington Gardens to Queen's Road, now Queensway, Bayswater, I could get a bus for a penny fare to Oxford Circus and walk from there. This I did each day; in the winter evenings when the Gardens were closed I had a much longer walk along the streets. Those were the days of horse buses which ran at regular intervals. There was a white bus, with an open roof, and I would get into the front seat level with the driver who sat up there controlling his two horses. It was always the same driver and we soon became fast friends. He was a red-faced, weather-beaten old fellow and I recall the talks we enjoyed together as if they took place yesterday. He seemed so wise and he let me tell him all about my doings at school. He encouraged me. When I was struggling to increase my speed at shorthand he would ask me 'Did yer get up to an 'undred yesterday?' I told him once what a horror Monsieur Pottier, our French master was, and my old driver would constantly comment: ' 'Ow's that old froggie, Potter, or whatever yer call 'im?' It was an incongruous but warmhearted contact, not particularly profound but it provided a basis for sympathy at a time when my life was rather isolated. I never knew his name nor he mine, facts which did not seem to have any relevance or importance. Now and again when

I was a little late my friend would scan the Broad Walk in Kensington Gardens as he came from Notting Hill Gate to see whether I was puffing along with my many school-books tied together in one hand and an attaché case in the other, containing my lunch. He would wait for me and ignore the peremptory pull of the conductor's bell, but when I got up to him and settled down, he invariably scolded me. 'I shall not wait for you again, m'lad,' he would say, but he did! Those morning chats meant a lot to me at that time, and I can see myself now, leaning forward in earnest conversation with my driver whilst he flicked his horses, urged them on or pulled them up. I felt I was on top of the world. I never let him down; if wet I would huddle under the macintosh cover provided. It was a very sad day for me when horse-drawn buses were abolished. I now possess a silver pass which allows me free travel on London omnibuses. This came to me as a director of Thomas Tilling Ltd, formerly an omnibus company, when its London buses were sold to the London Transport Board in 1949. I wish my old driver could know it! I think he would be proud, though no doubt a bit incredulous.

On the whole I cannot say I enjoyed Pitman's School very much, although let it be said emphatically that the training, which was entirely individual, was first-class. But we were never able to feel a part of, or pride in the school. We hardly did more than pass the time of day with our fellow students, for our noses were kept on the grindstone all the while. Looking back, it was a narrow life for a developing lad, and very concentrated. There were no organized games, no drama classes, no talks on politics – nothing – just a factory where we swotted and had the methods and machinery of business crammed into us. My studies, day and night, gave me some proficiency, and at the end of my three years at Pitman's I had numerous certificates, diplomas and medals, which I have never looked at from that day to this. When we move my wife loyally packs them up, although secretly she finds them a nuisance! I recall my anguish at failing to gain a gold medal for shorthand because they told me that in the transcription I had spelt 'fulfil' with two final 'l's.

So I came out of the sausage machine equipped for business, knowing the jargon a bit, with a grounding in modern languages, French and German and pretty advanced book-keeping, a shorthand speed of two hundred words per minute and the equivalent on the typewriter. I had also delved into French and German shorthand. Later, as a result of work in my spare time in the evenings, I became at the age of eighteen a certificated teacher of Pitman's shorthand and actually taught for a spell in L.C.C. Evening Schools for 7/6d. per session. I also did some reporting for a local newspaper in the evenings.

To have a command of shorthand is an asset. Apart from anything else, it teaches spelling and punctuation, and even today I frequently use it for taking notes, especially telephone talks. Taking dictation, however, as I did in my first job, I always found humiliating, and the typewriter I have always regarded as an unappealing instrument, so inflexible and unforgiving. Perhaps that is why I feel special sympathy for secretaries!

Looking back on my three years at Pitman's, I cannot fail to regret the absence of the arts and letters in the curriculum, although obviously at a business training school, they were not to be expected. A well-trained, cultivated mind, steeped in the classics and history has a foundation which enables it to turn itself in so many different directions. I saw this clearly during the Second War when I was serving at the Treasury: dons and historians took to the mysteries and complexities of exchange control, for instance, as if to the work born. I had no alternative to what is called a business education; the die was cast for me because the money for any other course was missing, but I often reflect what path I might have followed had the classics been more accessible to me in my youth. You do not develop quite the same taste for them later in life, or perhaps it is that in the *mêlée* of affairs the aptitude is missing and the time. Happily, conditions are today very different from those obtaining during my youth, for opportunities for good education now abound, and nobody need be deprived of following the path set by their natural talents.

As a boy, I was not animated by any conscious desire to succeed at all costs, though I am sure I wished to have success. This is the subtle difference. There was nothing fervent about it, although I knew I could help my family by any advancement I might make. I had no particular planned ambition as such, but as I grew up I tried not to miss any good opportunity which presented itself. I had a go at it, but never consciously strived to achieve this or that as a bit of long-term self-planning. I had no Dick Whittington dreams as a lad to see myself as Lord Mayor of London. Our home was too humble, and I rather distrusted my capabilities. My mother who might secretly have considered I was capable of some such achievement, would never have let me nurture such grandiose ideas, for fear I might have become too big for my boots. She was firmly against that sort of thing.

As a matter of fact, I don't much care for ambition. The Oxford Dictionary describes it as 'ardent desire for distinction', and it is the 'ardent' which does not appeal to me. I prefer 'progress' to ambition. The same dictionary says of progress 'move forward or onward'. That suits my way of thinking better. It is less conscious. 'Seething with ambition' describes for me someone rather unattractive. This does not mean I have never longed for things to happen. Indeed I have at moments passionately prayed that a certain event would come to pass, such as gaining the Campden Scholarship. I was at a crescendo of anxiety until I knew it had been secured, for it meant everything to me and to the family. But I think it was for the success of the idea rather than for personal success that I urged myself along. And there have been similar situations since, some of little significance, some more important, but I cannot recall that any of them have been thought out, or planned. I am a profound believer in right things happening if one is ready and expectant, having the lamps filled and trimmed. I have no doubt this attitude of mind attracts opportunities and can even make it unnecessary to go out to seek them. I believe firmly that activity begets activity, that ideas are the basis and source of everything, and that all that we do, every action we make or take has first to be in thought. I think I can say that I have mostly worked hard, endeavouring to do my best, hopeful always that the path would broaden. Waiting for an event one feels should happen, is sometimes an exacting experience, but waiting, and in doing so, knowing *why* one is waiting, is not a passive occupation, but in a sense an active one.

Reflecting on my boyhood days, I am most conscious of my mother's perpetual struggle to make both ends meet although, like all children, we took things for granted. Having nothing to compare my upbringing with, I believe I was reasonably happy. We went regularly to Sunday

School at St Mary Abbots Church. I was also confirmed at this church, and to this day I blanch at the awful swear-word which came as a cry from my heart when, during the Confirmation Service, an almost new bowler which my father had somehow procured for me was moved by one of my friends so that I flattened it completely when I sat down!

It is a little difficult, in retrospect, to analyse exactly what my attitude was then to religion. In all honesty I must admit that it made no profound effect upon me. I was orthodox and stereotyped, and probably a pretty 'pi' boy. I did not attempt to plumb the profounder things of life for myself, but was willingly and obediently guided by my dominant though never dominating, mother. She taught us to say our prayers, which we did every night, somewhat unmeaningly I'm afraid – unless we had some personal request to make, or when we thought we needed divine assistance, to pass an examination for instance or to fulfil some troublesome task.

I think my attitude was not untypical of many other young people of those days, and some perhaps of the present time. I believed in heaven and hell, and I went to church because I felt it proper to do so. God had no particular significance for me except as a sort of glorified person up in the sky somewhere, to give me things at times and to help me, to whom I was ready to render thanks and praise in gratitude for benefits received. As I have said, I attended Sunday School, and later took a Bible Class of my own; eventually I became a Churchwarden and served on the local Church Council of St Peter's, Bayswater. Although there was no depth in my approach to religion, the Church of England gave me a standard for which I shall always remain extremely grateful. As one old darling used to say to us, when she came to visit my mother 'Always haim 'igh', mixing her aspirates. Perhaps that was what I was doing, though all unconsciously, or probably I was merely following my leader in an undiscriminating way. Anyhow, I was accepting the teachings of Christianity in an unquestioning fashion as they were taught to me, not reasoning things out for myself. But I recognize I had a sheet-anchor of a valuable kind.

The tragedy of the present-day scene is that so many young people have little or no standard by which to judge. They seem to find the demands and the discipline of Christianity too high. Nevertheless young people certainly do show a definite quality of sincerity, and one of their great virtues is their speed at spotting anything in the least bit phoney or hypocritical. Yet spiritual values and the inestimable asset of their attainment, as well as their uses in life, seem inexplicable to them, and alas, the example of many of their elders leaves plenty to be desired. We were especially blessed because our mother always stood firmly by her beliefs. She lived what she felt was right, and this was surely to our great advantage.

However, as I was growing up I must have had some doubts, some feelings of hesitation, for I remember when I was at Pitman's I was persuaded by one of the masters to attend a prayer meeting once a week in a house in Russell Square when there were talks about God. After one more than usually appealing dissertation, the master whispered to me at the door as I filed out 'Are you saved?' Not liking to disappoint him, I replied 'Yes' and then dashed away feeling a dreadful hypocrite. But an unforgettably seraphic expression came over the master's face.

It was many years later, when I was already married, that these heart-searchings which had not abated, found their relief, when I became a student of Christian Science. Most people associate Christian Science with physical healing, but this is only one aspect of its teaching, though of course important. Its main purpose is to reinstate primitive Christianity as taught by Christ Jesus, and it is based on and interprets the Bible. It reveals that God is truly a God of Love, something I had always wished to understand, but which on analysis I had found quite irreconcilable with so much that I had experienced and saw around me. Christian Science has come to mean more and more to me over the years, because it is not only a form of worship but a way of life, and as a result Christianity is of far fuller significance and profundity. Instead of a spasmodic flicker it has become for me a steady glow. I have seen the possibility of bringing into effect in daily life the First Commandment, the Golden Rule and the ideals of the Sermon on the Mount, which I had always regarded as out of reach, and inapplicable, especially in business dealings. I have found that God has no material appendages and that Christian Science has a strong influence on character, outlook, and in approach to all problems. It has deepened my appreciation of things and people. It has encouraged me to trust in God with understanding,

My Father

not with just a blind optimistic faith; it has made me aware of divine law at work in my life, and indeed at work in the lives of all men: it has convinced me of the efficacy of the power of prayer when rightly applied: it has kept me in perfect health and released me from the medical anxieties which dog us. In short Christian Science has transformed my entire life.

I have pondered long whether I should refer in this book to my religious beliefs, and I have concluded that something which has assumed such supreme importance for me cannot be omitted. I have no wish to proselytize nor to preach, but I *would* like to make the point that Christian Scientists are normal, real people, not in any way odd as so many seem to believe. They can be afflicted by the same problems and difficulties as anybody else but they handle them from a different standpoint. This is not to say, of course, that Christian Scientists always succeed in living up to the high ideals set by their religion, but if they are honest and true, they ceaselessly strive towards them. In these paragraphs it is impossible to do other than make a brief reference to a subject about which I could write very much more, but I must put on record my unbounded gratitude to Mary Baker Eddy, the founder of Christian Science. Mrs Eddy was by any standards a quite remarkable woman, a thinker who has had a more ennobling and spiritually uplifting effect on mankind than any other woman.

The Fraser family was united and compact. There was no National Health Insurance in those days so it was fortunate that we were a robust family and my mother was not called upon to spend much on medical fees. Owing to my preoccupations at Pitman's, then at my City job and later the incidence of the First War, there was a minimum of interchange of views and boyish fun and pranks between my brothers and myself, and I being older than they were, the disparity in our ages naturally seemed to create, not quite a barrier, but some sort of incompatibility which was developed and encouraged by our own independence of outlook and individuality. We tended to go our own ways and although the family spirit was impartially fostered and exemplified by our mother and we still rally to the flag whenever necessary, the inclination not to lean on one another has persisted ever since. My brother Douglas and I, at the age when life was taking shape for him, saw practically nothing of one another, and as I have already recounted, he was cut off very early in his life. I knew nothing of his inner thoughts or hopes. My sister is the real heroine of the four of us. She went out to work as a clerk at the tender age of fourteen and laboured hard and consistently until she retired when fifty-five. She was my mother's constant and devoted companion. There was perfect understanding between them. My younger brother, Harold, is the most intellectual of the family, being a student by nature: he would have made a fine professor. He met his wife, Kitty McKie, when they were both living in Warsaw, and they have three splendid sons. After a long illness, Kitty, who was a most charming and intelligent woman, died in 1960.

I really hardly ever remember feeling young. I imagine I was a hard-working, industrious sort of boy, and maybe my temperament just did not veer towards 'feeling young'. Our outlook ran on rather austere lines, and the way seemed uphill most of the time. I was an avid reader of Scott, Milton, Shakespeare, Henty, Oliver Wendell Holmes, Conan Doyle, George Eliot and of course Dickens, and I remember sobbing over Little Nell in *The Old Curiosity Shop*. We used to get our books from the Kensington Public Library. But I have to confess there was at a certain period another, and quite formidable, influence in my 'literary' life – boys' weekly magazines. There was one called *The Union Jack*, which each week recounted the hair-raising adventures of Sexton Blake. There were also two other penny weeklies, one named *Gem* and the other *Magnet*. These last named had quite an effect on me, for they dealt with the lives of public schoolboys. They brought brightness into my rather humdrum existence giving me an insight into the hitherto unknown life of upper-class children.

Fortunately, my father also enjoyed them and bought them every week. I could hardly overcome my impatience until he had finished reading them and passed them on to me. They employed descriptions which until I got used to them, were altogether confusing. For instance, there were the School House and the New House, the Dorm, and classes that were called forms – they only had 'standards' at my schools – and one form had the curious name of 'Remove'. There were the different groups in friendly rivalry; the juniors wore Eton suits and one boy – a constant butt – even sported a monocle. They discussed their games, their crushes and their feasts, their experiences in what they called tuck-shops, their bloaters for tea, their study feuds and their dormitory spreads. This was a new world, a world of colour and adventure, and I revelled in it.

Harry Wharton and Tom Merry, the respective heroes of the *Magnet* and the *Gem*, became my idols and I longed to be like them. They behaved themselves so admirably, they were so clean-limbed, they set a high tone, yet were strong and brave, never bumptious or priggish, and they commanded my respect and admiration. I cannot remember when the magic disappeared, but the memory of that new world of the *Magnet* and the *Gem* will never pass. I am indebted to a wonderfully graphic broadcast by Mr Jack Overhill on the B.B.C. some months ago on 'Magnets and Gems' for bringing these magazines back to my mind, and recalling for me some of the names.

Before I gained my scholarship to Pitman's I was always working at something, either doing odd jobs or trying to pass some examination or other. My mother discussed family problems with me as the eldest son from an early age and this probably endowed me with a disproportionate sense of responsibility. Between the age of thirteen and sixteen I was particularly hard pressed, staying on at Pitman's three or four nights a week until the end of the evening session at 9 p.m. In consequence my home life was limited. During that period a kind friend of my father's gave me an old bicycle, on which I would trundle off and get as far as Richmond Park, which in those days was completely unspoilt and, as I thought, of unbelievable beauty. Those visits were very precious, probably because there was space and I was alone. Whilst still at St Mary Abbots there was an occasional game of cricket or football on the school ground near Wormwood Scrubs Prison on Saturday mornings – a long trek. I never showed any proficiency at cricket either with bat or ball. Even now I can feel the anxiety which gripped me when a ball was hit my way, in case I should drop the catch, or misfield, and then be slated by my companions. I am afraid that facing ferocious bowling never gave me much of a thrill. As for football, the ball seemed so much faster than I was. I never could catch it up, and when I did, my feet always appeared to be too big and uncontrollable for the contact to be effective. No doubt I missed a great deal in character-building by my hopelessness at games – anyhow the lack of opportunity to play them (though even those who have had this facility do not always acquire the poise which loses and wins with the same equilibrium). The joy which some derive from knocking the head off an opponent, just for the satisfaction of doing so, has never given me any pleasure. Maybe my outlook is gentler, or softer. One of my friends took up croquet when nearing the age of eighty and ploughed his way to the top. He was an experienced games player, right from early youth, captain of tennis, and goodness knows what. He told me his success at croquet was due to never giving up, showing determination, and letting the other contestants feel it. I suppose that is one way, but mine is more intuitive.

Although I took little active part in games, I followed County Cricket and League Football like a lynx. My own particular favourites were Surrey in cricket and Fulham in football. Tom Hayward and J. B. Hobbs were my heroes. I knew the status, and the batting and bowling averages of all leading players and was the proud possessor of a complete collection of cigarette cards with their photographs and accomplishments. When we lived in the Fulham Road I used to go along on Saturdays in the football season as often as I could to Craven Cottage, the Fulham football ground, to see the last ten minutes of the games, when the gates were thrown open and admittance was free. Once I took my brother Harold with me, and to my utter horror lost him in the crowd. I suppose he was about six. I passed through what seemed a lifetime of misery and anxiety during the next few minutes until I spotted him, serene and unconcerned. On my return home my mother was really angry with me: 'Gross carelessness,' she said.

In spite of my responsibilities I was a ridiculously sensitive lad. Certainly I was highly self-conscious – mainly due to the fact that I was over average height. It is said to be good to be tall. I agree, but not that tall. Six foot one or two should be the maximum! I exceed that by a couple of inches. The disadvantages are many. One is conspicuous and can never be incognito. I quickly found the drawbacks – Tudor cottages, sleepers in trains, scrambling into tiny cars, short beds in hotels, seats in theatre stalls and many other situations which a tall man must contend with. He inspires very little sympathy, and in a bus queue he is always embarrassed when he gets to the head to hear the cryptic comments of those behind. When doing my recruit drills before the 1914 war, and afterwards, I was the butt of the sergeant-major who would always be shouting 'That tall man, there, hold your belly in'; or 'that tall man, there, back a bit', etc. People ask 'What about the advantages of being tall, seeing over people's heads in a crowd and such like?' I am not very conscious that there *are* many advantages. Self-pity maybe: I wonder how I have survived! And I married a diminutive wife!

Another cause of worry in boyhood was that at the age of fourteen my hair started to go grey and over the next few years this caused frequent comment. Up to the age of forty it is said to be an advantage to be prematurely grey as it gives the semblance of more maturity. On the whole though, I feel that appearances are not all that important, and it is what shines out of a man that matters, whether he be fat, thin, bald or handsome. For a woman, I am banal enough to think that appearance matters enormously and that an attractive hat or hair-do can go a long way to compensate for other deficiencies. A wise woman always lets her husband help her buy hats.

My mother had a useful supporter in Mrs Willis the caretaker of our block of flats, a stout, comfortable, lovable and loving widow. Her youngest son, Garnett, became 'my mate' and we were constantly together. He also attended St Mary Abbots School. He had a superb treble voice and sang solos in St Mary Abbots Church, which was one up on me. We used to sing carols together at Christmas, but even with his appealing voice, we got little reward. However, we were a fitting partnership. I doubled up for him on the low notes and then detached myself to knock at the doors and collect the coppers. Late in life, after a great struggle in this country Garnett emigrated to Canada where he is the storekeeper for an English concern. He was the only true friend of my boyhood days and we still correspond regularly. Whether it was the constant moving from place to place, or whether it was the difficulty of entertaining other children in the restricted homes we occupied, I formed few schoolboy friendships. And at Pitman's there was no opportunity, more's the pity.

Pitman's shut for a brief summer holiday, two weeks I think it was, and during one of these sessions it was arranged that I should accompany an ex-St Mary Abbots boy, Philip Moffat, for a week's holiday alone at Brighton. I suppose I was about fourteen or fifteen. It was the first time either of us had been let off the family leash and it was something to get excited about, as can be imagined. We shared a room in a boarding house about a mile from the front and paid twenty shillings apiece per week for full board. I remember thinking the food was inferior to my mother's. I don't know what I expected. Neither of us could swim, so we sat on the pebbly beach all day. Moffat was older than I. He had been a senior monitor and was a studious, serious boy whom I held in respect. I remember he had a powerful beak of a nose which gave him a stern look. Imagine my surprise therefore when on the second or third day on the beach he scribbled a little note on a scrap of our daily newspaper suggesting we might go and sit with two young girls who were near by! Before I could say anything, he had screwed up the piece of paper and thrown it to the girls. Giggling happily, they opened it up and at once showed their acquiescence by nodding towards us. Whereupon Moffat conducted me over to the girls and gawkily and awkwardly we joined forces. A simple, harmless little incident, but it ruined the holiday for me, for Philip insisted on meeting the girls each day afterwards. I was not accustomed to female companionship outside the family and at that time thought girls were silly. I am still not sure whether it was because Philip attached himself to the pretty one, leaving me to squire the ugly duckling!

I have often thought of this question of school friendships, and have contemplated the blessing, and indeed the help, it is to be able to avail oneself of such an easy ready-made approach. I have frequently heard it said about some eminent person, 'Oh! George, yes, he was at school with me. He's all right. I am sure he will help.' Furthermore there is no doubt the intimacy of a friendship formed at school is very special and solid. It was one of the reasons which prompted me to work to send my two sons to Eton.

My mother had a deep faith in God and brought us up on this basis. I lived at home until my marriage at the age of thirty-five, and although my life was expanding all the while, and perhaps seeming to leave her behind, my mother never ceased to take a detailed and keen interest in all I was doing. Indeed, she was my guide in most things, and we all valued her insight and relied on her ability to help us to solve our little problems. Her wisdom was infinite, her interest unrestricting, so unjealous and so determined and objective in her desires for us. We were indeed blessed to have such a mother – she held us up when we were falling – she encouraged us when the outlook appeared bleak and she never failed to deflate us if she spotted any sign of cockiness. I think of her incessantly and am grateful to her for the high yet humanly attainable aims she set us. My sister tended her lovingly until she passed away after much suffering in 1949 at the age of seventy-nine. I particularly remember the last night spent at her bedside when together and alone she and I reviewed the situation of the family and she, mentally alert and firm as ever, but in severe pain, revealed her final and ultimate hopes for our happiness. I have failed her often but I remain everlastingly indebted to her.

Chapter 3

ONCE THE DECISION WAS TAKEN to leave Pitman's School before the end of my scholarship period, I lost no time in looking for a job. I had a tremendous sense of lightheartedness. Concentrated studying, swotting, learning – all that was at an end, I thought. I was going to be independent, to earn my own living, even to make an offering to the family funds. I would be able to give a small present here and there, out of my very own money. I might be able to go on holiday where I liked. I would be a free man. I would read my newspaper in the train. I was going out into the world.

I was naturally anxious to use what I had learnt at Pitman's, especially my foreign languages, accountancy and shorthand. But where? I was impatient. Usually Pitman's had enquiries in their Employment Bureau, but it seemed I was too immature at sixteen for the sort of job I was seeking. Anyhow they had nothing suitable on their books at the moment. Had I set my sights too high? Then I spotted an advertisement in the Personal Column of *The Times* which I had been advised to scan daily, so far without reward. It ran: 'Foreign correspondent in a small banking firm, French, German, shorthand and typewriting essential, if possible some knowledge of bookkeeping'. I could hardly believe my eyes, but the snag came as I read on – 'Age preferably nineteen to twenty-four. Apply in writing to Manager, Bonn & Co., 62½ Old Broad Street, E.C.' My heart sank, but I decided I would have a shot. My grey hairs were already fairly noticeable, I thought. And who knows?

So, with my mother's help, I composed and sent a letter setting out my qualifications and hoping to be favoured with an interview despite my youth. Never has a reply to any letter been more keenly awaited. However, I was not kept long in suspense, for the next morning a telegram arrived asking me to go for an interview the following day, Friday, 12 June 1911. I hardly slept that night, rehearsing what I should say and wondering how I could make myself look more grown up. Off I sallied, in my one best suit, clean shirt and collar, all carefully supervised by my anxious mother. This was the most momentous day of my life. The job seemed handmade for me. It was so essential that I should bring much needed money to the family coffers. Were there other candidates, more suitable, more experienced than I? My mind was in a turmoil due partially to anxiety lest I should not be good enough, and part wonderment if I succeeded in being accepted, as to what life in a City office would prove to be. All very natural in retrospect, but devastatingly worrying at the time.

We were then living at No. 6 Victoria Gardens, Notting Hill Gate, where incidentally, for the first time in my life I enjoyed the luxury of a room to myself. At least it was hardly a room, just a box, having once been a bathroom, but I was alone. Our home was a few hundred yards from Notting Hill Gate tube station, so I slid in there, emerging at the Bank Station only a short distance from 62½ Old Broad Street.

As my steps took me nearer and nearer, along Threadneedle Street by the Bank of England which seemed formidable and threatening to me that day, past the Stock Exchange, into Old Broad Street, alongside so many other scurrying people, my apprehension grew. My telegram had been signed 'Jacobs, Manager': so, at No. 62½ I mounted to the first floor, where passing through a swing door, I saw BONN & CO. in big letters on a brass plate on a door to my left. I went in and observing a bibulous looking man (not in uniform but in plain clothes, I was disappointed to note) sitting in a corner across an open space, I crossed over to him and nervously asked if I could see Mr Jacobs. I was elated at his reply, 'Yes, young feller, we're expecting you.' I thought that was very hopeful, as I was shown into a tiny ante-room and told to wait. Minutes passed, then to my surprise a tall, rather unattractive woman entered and said, 'Come with me. I have to put you through your tests.' It later transpired that I was to succeed her. She took me off to the tiniest cubbyhole, which she shared with the telephone operator, and standing over me, for there was no room to sit, she dictated to me some pro forma letters at high speed which I then had to type out. This satisfactorily

[31]

accomplished, she addressed me alternately in French and German, which I found vastly more difficult, having had so little practical experience of speaking. So I stutteringly replied in English. I thought this was my downfall, but no! The lady said, 'That'll do. Now you must see Mr Jacobs,' so I went back into the little waiting room slightly more confident.

If only Mr Jacobs liked me! He came in, smiling. I towered over him, and wondered whether he minded. I hoped not. He hardly asked me any questions, which I afterwards discovered to be in character with his own somewhat timid approach, but said he needed two references. Forewarned by my mother, I had secured these in writing, one from Pitman's on my record there, and one from the local parson testifying to my respectability. These I produced quickly from my pocket and Mr Jacobs read them approvingly, telling me I must now be seen by the senior partner, Mr Max Bonn. Subject to his agreement, I would be engaged to start on the following Monday. In view of my lack of experience and years, they could not pay me more than £70 per annum. Would that suit me? As it was more than I had ever dreamt of, I quickly acquiesced and was shown into the Partners' Room to be inspected by Mr Bonn himself. I was informed that the other partner Mr Walter Bonn, a cousin, was away that day. When eventually we met, I was to observe two men in striking contrast: Max Bonn was a Jew to his fingertips, of German origin, naturalized British, guttural, sensitive, warm, brilliantly intelligent, a trained international banker; Walter Bonn was, on the other hand, Eton and Cambridge, haughty, diffident, a country gentleman more interested in hunting and farming than banking, and who later had a most distinguished career in the 1914 War with the Welsh Guards. His old father, Mr Leo Bonn, whose English was execrable, and who had provided most of the capital to set up his somewhat reluctant son in The City, haunted the office from time to time.

Mr Max Bonn fits into my story later on. On this first occasion I found him terrifying. His dark eyes restlessly looked me up and down and the questions he put to me, though kindly expressed, tied me up in knots, so complicated and tortuous were they. However, I apparently passed muster, and with a warm smile which transformed his monkey-like little face, he said, 'All right, young man, see you next week'. Out I went, hoping against hope that I should never have to do work for Mr Bonn himself. Little did I know.

Feeling as if I had been crowned King of England, I stepped gaily back to the Bank Tube, so unlike my anxious exit an hour or two earlier. The train was exasperatingly slow and jerky – I could not get home quickly enough to tell my mother the joyful news. She was just as excited as I. The salary seemed huge to us, seventy whole pounds per annum. Later I asked if I might be paid weekly, as this was more convenient at home, so they settled on 27/- per week.

Thus I was launched into the banking world, and by sheer fluke. I might have gone into any profession, stockbroking, publishing, journalism, anything – if by chance my eye had hit on another advertisement where my qualifications seemed suitable. And if it had been some other occupation than banking, I am certain I should have accepted the offer with as much alacrity, and as much joy.

It was on 15 June 1911, my sixteenth birthday, therefore, that I entered The City at 62½ Old Broad Street, London, E.C. I was amused by and slightly ashamed of the '½', for it was a fair-sized, modern building, and I never discovered 62 or 63.

Many people who have reached higher status than I have started their careers as office boys, running messages and sticking on stamps. I did not have to do either, for with my training at Pitman's I had gained enough knowledge to get my feet just above the lower rungs of the ladder. It is absurd to regret this, yet in some ways I do, if only for the reason that during all these years, I have never really known my way about The City, or become intimately acquainted with the precincts, ancient alley ways and buildings, landmarks and other objects of historic interest which are to be found in such abundance in The City. Shame on me! I have only been to the Tower of London once, and that when I was about ten years of age; I have never climbed the Monument, and until I became a director of the Royal Exchange Assurance I had only been into the Royal Exchange once in my life, and that for an evening concert. There is no excuse, except that I never was an office boy. Time has flown fast, and my life has been strenuous giving me little time for sightseeing in The City. Much the same applies, if for other reasons, to most people who work in The City. They just 'work' there and rigidly abide by their working hours. But perhaps I should admit that in such matters – old monuments, cathedrals – I veer towards idleness.

As can be expected, I was still in a state of suppressed excitement when I left home on my first morning for the office. I had bought a season ticket, but on my mother's cautious advice, only for a month. 'Just in case,' she warned. This proved sound, nonetheless, for I discovered that a ticket from Queen's Road to Tottenham Court Road was half the price of one from Notting Hill Gate to the Bank, so I settled on this, and walked at either end. When I had been at the office for my interview three days earlier I had been too flustered to take anything in. I had been told to report to Mr Jacobs at 9.20 a.m. but when I arrived, he was not there, nor was the overbearing lady who had tested me. So there was nothing to do but wait whilst the others came in, eyeing me with curiosity as I sat on a tight little chair in the corridor. It was like going to a new school, that awful first day's initiation.

At last Jacobs arrived panting and apologetic, and greeted me warmly. I was to sit in his fairly sizeable room, which he shared with an international team, Rudolf Hohenemser, a German, and Robert Bonzon, a Frenchman. Jacobs took me round the office to introduce me to the other members of the staff. I was to become one of a very small unit. Only the counter seemed large and, by comparison, out of proportion. Those in the general office, perhaps ten altogether, sat on high stools and shook hands rather stiffly. I noted that the majority wore tail-coats and when they went out, they donned their silk top hats. I wondered when I would graduate to such a dizzy distinction.

It was all very free and easy. One of the clerks was doing handstands in the corner of the office. He afterwards left to teach physical training, and later became a quack psychiatrist. The warmest welcome came from Alfred Clermont, Manager of the Securities Department, which numbered two people besides himself. He bothered to seek me out later in the day and made me promise to come to him if I felt strange or at sea. 'I know how awkward and difficult the first few days are.' He and I were destined to become very closely acquainted as years passed, but I never forgot this endearing sign of thoughtfulness at a moment in my life when it was particularly consoling.

[34]

But your first day is relatively unimportant, for you are hardly conscious of surroundings; they still remain to be discovered, to become known and appraised. The real thrill comes later in the awakening to the possibilities that surround you and in understanding and overcoming problems.

I was delegated to do all the correspondence for Jacobs, Hohenemser and Bonzon, and a splendid training it was to prove. Each in his different way was very knowledgeable, and luckily I did not appear to irk any of them, and they were at pains to show me the ropes. Thus I soon got a glimpse – in a potted sort of way – of varying aspects of international banking. We had relations with all the leading overseas centres, by the very nature of the business, and names such as Heidelbach, Ickelheimer & Co., White, Weld & Co., and Kuhn Loeb & Co. of New York, Crédit Lyonnais, Société Générale and Arthur Spitzer of Paris, Lippman Rosenthal & Co. of Amsterdam, and Lazard Speyer Ellissen, Frankfurt-am-Main, rolled off my tongue as if they had been my special friends all my life.

Jimmy Jacobs, as he was known to his friends (although I never became intimate enough with him to be on Christian name terms), nominally ruled over the office, but his rein was very light, as he was constitutionally unsuited to take a lead. He had a kind nature, and the most beautiful handwriting I have ever seen, a rather characterless copperplate. His wife, a militant suffragette, whom he had married late-ish in life, was a handsome but determined woman. She ruled him, completely and absolutely, so much so that Jimmy always bore a hunted look, and having made a decision, wondered at once if it were correct, almost as if he needed his wife to help him. But nobody could have been more helpful to me or a better teacher, and I benefited vastly.

Bonzon, whose father was a distinguished banker in Paris, was striving to develop new business, both in the banking and investment spheres, in Paris and provincial France, relying on his father's reputation to open hitherto closed doors. It was an uphill task and never came to much. It meant, however, endless correspondence in French with minute banking firms or agencies all over France, which was good for my French and geography of the country, but highly unremunerative for Bonn & Co. Bonson never desisted, and if in the morning as he searched his mail there was an order to buy 10 Rio Tinto, usually at a prohibitive price, he would turn gleefully to Jacobs and never fail to exclaim: 'Leetle fishes are sweet.' Bonzon was a very testy man and terrified poor little Jacobs, who would even look to me for support in an argument. When on one occasion Jacob's business instincts forced him to doubt the value of some of Bonzon's journeys all over France, Bonzon fell on Jacobs, who cowered pathetically in the face of the Frenchman's furious volubility.

Hohenemser, the third member of the trio, was a solid lump of a German, with short curly hair, a great snout for a nose, rimless pince-nez, and immaculate Savile Row suit. His shoes, encasing tiny feet out of proportion to his body, were made for him at Lobb, he would proudly tell everybody. He used scent, and lots of it. This shocked me, but I was to grow accustomed to it. He watched our German interests and all overseas situations, except France.

I was thus especially favoured in my first essay into The City, sitting with three men of different nationalities and with such widely diversified points of view and approaches to problems. Later I was admitted into their discussions as I became able to understand the basic issues and could follow the various transactions through from their inauguration. The business of the firm was very good, if small, and its contacts were of the highest class. Its functions were in the usual banking fields – current accounts, borrowing and lending money in the Discount market, Stock Exchange transactions for the firm and for clients, financing industrial projects, mostly overseas, and investments. It was a typical small banking business, sound and with excellent prospects of development.

At the end of the year my pay was raised to £100 per annum, and I discovered a delightful habit amongst banking firms, of giving bonuses at Christmas according to the profits of the firm and the standard of the work done by each employee during the year. Apparently Bonn & Co. had had a smashing year, for I was awarded no less a sum than £20, in addition to my increase. This was announced at lunch time, so enabling me to rush out to Threadneedle Street Post Office and send my mother a telegram to give her my wonderful tidings, only to be rebuked when I got home for my extravagance in spending sixpence on a telegram. But I felt a salary of £100 per annum was real money, and I was over-joyed.

Occasionally, very occasionally, Mr Bonn would dictate to me, in perfect English, long letters on involved banking matters. I was more and more astounded at his complete command of the language, although at first the meaning of most of the complicated and involved operations he described passed over my head. I soon realized this was 'the goods', and that I was being offered a priceless opportunity of learning the business of banking from one who really knew. So, despite the anxious beating of my heart when summoned 'to the presence', I tried to follow Mr Bonn's highly ingenious ideas intelligently, and was glad when I found he was calling on me more and more.

All the same, my contempt for sitting down and taking dictation developed; I wanted to *do* something, to create, not to be subject to other people's thinking, helpful as that might be. It was to be a stepping stone, I felt, not a life's job, so despite the valuable experience I was gaining, I started to agitate to go into the outer office, to be a bookkeeper.

As a matter of fact, I was settling down very comfortably as a nobody in The City. I was just beginning to find my feet and to realize what some of it was about. It was never humdrum or routine, an aspect of City life I have always since been fortunate in avoiding. In fact, I never remember my life being dull or time dragging. There has always been something new to think of, to anticipate, some problem to solve, something to work for, somebody who wanted advice. And so it has remained until this very day – exciting, worthwhile, challenging, at times disillusioning and disappointing, but always varied and interesting.

In those early City days we were expected to work hard. Hours were longer than today, 9.15 to 6, and 9.15 to 1 every Saturday. Luncheon vouchers were unthought of, so I generally took with me a lunch of sandwiches or sausage rolls prepared at home, which I ate in Finsbury Circus whenever weather permitted. I thus got to understand the ways of pigeons, for they were anxious to share in my meals.

After the 1914 war, when I was better off, I used to lunch regularly but frugally at the Red House in Bishopsgate and some of us had our own table there each day, ruled over by Emmie, as attentive a waitress as ever existed. She was very tall and thin as a stick and sweet to us. She told us all her troubles in full detail and we heard how the 'old man' was bed-ridden. But she knew our every wish, and we were all 'dears' to her. I remember we used to leave 2d. or 3d. under the plate as a tip and had a good whip round at Christmas. Later Emmie had to give up work, as the 'old man' got worse. 'I can't leave 'im, yer know, but it'll break me 'eart to give up me gentlemen.' So we deserted the Red House for 'the Throg', Lyons's in Throgmorton Street, which occupied a distinctly higher place in the lunch-time hierarchy. Even the Government broker ate there. Nowadays most houses have their own luncheon rooms for partners and the bigger ones provide canteens for their staffs. But the office boys and girls still feed the pigeons in Finsbury Circus.

Banking houses have always been sensible and generous about holidays, and even as a junior I used to get three weeks. Staff relationships have changed considerably since I first started to work. Management now takes more interest in its employees and offices have an atmosphere of greater informality; the 'boss' for example is no longer the remote and unapproachable figure he was. These are changes for the better which are an encouragement for individual talent to blossom, so that those with ability can reach the top. Working accommodation, with ample heating and light and a greater sense of spaciousness, are amenities only a few enjoyed in the past. Despite all the new blocks constructed in recent years, there remain too many offices where working conditions are unpleasant.

I still led rather an isolated life, inasmuch as I formed no particular friendships. I used to get the international news from Bonzon and Hohenemser. They took *L'Information* and the *Frankfurter Zeitung* daily and I invariably peeped at them. Those two newspapers, especially the latter, gave a unique coverage of world events. Our talk together was usually about the international scene but at that stage I cannot remember having any particular views on the political outlook. I was very impressionable and receptive. Political and economic movements are felt in City circles much quicker than anywhere else as fingers must always be kept on the pulse there for the ensuing reactions.

Soon the gathering clouds of the 1914 war began to cast their shadows in Europe and business fell away. Hohenemser was restive to get back to his homeland and the feeling between him and Bonzon was becoming tense. Eventually Jacobs and I were left alone. I was given a high stool in the outer office as a bookkeeper. I did not yet qualify for a top hat and

C.E.F. as Air Raid Warden 1939

tail-coat even though the others wore them. My immediate boss was a German Swiss, Fritz Gamper, a splendid man who later became Manager of Helbert Wagg. I soon realized that the bookkeeping I had learnt out of a book at Pitman's, whilst helpful, was totally different from the practical work I was set to do at my new desk. Gamper took little time to spot my defects. I don't know why it was but I never could balance my books first go. They were never much out, usually in fact a mere penny, but that was far more difficult to 'find' than £100,000, and Gamper and I spent agonized hours at night, at balancing time, searching for that infuriating penny. He got very cross with me and I was tempted to produce it from my own pocket, though I knew that would not solve the problem.

Next to me sat Willie Harman, a younger brother of the Martin Harman of Lundy Island. Willie was a fine fellow, tall and intelligent. We had a lot of fun and often fed the pigeons together in Finsbury Circus, having surreptitiously taken our lunches from under the flap of our desks. My mother always wrapped mine up in a towel, 'to keep it moist'. One day Harman introduced me to his elder brother Martin and I discovered what highpowered salesmanship was for the first time. Martin Harman was an agent for an insurance company, as a side-line, and before I knew where I was, I had agreed to insure my life on an endowment policy for £500. That was my first attempt at saving money, but thinking I saw the sense of endowment insurance, my appetite was whetted, and it became almost a habit with me, partially I think because I got a kick from being declared a first-class life. Sadly, my Harman was killed in the 1914 war.

Being in the outer office, and not shut up in the somewhat more formal atmosphere of the Manager's office, I became more closely associated with the members of the staff, although Max Bonn used to drag me back now and again to do special letters for him. But business was very slack, and these letters became fewer. I was of course also working at odds and ends of other things in the evenings, teaching shorthand and doing a bit of reporting, and Clermont had drawn me into the Boy Scout movement.

This was already flourishing in those pre-1914 days under the leadership of its founder, Lord Baden-Powell. In Paddington, where Clermont

D

lived, there were many troops. Ours, the 28th West London (the Earl of Chesterfield's Own) was the biggest in the area and I was one of the Assistant Scoutmasters: we were at one time one hundred and twenty strong. It had been founded by Alfred Clermont, who was an excellent citizen and gave his life to work amongst boys, particularly the Boy Scouts. My brothers and I took an active part because we realized the immense benefit it was for lads at such an impressionable age to be kept off the streets by the attraction of other interests. Hardly an evening passed without some sort of engagement and Saturdays were fully occupied with parades on Hampstead Heath and further afield. Our Headquarters, in an old school off Westbourne Park Road, was a hive of activity, with classes, and instruction in various useful occupations.

It was a testing task by any standard to keep so many lads busy and interested. There were annual camps, mostly at Walton-on-Thames, troop church parades and district parades too; annual sports, football, cricket, boxing, concerts and plays all helped toward character building. Clermont supervised everything and he persuaded many young men of quality to help him in his work. He was an important influence for good in the district, and many a man who passed through his hands must even now look back on those days with gratitude. They are distributed over numerous parts of the world and I know of several who have won their way up the hill. I have always been a strong supporter of the Boy Scout movement and all it stands for. Its motto 'Be prepared' has great significance, and when boys' imaginations can be fired to understand the high motives of the movement, so practical and appealing to the young, its value to the youth of the nation cannot be over-estimated. One of the requirements of a Scoutmaster is that he should exert a good influence over his scouts. Before the 1914 war there seemed no reason to think that my influence was other than reasonably favourable but in the disturbed times of the post-war period when I was fully occupied and had to travel a great deal, I retired from the movement. I imagine such misgivings must assail everybody who takes part in 'good works'. It is the challenge to one's highest qualities, as well as a discipline. Perhaps in retrospect I was splitting hairs, but if one is to lead, one must set the example.

Chapter 4

In JANUARY 1914 I had joined the Territorials, the London Scottish. Admission to this regiment was the only direct benefit I ever derived, as far as I know, from my father's ancestry, because in those days one parent had to be Scottish. I shall never forget the glory of my first and only annual inspection parade in Hyde Park in July 1914: full parade dress, plaid, white spats, pipe band and a perfect English summer day. How thrilled I was! There was, however, one awful moment. Our Commanding Officer gave the Battalion the order to slope arms, when we were already at the slope! Not a man flinched and the Colonel corrected himself immediately, when he said: 'I beg your pardon, Gentlemen, Order arms!' When we were back in the privacy of our own Drill Hall, he thanked us fervently.

I have always been rather a fire-eater by nature but I cannot truthfully say that patriotic reasons animated me when I joined the Territorials. The London Scottish enjoyed, and has always enjoyed, the highest reputation as a Territorial regiment, and I was more than proud to be accepted by the Regiment. I regarded joining up with them rather like becoming a member of a good club. It was in no sense anticipating the war, although when it came, I was glad to be those months of training ahead of others.

I worked hard to complete my recruit drills and do the necessary Bisley shooting to qualify me for the summer camp which was to be held on Salisbury Plain during the first two weeks of August 1914. I was no great shakes at shooting or drilling but I scrambled through. We actually arrived at the camp site, but before we could pitch our tents, the order came to return to London as mobilization was imminent. I shall not easily forget that trek during the night over the plain to Ludgershall

Station or the sleeplessness of the return journey in the train to Waterloo, the forebodings and the doubts. The next day I was mobilized, and thereupon became Private Fraser, No. 2049 C Company London Scottish, destined to wear the hodden grey kilt for a long time, longer than we thought, for all of us believed the war would be over by Christmas.

There was a grim reminder of it wherever one went. Kitchener's Army men were soon drilling in make-shift uniforms, and regulars and territorials were all over the place, with guns, limbers and wagons. Conditions then were so different from the Second World War. The preparations were obviously more amateurish, but there was a tremendous sense of urgency as our Regular Army was in action almost from the opening. Bloody battles were already taking place in France, and the wounded began to arrive back in this country.

As for us, after a miserably uncomfortable ten days billeted on surely the hardest, most unyielding floor possible in the Drill Hall at H.Q. in Buckingham Gate, during which we were daily exercised by route marches around the streets of London, full of cheering people, we took the long trek to Leavesden Asylum, the other side of St Albans for concentrated training. This was my first route march with rifle and full pack. When we had gone half-way, about twelve miles, we bivouacked for the night in a field. The cool earth was soft and inviting to our tired bodies after that march and especially by comparison with the floor of the Drill Hall. But this march was but a fore-runner of much worse to come. Arrived at Leavesden, we found the inmates were still there. We, the other lunatics, were put through our paces on the asylum cricket field in no uncertain manner. Fortunately I was very fit and so able to adapt myself to this hideous and unwelcome translation to tough army life. Frankly I did not enjoy it. The companionship and the camaraderie had their appeal and there is no difficulty in assessing who's who and what's what in such circumstances. But I am too sensitive and finicky for communal living, so that most of it was a sickening burden for me and a constant demand to conform, which I resented. I suppose I am basically a rebel and like to take my own line so that army discipline, the blind obeying of orders, did not come easily to me.

Apart from my strong constitution, I attribute some of my hardiness to Mr Price who was our neighbour at our little house in Victoria

Gardens, Notting Hill Gate. It was 'his joy' (so he called it!) to take a dip in the Serpentine, summer and winter, each day, wet or fine. One day he asked, 'Why don't you accompany me?' So I did, although I could not swim. He and I used to trot side by side from Notting Hill Gate across Kensington Gardens to the Serpentine in Hyde Park. It became a habit. I did it for three years until the war came. We must have looked a curious couple, he white-bearded and tiny, and I long and lanky, with our towels round our necks. I soon taught myself to swim, and Mr Price and I went on and on, throughout the winter; we could not stop. We were pioneers, almost curiosities. Swimming in the Serpentine in those days was not nearly as popular then as it is now, nor as comfortable. There were no facilities of any sort for undressing, no shelters and no protection from prying eyes nor from the icy winds. Mr Price and I did not have the benefit of the arrangements later introduced by Mr George Lansbury, the enlightened Labour Minister, who had huts built and created what is known now as the Serpentine Lido where many thousands of people can swim in freedom and comfort. Mr Price and I each took with us the previous day's copy of the *Daily Mail* which we spread out near the edge of the lake, securing it under the legs of a Park chair on which we had a season ticket. Thus we emerged from the water, stood on the newspaper, and did our drying with the minimum of trouble and fuss. In summer we would swim across to the other side of the lake and back. In winter, however, we confined ourselves to a dive from the board before making for the shore and friendly newspaper as quickly as possible. Twice we took part in the Christmas Day race together, without any success, but we were very healthy. I shall always remain indebted to Mr Price for his introduction to the Serpentine. It became such a habit and so much part of my routine that when I was away or prevented from going for one reason or another the day was not the same. I am convinced it set me up for that grim first winter of the war in Flanders and Northern France. The odd thing is that I remain to this day one of the worst swimmers imaginable. I attribute this to being self-taught too late, and to my general ineptitude for any kind of sport or games.

All the same, I have had the satisfaction of rescuing a very frightened, if not an actually drowning woman. Just after the 1914 war, I was at a small deserted beach at Highcliffe in Hampshire. It was lunchtime. I was sitting on the sands reading, unconscious of any other person around me, when suddenly I heard a woman scream, not very far out; she threw up her hands and went under. I was terrified, but realizing I must do something I waded in. I am tall and she was short, so that when the water was up to my neck and I was still standing, she was out of her depth. At that point I reached her. No woman has ever embraced me more tightly. The tide was going out and we both went under. I thought my last moment had come and that we should be drowned in fairly shallow water for I could no longer feel the sand beneath me and I was a wretched swimmer. But after more struggling and shouting the lady, who was no chicken, saw the point. She relaxed and let me get hold of her. Just a little pushing, then a bit of dragging on my back and we were safe. There were no witnesses of this ignominious episode, which would hardly qualify for the Royal Humane Society medal for life-saving! But there was a happy conclusion. The lady reported the matter to her husband who happened to have a small watchmaker's business in the village. He sought me out the next day on the beach, and in a burst of emotion, undertook to repair my watches and those of any member of my family, free of charge, for the rest of his life. I am afraid we never availed ourselves of this magnanimous offer!

On 15 September 1914 the London Scottish left the St Albans neighbourhood where we had undergone the most gruelling drilling and training, night attacks, day attacks, shooting, and lengthy route marches, and we crossed the Channel on the s.s. *Winifred*. We were the first Territorials to be sent overseas, and the first troops to land at Le Havre. We were ecstatically received by the French, especially by the ladies none of whom had seen soldiers in kilts before. They all asked us the same question! 'C' Company travelled in cattle trucks to guard the railhead at Villeneuve Triage, outside Paris where we occupied a railway shed on the main line. At every stop there was the same clamour of hospitality. On the less cheerful side we came upon hospital trains, no more than converted cattle trucks, full of our wounded and mutilated on mere stretchers, suffering agonies because inevitably the medical arrangements were as yet inadequate.

Eventually we were ordered up to Ypres which was just being

hurriedly evacuated by civilians. Shelling of the city, later to be deci-mated, had just begun. The horror and plight of the civilian popu-lation, so often witnessed later and even more markedly in the Second World War, left its memory on me. After passing through the city, with its shops full of goods but without owners or salesmen, we were deployed outside the city near Messines. This was being shelled by long-distance artillery, throwing over what we nicknamed 'Jack Johnsons' after the world champion boxer. The noise of their approach was terrific and the thud they made on landing shook the earth: the craters were colossal, pushing up tons of earth. If they achieved a direct hit, it was good-bye for ever, but it was the demoralizing effect they had on us new troops which told. It was at this moment that I fell for my first taste of intoxicating liquor – rum. It was hardly a taste – it was a deep draught, drunk out of a mess tin. I felt it trickle down to my very toes. I did not ask myself why I had succumbed nor what my dear mother would say. I knew the answer to both questions! We went off to rest in a farm house, and next morning, for the first time, there was nothing between us and the enemy. It was an uncanny feeling. We had been informed that the Prussian Guards were facing us. We could hear their bands in the far distance and later we were told the Kaiser himself had been behind the German lines, encouraging them to capture Ypres. Before the attack we were subjected to a further dose of ghastly shelling. I am sure it was trivial by comparison with what came later and in the Second War, but it was a fresh experience for us and we hated it.

It was 31 October 1914, Hallowe'en, and we were lying in open order in a beet field. Afterwards the British Army was referred to as 'The Long Thin Line' stretching between the Germans and the Channel Ports and that was an accurate description of the state of affairs that night: we had no reserves between us and Ypres and our troops were so thinly spread that my next-door neighbour was at least ten yards from me. Nothing behind us. All day we had been under heavy shell fire. I tried to create some protection for my head by scratching up earth against a beet, but of course it was just a sign of the desperate state I was in. At dusk the attack materialized as expected and I could discern in the half light of early evening, in solid formation, helmeted and with bayonets fixed, an over-whelming force of Germans bearing down on us from about two hundred yards away. Nothing could have been more calculated to strike terror into us, after the day we had endured without food or refreshment. Somebody shouted 'Fire!' We obeyed, but apart from dropping an odd German here and there our efforts were quite paltry and did not stay their advance for an instant. Frankly I was petrified and hearing the word 'Retreat', or imagining I did, I skedaddled. We all did. I have been ashamed of it ever since, but at that moment there was no apparent use in waiting. My bare knees were knocking together, and the cold was not the cause, since kilts are notably warm garments. Presumably the Huns were as frightened as we were for why they did not run straight through us will never be known. That was one of the mysteries of the war. We fell back to the shelter of our overnight farm, and whether the Germans in our sector had advanced ahead of their comrades and found themselves enfiladed and so retreated, I am not sure. It was a great jumble. Whatever the reason, the enemy was luckily not so numerous when we reached the protection of the farm's haystacks. We dodged around them, like a game of hide and seek, chased at the point of the bayonet, and in sheer self-defence I gathered enough courage to retaliate now and again – not with any satisfaction but in utter black fear; a bayonet is a dreadfully ominous and threatening instrument. Happily for me, this was the only occasion when I was actually engaged in hand-to-hand fighting during the war. It was certainly enough. I wondered, had Hohenemser been there, what we would have done to one another. I realized I had nothing against him personally. I did not even hate the Hun, as such, yet here we were engaged in the biggest 'civilian war' of all time and we could do nothing about it, except what we were told. There were few, if any, ideological or patriotic reasons motivating me and many a time in the filth and mire of life in the trenches, I asked myself what it was all about, what we were fighting for. To kill the Kaiser? To rid the world of him? It seemed a small task for all the bloodshed. But probably, all unconsciously, we were fighting so that 'Britons never, never, shall be slaves'. But at the time, I was not sure.

Others more heroic did better I expect, and got their bayonets into more German bellies, or died or were taken prisoner. Anyhow, the attack was stemmed and Ypres was saved from German occupation. We had retreated so far that we ran into the Corps Commander himself and his staff. Immediate orders were given for a counter-attack. I shall never forget his steadiness and the distinguished aura he created even in the black of that winter night. Some companies of the Battalion – not ours – then carried out the counter-attack, in which they made a most gallant charge at Messines which will for ever rank as a decisive step in the defence of Ypres and the Channel ports. The losses were cruel in killed, wounded or prisoners. To this day I remain conscious of the inglorious part I had played on the occasion of my baptism of fire.

This was the foreplay of the first Battle of Ypres, which soon erupted over us – cold, hungry, and miserable. With two others, I was in a trench in Zillebeke Wood, a few sandbags as protection for our heads, with poor Ypres, shelled and shelled behind us. Two of us were on duty and one rested in the mud. We stayed there for twelve days, sniping away at German soldiers dodging between the trees in front of us. I know I was praying all the while I could shed six inches from my height and not have to bend so much. Army discipline insisted we should shave each day which we did from the moisture of the dregs of our tea in our mess-tins. We could ill spare our clean water. It was all one long nightmare with the dark made eerie by the Very lights constantly being shot into the air, disclosing ghostly figures flitting about – probably just as scared as we were.

We fired so many bullets that we hardly knew what to do with the cases. I stuck mine into the parapet in front of me patterning the names of all my girl friends, wondering whether I should ever see any of them again! It was a mighty risky thing to have to climb out during the day and for our own sakes we restricted our needs to the absolute minimum. Heroic Army Service Corps men brought us skimpy rations at night and our own cooks sometimes sent some hot soup to us, but it was mostly bully beef and biscuits. When we were relieved, I believe by the Oxford and Bucks Light Infantry, we could hardly use our legs. But when a few hundred yards ahead out of earshot of the enemy, a piper struck up, we were galvanized and fell at once into step. There is nothing to beat the bagpipes on such an occasion!

After a short respite, we were destined to settle down for the winter with the rest of the Army, in and out of the trenches, sometimes for short periods in the front line, sometimes longer. When we were sent back to rest, we had a thorough clean-up and were able to attack our most annoying enemy, the louse, and we would burn with our cigarette-ends some of the hundreds in the pleats inside our kilts – a fine hide-out for them. Sometimes we were in billets, sixteen or so of us on the stone floor of a farm kitchen. We got to know the 'cushy' billets, where the farmer's wife would satisfy our insatiable desire for omelettes and not sting us too much. One good lady, a spinster, was our special favourite and we were fortunate enough to be with her two or three times. I was the Corporal in charge at one visit, and she liked to spoil me, calling me 'Mon grand bébé' which was at once adapted in the section in another sense. I went back after the war to visit the sweet old thing, but found the bed in her spare room much less inviting than the stone floor of war-time. We all had 'pen girls' and much to the amusement of our officers who had to censor our letters, we wrote practically identical things at some length to them all. We used to receive wonderful parcels from home. My mother's home-made cake never went far: it was very popular.

That first winter, spent in trenches and dug-outs, had few, if any, compensations; the mud, the rats, the shelling, the hand-grenades, the battles of Givenchy, Festubert and Neuve-Chapelle. The London Scottish were brigaded with the 1st Coldstream Guards, 1st Scots Guards, 1st Black Watch and 1st Cameron Highlanders in what was known as The First Guards Brigade. Due to wounds, deaths or sickness I found myself in early 1915 promoted from private soldier to Lance-Corporal, Corporal, Lance-Sergeant and finally Sergeant – all within ten days. Finally I was appointed Acting Bombing Sergeant of the 1st Guards Brigade – the nearest I have ever been to the Guards. Apart from their disciplined bearing at all times and under all conditions, my outstanding recollection was the remarkable, if very repetitious, variety of swear-words Guardsmen can contrive to insert into even the shortest sentence.

Sometimes our lines were only ten yards from the Huns and we used to keep them hopping, by skying jam-pot hand-grenades over at them and then darting speedily off behind a redoubt or down a dugout before the retaliation came. Although many of my comrades had either been killed, wounded or fallen sick, Spring of 1915 still saw me surprisingly unscathed and in excellent health but with a strong attack of *le cafard*. I often used to think of my blasé approach to the risk of death then, compared with my stark fear a few months previously. It just shows what one can get used to! Nothing at all to do with bravery.

In July 1915 came my first leave after ten months overseas. My mother's overwhelming relief at seeing me again induced me to try and get a commission, in order to stay in England for a bit. This I did not find difficult and at the end of six days I returned to the Front, armed with a War Office request to my Commanding Officer to release me for a commission. The Colonel was very angry, telling me that whilst I was on leave I had been recommended for a commission in the London Scottish, and that alternatively the Black Watch had expressed interest in me. Memory of his disgust remains with me even now. 'You, a sergeant in the London Scottish, going off to an English Regiment!' What chagrin for me! How I cursed my precipitate action at home, which meant I must decline an honour anybody would covet! But my new Commanding Officer would not, or could not, release me despite all my entreaties, and so six weeks later back I went to London, a very forlorn commissioned officer.

The War Office allowance for the provision of full officer's uniform and kit such as camp bed etc. was only £50. I was therefore very distressed when I was informed that our new Commanding Officer insisted upon our ordering our uniforms from one of the most expensive Bond Street tailors. We all had to dig deep into our pockets in consequence. I found my new association generally distasteful and I do not doubt my feelings were reciprocated. After six weeks as a 2nd Lieutenant, I put in to be drafted to the Dardanelles where the 1st Battalion of the Regiment was fighting in the famous 29th Division at Suvla Bay. We had been billeted at Beckenham in Kent, which made London, home and the theatre accessible. George Robey and Violet Loraine were cheering us with 'If you were the only girl in the world'. Gerald du Maurier was acting in *Dear Brutus*, Barrie's famous play, and I re-visited it many times; *The Lilac Domino* was playing, a glorious musical comedy, and there was Dennis Eadie in *The Admirable Crichton*. I do not recall very much of war-time London in 1914–18. There was this superficial gaiety, but actual living was much harder for Londoners in 1914 and after than during the Second War, despite the bombing. My

[49]

memory is of very severe rationing, having to eat horse meat, and unlike the Second World War, we even had to give up coupons in the restaurants. This was a rigid law. I was so downhearted at this period, mostly because of thoughts of where I might have been, that I became somewhat wild, and mess nights were riotous affairs for me. Once I tipped the Regimental Sergeant-Major's cap off his head, as he was being given a drink in the Officers' Mess – hideous offence! Deservedly, I was severely reproved. When at last my request to be sent overseas was granted, life took on a new zest for me, and the Colonel was glad to be relieved of a disgruntled rebel.

Accompanied by two other officers of the regimental draft, I joined nearly 6,500 reinforcements on board the old s.s. *Olympic*. The journey which took us twelve days, was my first experience on a big ship. I shared a small cabin with an Australian captain who was returning to the Dardanelles after a slight wound sustained in the landing. He was a powerful fellow, a cattle rancher, very disdainful of young British officers, and called us all 'War Babies', which enraged me after my considerable period of service in France. However, we were all war babies to him, and I could not budge him.

Alas! When we got to Suvla, the Battalion was severely weakened and disorganized by a serious attack of frostbite of all things, and with the remnants I was eventually sent into reserve on the island base of Mudros. We spent only a matter of a few weeks at Suvla and never returned, since almost immediately the total evacuation of the Peninsula was ordered. I was however at the Dardanelles long enough to see the utter hopelessness of our position once our original attack had failed on landing. We were all shipped to Egypt, to a camp in tents at Wardan, some forty miles in the desert outside Cairo. At the age of twenty the desert brought things out of me. I loved its peace and loneliness, and the walks I took by myself afforded me relaxation and allowed me time for reflection. I was calm again. I started to read poetry. It was also my first contact with Arab life and I was able to visit Cairo, the Pyramids and Alexandria, all of which naturally made a profound impression on me. In those days such historic places were surrounded by mystery and glamour. We were always tantalized by the scurrying figures of the native girls in the village not far from our camp, who once out of range and their faces protected from our vision, could be observed watching us round the corners, consumed by curiosity.

Cairo in early 1915 was much as it was, I imagine, in the Second War: a centre of fun for those relaxing on leave. I did not enjoy it much, for the Gippy native was not by any means one of my favourites, and I suppose he has not changed greatly since. All the same, war-time Cairo gave me my first taste of night life and opened my *ingénu* eyes. I was gradually growing up in this new world in which I found myself.

But I was soon to be disturbed. I had been appointed Machine-Gun Officer of the Battalion and was delighted at this opportunity at last to show some individuality. Alas, while playing football, at which I have already confessed I was useless, I badly damaged my left knee. I remember a friend of mine in the London Scottish once saying that on the field I never seemed to be anywhere near the ball, but this time I was! Wishing to stay with my newly formed machine-gun section, I begged the medical officer not to persist in sending me to hospital. He relented and I remained hobbling about in camp giving lectures. But the knee deteriorated, the leg stiffened, and I was eventually despatched to Mena Hospital in Cairo where I stayed for many weeks, just when the Battalion was ordered to France. This was a crushing blow for me, but worse was to come. I was sent back to England on a hospital ship, was operated on in London, and was eventually discharged from the Army as unfit for further war service. By then my leg seemed to have become permanently stiff. However, it gradually got better so that I could walk with comparative ease. But to this day I have regretted my mulishness in declining to have what was originally a trifling trouble attended to immediately.

Chapter 5

Thus I was a civilian again, having had so far a very active war, mostly overseas. What ignominy! How inglorious! I became very restive indeed. I disliked being in civilian clothes, doing nothing for King and Country. Whereas I was in fact one of the 'Old Contemptibles', I was, ironically, given a white feather, which I used to treasure with some amusement. The donor, a tweedy old maid, went scarlet when I told her I had the much prized Mons star, which signified that the wearer had seen service overseas in France before 30 September 1914. In 'my' war, medals were much rarer than in the second war.

Then suddenly everything was transformed. Quite by chance I met Claud Serocold. He was a leading stockbroker, an intimate friend of Max Bonn and had been a regular visitor to the office before the war. It transpired that he was Personal Assistant, with the rank of Commander RNVR, to Admiral Hall, the Director of Naval Intelligence, the famous admiral known to everybody as 'Blinker' Hall. I told Claud my sad tale. He said, 'You know German, don't you?' I replied that I did, but it might be rusty. 'Never mind that, they can do with you in Room 40 O.B. at the Admiralty, I am sure. I will arrange for you to be interviewed, and if they like you, there is an exceptional job for you there.' All went well. I was vetted and accepted, was re-gazetted to my old Regiment and seconded for Special Duties at the Admiralty. By then I had two pips. This was my highest Army rank, although I faintly recall that whilst in Egypt I was once promoted in Company orders to a Captaincy. But this only held good for a few weeks. However, now I was back in uniform again and able to look everybody in the eye! This amazing stroke of good fortune changed my whole life. No wonder I remain deeply and permanently grateful to the memory of Claud Serocold!

What was this Room 40 O.B. and what was the nature of its work? I was soon to discover that it was in effect a cluster of several rooms and, curiously enough, on each door there was marked 'No admittance' in big letters on a brass plate. Intruders were summarily dealt with. Room 40 was never empty during the whole war. It was only given over entirely to the charwomen for its first good clean after the armistice in November 1918. I had been told that the work was highly confidential, and I had a clue it was so-called secret intelligence work, but what was it? It was, in fact, the room to which were sent all intercepted wireless signals put out by the German Navy. Its function was to crack the ciphers and decode the messages, carefully studying them for any significant points. Since those days its fame has become world-wide and the results of the work of Room 40 are recorded in every authentic history of the 1914 war. It altered the entire course of the war, for not only did its occupants concentrate on German naval messages, but they procured, by devious and often ruthless methods, by brilliant ruses and by ingenious interception, German diplomatic dispatches and telegrams, which, once in the skilled hands of those in Room 40, were deciphered and their contents put to good use.

The outstanding example of this was the Zimmermann telegram. It will be remembered that this telegram was dispatched early in 1917 by Zimmermann, Under-Secretary at the German Foreign Office, to the German Ambassador in Mexico instructing him in substance to complete an offensive and defensive alliance with Mexico, which was to declare war on the U.S.A. and so prevent that country from coming to the aid of the allies in Europe. The telegram also promised generous financial support and gave an undertaking on Germany's part that Mexico should reconquer her lost territory in Texas, New Mexico and Arizona. It was tied up with Germany's intention to start, on 1 February 1917, unrestricted submarine warfare calculated to compel England to sue for peace in a few months.

It was the direct result of the disclosure of the contents of that telegram that the United States declared war on Germany on 6 April 1917. The Zimmermann telegram can, therefore, legitimately be called the most famous in history. The deciphering was accomplished by two men, Nigel de Grey, once a publisher with William Heinemann and later a director of the Medici Society, and the Reverend W. Montgomery of the Westminster Presbyterian College, Cambridge. I believe de Grey got an O.B.E. for his war services and Montgomery, nothing. Puny recognition!

The book *The Zimmermann Telegram* published a year or so ago by the American writer Barbara Tuchmann gives the complete story. The original message marked 'Keep under lock and key; only one copy', signed by Hall, is, I believe, framed in the Admiralty.

To understand and to appreciate the delicate details involved in the thoughtful planning and preparation, the handling of the sensitive personalities involved, the verification of the Zimmermann telegram, the protection of Room 40 so that its work should not be placed in jeopardy, I also recommend Admiral Sir William James's biography of Admiral Sir Reginald Hall, entitled *The Eyes of the Navy*. Therein will be found not only all the enthralling details concerning the Zimmermann telegram, but a full account of some of the other fantastic achievements of Admiral Hall himself, including the Casement arrest. The author was not only an intimate associate of the Director of Naval Intelligence, but was also in command of the whole operation of Room 40 and responsible for its vital development and exploitation for the war effort. In his book, Admiral James quotes a letter sent in March 1918 by Dr Page, the American Ambassador in London, to President Wilson, in which he says about Admiral Hall, 'He is one genius that the war has developed. Neither in fiction nor in fact can you find any such man to match him. The man is a genius – a clear case of genius. . . . I shall never meet another man like him: that were too much to expect.' High praise, but in no way exaggerated.

Those of us who worked for Admiral Hall all revered him. We knew we would be his slaves, come what may, such was his magnetism and our blind devotion. Room 40, under Captain James as he then was ('Bubbles' of the famous picture by Millais), was a section, and a very important one, of the Naval Intelligence Division over which ruled 'Blinker' Hall. It was the latter who, through his genius and insight, made realities of and dealt with the extraordinary situations which opened up from our deciphered messages. In consequence, he was inevitably a man who wielded vast authority and power and whose views

(*Above*) Drawing of 41 Threadneedle Street.

(*Right*) First of a series of cartoons in the *Evening Standard*, August 1957 – 'Mr Lionel Fraser, head of Helbert Wagg, The City bankers, has taken a country house for an away-from-it-all holiday. There is a big garden and a high wall. But it still has a telephone.'

were sought and respected by members of the Government on both sides of the Atlantic. I doubt whether he disclosed many of his secrets to them! He knew so much. He had direct access to Cabinet Ministers who would seek his advice on matters far distant from naval affairs. He was allowed to go to work to solve his problems in his own way, tricking the enemy, laying his traps for them, taking enormous chances at times in case his interpretation of a situation, resulting from his amazing second sight, had let him down. He was a gambler if you like, often audacious and unorthodox but mainly brilliantly successful. It was Admiral Hall, with the assistance of Captain James, who collected around him the men of brains whose particular skill and facility it was to be able to break the German ciphers and decode their messages.

The work was obviously of a top secret and highly important nature – therefore a certain standard was essential, as well as an intimate even colloquial knowledge of the German language. Intercepting wireless signals and attempting to read them had not been thought of before the war, and when the small band of pioneers under Sir Alfred Ewing discovered the cipher key and began to read German naval signals, it was vitally important to keep this unique source of intelligence a profound secret, and throughout the war it remained so, only known to the Operations Division and some members of the Board of Admiralty.

But by the time I joined Room 40 in October 1916, our Allies, as well as our enemies, had realized that the best means of obtaining intelligence was through wireless traffic. We discovered the efficiency of the German Room 40 when they read Jellicoe's signal to the destroyers on the evening of the Battle of Jutland, and repeated it to the German C.-in-C. Room 40's achievements ceased to be a secret when the war ended, as the official Historians could not perform their task without quoting deciphered signals, and diplomats were unable to give a faithful account of their stewardship without quoting the deciphered diplomatic messages.

A book entitled *Room 40 OB or How the War was Won* and a biography of Ewing entitled *The Man of Room 40* left little untold about the remarkable growth and achievements of an organization which had been such a carefully guarded secret, and there are good accounts of

Room 40 and cryptography in the 1914–18 war in the standard Encyclopaedias.

I found myself – by far the youngest man and the only officer in army uniform – amongst a body of distinguished men from many walks of life, though mostly academic. There were peers, professors, fellows of colleges at Oxford or Cambridge, leading schoolmasters, as well as the reverend gentleman I have already mentioned. Those who were of military age were at once plonked into the uniform of an officer in the RNVR and given two stripes. There were many odd incidents when these professors, masquerading as naval officers, untrained in naval discipline and such things as saluting a senior officer, met an admiral in the street. Once one particularly absent-minded professor set off from home without his cap! And another wore it back to front!

My academic knowledge was as nothing beside theirs, and so to a lesser degree was my knowledge of the German language but perhaps this was balanced by a more acute approach, or perhaps I saw situations more quickly than some of the professors who had inhabited ivory towers for so much of their lives. I made some close friends, the chief of whom was William Clarke, the son of the famous Q.C., Sir Edward Clarke. It was due to his deciphering of a message at the time of Jutland that the British Navy was able to make its dispositions which, as is well known, led to the reverse of the German Navy on that occasion. He also was awarded an O.B.E. – but belatedly! Clarke was one of the 'originals', as was Alastair Denniston, an ex-Osborne schoolmaster; F. E. Adcock of King's College Cambridge fame; Dilly Knox, Professor of Greek, as well as his brother Monsignor Ronald Knox; Frank Birch, a don and distinguished dramatist; Francis Toye, once Music Critic of the *Morning Post* and Bullough of Caius who was married to the daughter of Eleanora Duse. These were important characters; later we were joined by such a luminary as Frank Tiarks, a leading City man, Director of the Bank of England, whose son, Henry, was later one of my partners. Frank Tiarks was specially kind to me. And Captain Edward Molyneux, who established himself in Paris in 1920 and became one of the world's most renowned *couturiers* was amongst the actual occupants of Room 40 itself. In adjoining, unnumbered rooms, the Political Section was established, under the diplomat Sir George Young, who had with him Nigel de Grey and Montgomery, as well as Ben Faudel-Phillips, Desmond MacCarthy, the famous literary and dramatic critic; Lord Lytton, a former Viceroy of India; Lord Monkbretton, and a most curious little figure, an ex-Foreign Office man named Somers-Cocks, who could almost quote the *Almanach Gotha* by heart. There were also others, men and women; their brilliant work in a very difficult field yielded a rich reward.

I felt very humble and unequal. At first I was given lowly jobs to do, but soon I was drawn into the inner circle and stayed there until the end of the war. I was originally posted to the Political Section under Faudel-Phillips, but this demanded very involved translation and my inadequacy soon became evident. I was therefore passed over to a 'watch' in the Naval Section, inside Room 40 itself, twelve hours on duty and twenty-four off.

Curiously enough, the original German signal-book on which the entire Room 40 organization was constructed came to us via the Russian Admiralty and we were of course in close touch with our opposite numbers in the Room 40's of our Allies. The key to the code used to remain unaltered for periods of three months when I first arrived, but as the Germans became more alert it was later reduced to every month, and eventually it was changed every twenty-four hours. So at midnight each day messages became unreadable: after applying the key to 'the groups' in the incoming signals, there was no counterpart in the signal book for the resulting groups. It was the task of the watch before going off duty at 8 a.m. to try to discover the new key. This was mostly accomplished after we had picked up the daily routine messages of certain well-known units in the German fleet, outpost boats for instance, indicating (which they did every day) that they had taken up their position, or appeals from other enemy ships begging for lights to be shown to enable them to locate themselves. These repetitious signals mostly gave us our clues, but of course sometimes there was silence from these normally loquacious units. At such times we had to use our agility, based on our close study of all German naval movements, to try other methods. It was a perpetual challenge to each watch who hung their heads when relieved if they had not succeeded, but who also had a glorious sense of triumph once the key was found and messages were again being deciphered.

An even greater challenge came when the Germans introduced a new signal book. It was then that the knowledge of German signals and routine movements, which had been accumulating over the years, was invaluable. Fortunately for us, our directional wireless stations were always able to fix the position of any ship that made a wireless signal.

I specialized in the 'High Sea Fleet', i.e. the battleships, cruisers and destroyers; others in submarines, and others in Zeppelins. It is not difficult to estimate the indescribable value Room 40 was to our war effort. Posterity will bless Admirals Hall and James, but, the British being what they are, I doubt whether full credit will ever be awarded them. I heard the other day from Admiral James, now over eighty I believe and living in Scotland, still full of life and fun, telling me he had recently joined the Royal and Ancient, St Andrews, the oldest new member ever. At his age he said he was interested in obituary notices, and he thought his would read better if it contained a reference to his new golf club, joined at such an advanced age.

Strange as it may seem, there was a certain amount of mistrust from the operational side of the Admiralty in the initial stages concerning the truth, and value, of the information provided by Room 40. There was a tendency to look askance at the work of a bunch of professors with no experience of naval affairs and it took all the tact of Admiral Hall to get these doubts erased. His case was helped by certain specific, and verifiable, pieces of information, which made the Operations Division prick up their ears and have more faith. When an Intelligence Centre within Room 40 was decided upon (I was one of the original members under Frank Birch), it became no longer just a cryptographic bureau, passing on messages to the naval staff without comment, but it issued daily reports, giving its own interpretation of events in the German Navy, based on deep and careful study of past movements, and precisely what it thought these events signified.

As confidence was firmly established, so interest in us increased, and we would often get a visit from Admiral Jellicoe before he went home, usually asking 'Can I count on a quiet night tonight?' And Admiral Beatty also came along to see us when he was in town. Two very contrasting characters; Jellicoe quiet, delightful, unassuming, almost diffi-dent, and Beatty more brusque, more firm, a more obvious personality. Other Admirals who visited us were two a penny.

For me, Room 40 provided a rare opportunity and a challenge. Not only had I the satisfaction of participating in work of supreme importance to the war effort, but I was jet-propelled, for the first time in my history on level terms and into close association with prominent people, highly cultured and highly educated. To this day I am staggered how I held my own, if I did. Much goodwill was shown towards me, and as I said, I made some close friends, few of whom, sad to relate, still survive. I was shown a life which had been closed to me hitherto. Outstanding in my memory are the musical parties in Edith Grove, Chelsea – home of the intelligentsia – given each week by Frank Birch, Dilly Knox and Edmund Green, an ex-Osborne schoolmaster also in Room 40 (three strangely differing characters) where Suggia, the renowned cellist, their next-door neighbour, would thrill us by her unrehearsed performances. Another friendship was with Marjorie Haggard, niece of Rider Haggard, whose brother, having had a leg shot off at Jutland as a snotty, was in Room 40. Marjorie Haggard, later Mrs Charlton, used to accompany me on Sunday afternoons to the Albert Hall, where my knowledge and greater appreciation of music were actively developed, if not, I am afraid, any deep understanding. Clara Butt and Solomon inspired some of it. Enjoyment of music grew as I got older.

I owe most, however, to one man in particular – Sir Benjamin Faudel-Phillips. He was an odd-looking little man, a bachelor, with a rather rasping voice, a Jew, but not orthodox. He had protruding, penetrating eyes, a pot belly and carroty, thinning hair; he generally wore an old Etonian tie and had, I believe, been in 'Pop' there. He was widely travelled, a fine linguist, a skilled gardener, and had a heart brimming over with kindness. He certainly poured it out on me. His mother was originally a Levy, changed later to Lawson, and they owned, if not all, at any rate a large part of *The Daily Telegraph* from which the family fortunes were mainly derived. The Faudel-Phillips's had a family busi-ness of their own, Faudels Limited, an import-export business dealing in toys and such like goods. Ben singled me out and took me under his wing, and literally enveloped me. He taught me some of the intangible aspects of life, those things which come naturally to the well-born, but which can cause the rest of us acutely sensitive moments: how to conduct oneself, how to handle one's table napkin at dinner, how to eat one's soup, how to appreciate beautiful things, furniture and pictures. Ben taught me all this. When I visited his lovely house, Balls Park, Hertford, he would din his ideas into me. We would stand before his fine old masters and his museum pieces of furniture whilst he would ground me in their salient points. He taught me feeling for the best features of life, not luxury, for he hated ostentation, but the things which really mattered. Ben had a valet, Renard, a Belgian, who was his close confidant and retailed to him all the house gossip, about the domestics as well as the guests. As a special favour Renard was put on to valet me – an attention to which I was in no way accustomed and which I would happily have done without. As he gently tended my threadbare underclothes and laid them out in the mornings, I would hide my head under the bedclothes in shame for the holes and their general shabbiness. He was too good a servant to indicate that he had observed these flaws, but I *felt* he had, and that was sufficient.

I hope I have said enough to show my gratitude to Ben. One story I would like to tell about him concerns his generosity as a host, for his table was unsurpassed. He always confessed he was a greedy man. His week-end parties, after the war, were superb. He once showed me a letter from one of his guests after a particularly exotic wine and food week-end. It ran: 'I write with a full heart and a distended stomach to thank you . . .' etc. That just about summed it up.

Ben was not a strong man physically, so he did not hunt, shoot or fish. Had he participated in these sports, he might have whetted my appetite at least for shooting and fishing, although I doubt if I should ever have wanted to indulge in hunting. Maybe I have missed a great deal by never having shot or fished, but neither came my way. I often note the pitying, sometimes scornful, expressions on the faces of my friends when I admit I have never taken part in these sports, but I must put up with them. However, I do think I have really missed something in not having skied, for that sounds thrilling. But then, I do not like mountains much – they menace me. I was bred a town bird. I love London – its beauty, its grandeur, its theatres, its museums, its parks and its art galleries – and I love it especially during the week-end when most of my friends are chasing something, firing at something or killing something and returning to town in cars, nose to tail, exhausted and irritated. I agree with Dr Johnson when he said 'When a man is tired of London, he is tired of life, for there is in London all that life can afford'. It was the 'wonderful immensity' of London which attracted him so forcibly and which never ceases to hold me too. Of course I love the country also – to visit, but not to live in – too many strange noises, cows, birds, cocks, too many draughts, too many demanding neighbours, too many drips from the trees and too much mud when one sets out to the pillar-box to post a letter at 4.30 p.m. on a dark winter evening. No, give me London every time, where I can live and think, with everything accessible to me, and heaven protect me from ever becoming a commuter, or from having the burden of a cottage in the country!

At last the Armistice came. I was on duty that morning and like so many others, I went into Whitehall to give vent to my feelings. Being truly British, the crowds were too shy to shout or dance or do anything much, so they just stood and swayed. I felt frustrated by all this, so I mounted a bus and went on to the open roof. For the rest I will quote from *The Indiscretions of a Naval Censor*, by Sir Douglas Brownrigg:

'The situation was saved by a young subaltern. As the speed of the bus was reduced to rather less than foot pace, he solemnly stood up at the back of the roof, and beating time with his cane, he started three cheers which lifted the safety valve of the crowd, and they began to give voice to the ferment of joy that was inside them. The subaltern was an extraordinary sight. He travelled to and fro many times on buses, keeping the crowd yelling and cheering in a perfectly orderly manner, his face remaining sphinx-like with not a trace of a smile on it. He did good work that morning.'

I remember vividly the occasion of the surrender of the German Fleet. The main ships made for Scapa Flow and sank themselves there, but the submarines were ordered to hand over at Harwich. Frank Birch and I were detailed to act as interpreters as they came in. So we motored up there one morning at dawn in time to see the German submarines entering the harbour one by one. It was a joyful moment for us, but hardly for the dejected and miserable officers and men – and I shall

[61]

always recall this second face-to-face meeting with the Huns since the beginning of the war; the former being my bayonet contact at Messines in October 1914. This presented something of a poignant contrast.

The Naval Intelligence Division decided to have a party at the Savoy to celebrate victory. I felt like Cinderella, for I had never been to a dance or indeed ever danced a step, but I naturally wanted to go, and invited Joan Harvey to accompany me, making her at the same time acquainted of my total inability to waltz or foxtrot. She said, 'Never mind. Come home this afternoon and I will teach you, if only I can persuade father to play the piano.' Father proved to be no other than Sir Ernest Harvey, Chief Cashier of the Bank of England, but he willingly fell in, and so, with the drawing-room rugs rolled back in their house in Cranley Gardens, I had my first dance lesson at the age of twenty-three. I believe I got through the evening without too many disasters. In its way that party at the Savoy was another rung up the ladder for me – it was something novel in my experience and a part of my social education. Joan Harvey was one of the young ladies of Room 40 who were imported later in the war to assist on the clerical side. Their chief was Lady Hambro, the distinguished mother of a distinguished son, Sir Charles Hambro, and she was the first lady I ever saw smoking cigars. The only other ladies whose names I can recall as serving in Room 40 were Margy Bayley, wife of the medical officer of my Battalion at the Dardanelles and in Egypt – one of the first ladies to 'shingle' her hair, much to the consternation of her many male admirers; Bea Speir, who was mostly famous for the variety of the bandeaux she wore round her head – every day a different one – and Rhoda Welsford, a beautiful blue-stocking and a magnificent dancer. But there were many others, and indeed the ladies made an important contribution to the work of Room 40.

Chapter 6

ONCE AGAIN I WAS CONFRONTED with the problem of what to do. Should I return to The City to my old job or try somewhere else? The Admiralty wanted me to stay with them but I did not fancy becoming a permanent civil servant.

At that time the Minister of Munitions invited Ben Faudel-Phillips to undertake a mission to Barcelona to try to cancel a contract the Government had made with the Hispano-Suiza Company for the manufacture of a quantity of aeroplane engines, which were no longer required. Ben agreed, provided he could take me as his assistant. I welcomed the idea, having nothing else on hand, so we went by train to Paris, which I was visiting for the first time. We stayed at the Ritz Hotel, which it is not difficult to believe I found to my entire satisfaction! The first night we went, guess where? To the Folies Bergère! I saw the incomparable Mistinguett.

Barcelona, when we arrived, was in the middle of a syndicalist riot, with troops occupying the main square, the Plaza de Cataluña, and no bull-fights! Our mission was a total failure, but a lot of fun. It was the first really big negotiation I was to have a hand in. It involved masses of meetings, but the Hispano-Suiza Company insisted on full payment at that time and were quite unmoved by our tale of financial stringency. We were showered with invitations, cars at our disposal, etc., but Ben refused them all, which was right, and typical of him. It was very tempting, but we never left the hotel, except on foot, for there were no taxis due to the riots. The Cathedral, the Avenida de las Ramblas with its beautiful flower stalls and Mount Tibidabo, powerfully dominating the city, were my main memories. I have never been back since. On return to London, Ben presented me with a half-dozen shirts from Beale &

Inman – my first made-to-measure – and a malacca cane with my initials on a gold band. I felt very smart. I still have the stick.

Back at home, nobody seemed to be rushing at me. Ben introduced me to the Chairman of the Colonial Bank for a job in Sierra Leone, but I declined his offer. The Gold Coast was then called the White Man's Grave. Having tasted a new life, I wanted to live. Anyhow the pay was not attractive. So I sought an interview with Max Bonn who had not at all enjoyed the war but had done some extremely valuable work behind the scenes. When I was mobilized in August 1914 my pay was £4 per week. He offered me the same salary if I returned, saying that from the business angle he was doubtful if I was worth it but in view of my four years' extra experience he was prepared to go that far, although there was no real job for me. This was bitterly disappointing to me. My pride was hurt, for not only did I modestly consider that my outlook and stature had grown during my war-time career, but my Army pay and special allowances had totalled nearly ten pounds a week, and I did not relish such a substantial drop. However, Frank Birch, who had become a great friend, had at that moment been commissioned to write the war history of Room 40 and was authorized to invite me to assist him, offering me £3 a week for evening and week-end work. This I gladly acceded to and at the same time accepted Max Bonn's offer. I have since realized the wisdom of his stand against my inflated ideas, and that he administered some good medicine to me in giving me the chance he did. It proved to be a vital decision – one of the most important of my career, as it turned out.

So I returned to my former desk at 62½ Old Broad Street, a bit apprehensive but not without hope. Walter Bonn had decided to retire after his tough experience in the war, apart from his natural preference for a country life rather than The City, so Max Bonn was left alone as the sole partner. Jacobs had been carrying on practically single-handed during the whole war and welcomed some companionship. In fact he soon invited me into his office to sit opposite him, where before the war he had been faced with Bonzon and Hohenemser. The former had been cruelly wounded: we never heard anything more of Hohenemser. But once back, I had to occupy myself. Most of our current business had gone and it took time to re-establish our foreign connections which were in disarray. In the meanwhile, we had to live and earn money, so Jacobs conceived the idea of trying our hand at dealing in foreign exchange.

At that time the currencies of the world were beginning to sky-rocket as an aftermath of the financial disequilibrium caused by the war, and there were many opportunities for making money by means of arbitrage. Webster's definition of 'arbitrage' is: 'purchasing in one market for immediate sale in another at a higher price'. The last four words do not always follow as a profit is not exactly inevitable, but at any rate it constitutes an arbitrageur's aim.

Arbitrage flourishes most strongly when communication is difficult, i.e. when telephone or cable contact is infrequent. This allows price discrepancies to appear between one centre and another, caused by abnormal local supply or demand, and the resulting margins are only regulated or absorbed according to the speed or slowness of communication. Nowadays the margins are minute since communication is almost instantaneous. A cable to New York giving an order to buy or sell produces a reply within three minutes, or by telex in one minute, with the execution duly completed. Not much scope for arbitrage there! But after the 1914 war, cable and telephone communication was haphazard and chaotic. With an active, alert counterpart at the other end it was almost money for jam. Jacobs and I felt our way gently at first and gradually we built up a small but remunerative business. The trouble was that nobody was precisely sure how strong Max Bonn was financially, so our operations were not of any size. However, whilst we were still getting into our stride, we learned that important decisions had been taken for the merging of Bonn & Co. into Helbert, Wagg & Co. Ltd. This took place in May 1921 and changed the entire outlook. Gamper and I were offered jobs at Southsea House, the then offices of our new friends, and Max Bonn joined the Board as a Managing Director. Some others including my sister and Miss May Howcroft, of whom more later, also came with us. Jacobs returned to Lazard Brothers whence he had come before joining Bonn & Co. in 1910.

This was a momentous event for me and for my future. Albert Palache, who was foreign manager and destined to become a partner of Helbert Wagg, interviewed me and told me that the decision had been taken to inaugurate a foreign exchange department for my new firm and that I was to be appointed manager in sole control. Here was another remarkable opportunity – manager of a foreign exchange department at the age of twenty-five, with an assured future ahead of me if I succeeded. Palache left it to me to choose my deputy from the existing staff of the firm, but promised to second to my department as my chief bookkeeper a young man, the brightest star in the book-keeping department.

This proved to be George Bolton, now Sir George Bolton. He quickly graduated to a dealership with us, later became the chief cashier of the firm, and, being lent to the Bank of England in an emergency, never returned. His is an exceptional career, very influential. He is the original of the now much used adjective 'dynamic', pouring out new ideas incessantly. He is a brilliant, forceful and creative banker. If any man has made his own success, and still remained completely unspoilt and without conceit, it is George Bolton. We have maintained close friendship, and incidentally I was his best man some thirty years ago when he married Miss May Howcroft, a highly intelligent woman. She and I have been friends since those days long ago when, at the age of fifteen, with long black wavy hair falling down her back, she used to play the piano at the concerts held in aid of my Boy Scout Troop.

James O'Brien, who had an important but rather humdrum job in the Securities Department seemed the most likely candidate for my No. 2 and he gladly seized the chance of adventuring into new fields with me. He became adept at dealing, and although at first it was a rather slow process of learning by experience, I think I can say in all modesty that we developed into a thoroughly workmanlike team. Later, O'Brien became a partner with special charge of our Investment Trusts where his knowledge of securities both here and in the U.S.A. soon became widely acknowledged. L. W. Turnham, our trustworthy recorder of transactions, was later to become our dealer. Both have recently retired.

Dealing in foreign exchange is essentially a matter of mutual trust. Most transactions are conducted on what is called a 'Here and There' basis, i.e. the foreign currency is paid over on a prearranged date, usually after two days, whether it be for instance, in Rio de Janeiro or New York, and payment for the countervalue is made in London on the same day, confidence in the undertaking of one's counterpart being the only assurance that the countervalue has actually been delivered. In present times when banking houses are mostly strong and sound, little danger exists, but in the rackety days of the early 1920s, there was grave risk, and one had to be particularly careful that one's counterpart was secure and good for his engagements. There were some major banking catastrophes in those days in Berlin, Vienna and Milan, and London itself did not escape some failures. It was essential to be extremely wary not to get caught long of balances with a defaulting foreign bank, or to have an unliquidated transaction with them. I remember once noticing a remote item in the newspaper that a queue had formed outside a certain Italian bank with which we had our account in Milan. We thereupon disposed of our balance, for delivery the next day. The bank closed its doors a few days later. Obviously even greater attention had to be paid when dealing in the forward market, for radical depreciation could emerge in a firm's standing even in the short period of three months.

The firm of Helbert Wagg had left The Stock Exchange only in 1912 to become bankers. Thus with the interval of the war, there had been little occasion for them to make their mark in their new sphere, and when in 1921 we were all prepared to open more or less substantial operations in the foreign exchange market, many enquiries were instituted to elucidate who we were, what was our standing. It was often an effort to have our name 'accepted' for even comparatively unimportant sums of foreign currency. As for dealing in the forward market, that was entirely closed to us. However, little by little, as we always faithfully fulfilled our contracts, as business increased and we were recognized as serious people, it was possible eventually to operate in unlimited figures, both for 'spot' as well as 'forward' transactions and no difficulties were presented by even the most conservative banks. I can state, therefore, that Helbert Wagg's entry into the realm of foreign exchange dealing made a helpful contribution towards getting us established amongst bankers all over the world. I do not say that with the unimpeachable personal reputation of the partners it would not have eventually happened in any case but I do say that my department accelerated the process and effected the launching. It made the name prominent in all the leading banking circles. I estimate that ultimately we ranked, for activity and importance, certainly in the first six banks or banking houses engaged in the foreign exchange market, which, starting from scratch, was not bad.

The buying and selling of foreign exchange results from the requirements of merchants who buy and sell goods abroad, or from 'invisible' earnings derived from abroad, such as from insurance, shipping or speculative operations. Thus the big banks and the leading merchant banks automatically picked up foreign exchange business as a result of executing orders on behalf of their many customers. In those days we in Helbert Wagg had none of this 'ready-made' business. Whereas the operators for the banks would start the day with numerous instructions to buy or sell, my desk was invariably blank. We therefore had to create business either by persuading our contacts abroad that we could give better service than others, or by searching ceaselessly ourselves for disparities in the rates between one centre or another. This meant constant telephone communication abroad with Paris, Zurich, Brussels (where we had a specially attractive account), Amsterdam, Milan and Berlin, ever on the lookout to scrape up a profit. By lightning reference to the calculators in front of us we could immediately ascertain whether a margin existed between the two centres. If so we would act, buy or sell, and undo the transaction in our market here.

Our London business was always with foreign exchange brokers, with most of whom we had direct lines. At first we had multifarious separate instruments on our desk and it required a delicately attuned ear to detect which particular bell was ringing. Later these lines were concentrated on to a wonderful silent switchboard, with red and green signals, imported from France. It still remains in our office today, and functions perfectly after forty years of service, but in those days it was the latest invention and was visited by many V.I.P.s. Indeed, the foreign exchange department was the pet show piece in the building! The principal broker in those days was Harlow and Jones, but there were many, many others. Theirs was a very lucrative business. At this time numerous banking institutions of smaller or greater importance came into the market, and made the position highly competitive. Most have long since merged, been absorbed, or ceased to exist, but for the record, and for sentimental reasons in case they strike a chord somewhere it might be worth mentioning some of them: J. Stamm & Co., London and Eastern Trade Bank, Im Thurn, W. Ladenburg & Co., St. Phalle, J. Wassermann, Bernhard Scholle & Co., British Overseas Bank, Frederick Huth & Co., and Cull & Co. The last four named were of considerable importance and dealt on a big scale.

On one occasion we were operating in French francs with Lloyds and National Provincial Bank whose offices were opposite ours in Threadneedle Street. We had bought one million francs from them through a broker, and, wanting to increase the amount, I stepped on to the small balcony outside our dealing room, attracted their attention and using 'tictac' signs, I increased the deal to two million francs and then three million. It was all rather *opéra bouffe*, done for fun rather than to save the brokerage.

It cannot be said that our business was of a speculative nature, for we always endeavoured to close the day with our book square. With the violent movements it was dangerous to do otherwise! It was a wild game but for those who were participants it was anything but wild. They had to be ice-cold and bank on the spot all the time. It was easy to get burnt fingers.

Similar situations were arising all the time in the early 1920s in the Central European countries, especially Germany, Hungary, Austria, and Poland. Even Russia was plagued with the same disease, a rampant uncontrollable inflation. The collapse of the German currency had its origin in the Allied demands for the transfer of impossibly high amounts of reparations, and the resulting necessity to print more and more paper money. In 1926 there was the reverse process in France, for when Poincaré, the then Prime Minister, introduced timely measures for the salvation of the franc, the bears covered their outstanding commitments so quickly that within twenty-four hours the franc had doubled in value! Confidence returned and refugee money came back with it.

I remember we once sold half a million German marks to a certain furrier, through a broker. When the bargain came to be settled two days later, marks had depreciated considerably and the furrier wished he had delayed his purchase. He pretended to be aggrieved with us and tried to avoid settlement using the Gaming Act of 1802 as his loophole, claiming that we had scooped the profit. We naturally challenged this dodge as our operation was done in good faith, and as a part of our normal business was covered straightaway at the time. The case was to be heard at the Guildhall and I was our principal witness, in fact the only witness. It was my first court appearance since listening to Uncle Bert at Petersfield when I was a small boy. And happily my last, so far. The result was a foregone conclusion, as it soon transpired that our opponent had himself been having 'a spec', not needing the marks for genuine business. But I had to submit to a scurrilous cross-examination by a horribly insinuating barrister, who attempted to discredit me with irresponsibility on account of my youth. I cannot say our own counsel exhibited particular skill in the matter of the technicalities of the foreign exchange market as he posed some questions in cross-examination of me, which were embarrassingly unhelpful. Perhaps he had not prepared the case very well, or properly digested his brief. However, we won our case, which was the main thing.

In those days, I was able to have my finger on the pulse of world banking and could make accurate assessments of the standing of individual concerns, AA1, A1, 2 or 3. One had to follow, very closely, the economic and financial movements of one's own country and also keep a tight tag on the affairs of other important centres overseas. Adverse or favourable happenings would be reflected immediately in the foreign exchange. My judgment was very sensitive. To this day the standing and activity of banking houses all over the world has remained one of my special interests.

I was called upon to make regular visits to Europe to confer with our opposite numbers. My round was usually The Hague, Amsterdam, Antwerp, Brussels, Zurich, then Paris and home. I certainly became acquainted with the Continent at an early age, and in exotic circumstances. Yet there was a hopelessness in the atmosphere, smacking, even in business, of the 'Eat, drink and be merry, for tomorrow we die' mentality. Nevertheless, that period had a great gaiety, laced as it was with parties, champagne, Noël Coward's success, Cochran's revues, Ivor Novello's haunting tunes, Hutch, Paul Robeson, night clubs and laughter. Superficially merry, happy days, which, however, I enjoyed to the full. My foreign exchange duties especially in their instability and tension reflected the conditions in which we found ourselves.

Altogether, it was killing and frenzied work, and except that the department was able to make a substantial contribution to the profits of the firm, I found it difficult to persuade myself that we were doing anything particularly constructive or helpful in those very disturbed times. Indeed I was not sorry when activity in the world currencies subsided, and we found diminishing scope for our skill. It is a fascinating thought that George Bolton who was taking part with us in this unrestricted jungle warfare of the foreign exchange market had put into operation at the Bank of England the highly effective control system of the last war. I wonder what he and I would now be doing if there had been exchange control in 1919, robbing us of our first priceless steps up the banking ladder. Life would have been duller and calmer, I am certain, and less adventurous.

There were some outstanding personalities dealing in foreign exchange in those days, many of whom later achieved leading positions in The City. I remember particularly Ellerton of Barclays Bank, later Sir Cecil Ellerton and now dead, who was a highly skilled operator and always kind and helpful. He came up through the ranks and by his character and his unsurpassed knowledge of banking became Deputy Chairman of his Bank, respected and loved by hundreds of friends.

There was also Basil Bebb, later to become a partner in Hoare & Company, stockbrokers. His firm was then Bernhard Scholle & Company and they were active dealers. Having a New York office of their own, they were amongst the latest to cease work each day and many was the interesting deal we were able to do with them when most of our other competitors had gone home.

I remember with particular affection and gratitude, Daniel Dreyfus of Louis Dreyfus & Cie of Paris with whom we had a most profitable joint account for many years. Although having the same name he was not related to the Louis Dreyfus family for whom he worked. He was of course a Jew, a man with a philosophical approach to life, keenly musical and artistic, and appreciative of the theatre and opera which we enjoyed together. He showed his discernment by buying Picasso and Dufy pictures long before these artists became famous. He loved his food and wine, and had a constant battle against increasing girth. We spent many holidays together before his marriage, regularly visiting Fontainebleau for the Quatorze Juillet each year, and Cabourg, in easy reach of Deauville, which was then enjoying enormous popularity. He was an extremely keen golfer and we played together on most of the French courses – Morfontaine and St Cloud outside Paris, Biarritz, Chiberta and Chantaco at St Jean de Luz. He was my most intimate friend on the Continent. I was leading *garçon d'honneur* at his wedding in a Paris synagogue over thirty-five years ago, and my wife and I loved his wife, Gilberte, just as much as Daniel. She shared his interests, and herself played golf for France, to which poor Daniel certainly could never aspire. Sadly he died last year, not a happy man: he had not caught up with the modern world. We miss him immensely. His friendship was one of the most attractive connections resulting from my foreign exchange days.

Chapter 7

I T WAS AROUND THIS TIME that it entered my head to see whether
I could somehow manage to visit New York, ostensibly to establish
contact with my uncle Tom, my father's younger brother who had been
sent there as a babe in arms after the death of my paternal grandparents
and been adopted by a family named Rodman who had given him their
name. Since my father's death my mother had kept up a desultory
correspondence with him and he appeared keen to see his nephew. He
was reputed to be of more than adequate wealth and I was mercenary
enough to think that his relations in England, especially my mother,
might be able to share in some of his affluence. Like so many other young
men I had a hankering after the New World and it was tempting to be
able to reconnoitre the possibility of setting out one day to make a
fortune there, which then seemed so much easier than in England. But
how should I manage it? Max Bonn had the answer. He offered to lend
me up to £200 and at the same time fixed for me to share a cabin with
Helbert Wagg's New York representative, paying one-third of the cost
out of my own pocket and taking my summer holiday, plus an additional week, for the purpose. This was a happy arrangement for me and
off I sailed in August 1923, thrilled at the prospects ahead.

We were in the s.s. *Berengaria* which was formerly the German owned
Imperator, and she was full of American hostesses taking back their
daughters after doing the season in Europe. I had a roaring time and am
not now sure whether by the end of the trip I had, or had not, asked for
the hand of a beauteous creature from the deep South, whose lilting
southern intonation I found most attractive. However, I was soon
brushed off by her parents.

Arrived in New York I put up for the first night at the McCalpin

Hotel on Sixth Avenue, long since torn down. The heat was colossal, no air conditioning of course, and in my tiny room I lay all night in pools of perspiration with a small electric fan blowing what seemed ever hotter air on to me. In addition, just outside my window ran the overhead street railway – a monstrously noisy invention of the devil, which by itself would have destroyed any possibility of rest. I thought if New York was like this I preferred good old London. That was, admittedly, a first very quick view, but after many visits since, I have never ceased to wonder at the patience and stamina of New Yorkers who can endure and seemingly flourish in such inordinately violent extremes of heat and cold.

Next day I took a taxi and presented myself to uncle Tom and his wife, aunt Cora. They lived across the river in Brooklyn and until that visit I had never appreciated what an overcast look steals into the expressions of New Yorkers at reference to Brooklyn; they made me feel there was something contaminating, and definitely low class about the district. It was almost as if as a Londoner one lived in Whitechapel or in the Mile End Road. A change has taken place since, but not much, and until quite recently even humble New York people would smirk when I told them I had once an uncle who lived in Brooklyn! They couldn't believe it.

Uncle Tom received me rapturously; not so aunt Cora who indicated without any delay that uncle Tom had powerful commitments to her family. She did not welcome this intruder from London. 'Your uncle Tom is happy for you to stay with us a few days, but we cannot make it any longer than that.' She was kind but firm, but with this frigid reception I realized that there were to be no roots established for me in their home and that I should have to look elsewhere for a *pied à terre* if I decided to take up residence in the States. It was therefore only natural that after three or four days with them I took my leave and crawled back to the discomfort of a back room in a New York fifth-rate hotel. That little episode was over and all the anticipated romance of making contact with someone of my father's family missing.

The heat in the city was still unbearable and I am not sure whether it was for that reason, or owing to the disappointing reception at my uncle's, that I have no definite recollection or firm impressions of

[74]

New York on this first visit. I did not go again for about twenty-five years, but I know I did not like it. The noise, the restlessness, the jostling rude people, the climate, rebuffed me and I never got much beyond that. I did not feel at home, even the skyscrapers failed to impress me and when I had somewhat tentative talks with one or two Wall Street Houses, any previous enthusiasm I might have had for a future there faded away. I did not feel I could ever be part of a place which had so little tradition and where the business leaders appeared to have a restricted sense of duty towards employees – at times amounting to ruthlessness. My visit was at the height of prohibition and gangsterism. The deceit and the bribery undertaken by almost everybody to obtain strong liquor made a mockery of the unenforceable law and reduced normally high-minded men to the level of cheats.

So, conscious of an unrewarding visit, I again boarded the *Berengaria* and sailed for home, this time in the tourist class, having no Helbert Wagg colleague to share the cost. No debs, but heart-whole, and confident, as in the song, that 'England, England that is the place for me!' Needless to say, after many visits to the States my early views of the country and the people have undergone a fundamental change for the better. I would still never wish to live there permanently, but I have many good and interesting friends in the States who receive my wife and myself with charming hospitality and ensure that our journeys are not only worth while but stimulating. And I have long since been a strong advocate of Anglo-American co-operation as essential to world peace and progress.

Chapter 8

I FEEL IT WOULD NOW BE APPROPRIATE to paint a picture of this firm called Helbert, Wagg & Co. Ltd, situated in the very heart of The City of London in one of its most famous and well known thoroughfares – Threadneedle Street. Up to April 1925 the offices were in Southsea House, when we moved into our own building at No. 41 Threadneedle Street. There are two entrances, one in a little courtyard and one, never used, in Adams Court at the rear. There are two ground landlords, Emmanuel College and Christ's Hospital, and the great fortune, much envied, of standing room for two cars outside the doors.

The site of the present building was, in remote times, occupied by the Hospital of St Anthony, and it is curious to note that Threadneedle Street, a centre of opulence, was once called Pig Street – so named, some say, because the animals belonging to the hospital used to run about the street to be fed by the passers-by. Others tell me it was so called because St Anthony is also the patron saint of swineherds and 'an anthony' is the smallest piglet in the litter.

The National Provincial Bank – the adjoining neighbour, was erected on the site of an ancient inn called 'The Flower Pot' in 1865, and the site of the Westminster Bank down the road, erected in 1925–26, was once occupied by a French Protestant Church, and then by the Hall of Commerce, built in 1842. This hall was designed to rival Lloyd's and the Baltic, but it soon languished. Lloyds Bank, almost opposite us, marks the site of the Church of St Martin Outwich, demolished in 1874. For many years Helbert Wagg have paid a parish levy to St Martin Outwich.

When I first became associated with Helbert Wagg, I was struck by the oddity of the name. It was not as well known and esteemed then as it is now, and when in reply to a question, I said I was working with Helbert Wagg, eyebrows would be raised and I would invariably be asked to repeat it slowly. Nobody could believe it was not at least Herbert Wagg, or at any rate Albert Wagg and there were many other confusions, the best being a letter we once received addressed to Albert Wagon Co. Ltd. Actually I believe the name Helbert was originally derived from Halberstadt, a town in Germany, in the days when people did not have surnames. The name Wagg derives from Waage which means a weighing machine in German. Our Wagg family had owned a small jeweller's shop and this was a sign of its trade.

Helbert and Wagg came together in partnership in this country in 1804 when they established themselves in business as stock and share brokers as Helbert Wagg & Company. Mr Alfred Wagg who reigned as Chairman from 1922 until 1954 is the grandson of the original Wagg. Helbert Wagg retired from The Stock Exchange in 1912 to become bankers after a difference of opinion with The Stock Exchange Committee of which Mr Arthur Wagg, Alfred Wagg's father, was then a member. The firm had a flourishing Stock Exchange business, acting as official brokers to the great and all-powerful House of Rothschild. Those were the days, they would be the first to admit, when the obtaining of orders was not such a discriminating business as today, being then largely based on the 'old pal – slap on the back – you must have a go at this' method; the market was largely dominated by the professional operators, who were more or less 'in the know', and could act accordingly.

No description of the firm can be attempted in which the personality of Alfred Wagg is not all-prominent, for it was he, still going strong at the age of eighty-six, who was the true creator, or perhaps I should say, the re-creator of the firm. It was his vision and his leadership which formed the foundation on which the firm was built. Originally destined to go into the Foreign Office, he found himself a reluctant member of the staff of his family firm, and later a partner. A tall, pale man, of ascetic appearance, with the kindest pair of eyes I have ever seen, and a delicious sense of humour, he would be the last to claim any particular brilliance, yet he has a shrewdness and a flair for business which are quite unusual. He is a bachelor, who swears he has never had the nerve to propose marriage not realizing, curiously enough, that that is not always necessary. Of course he had the good fortune to be born with a silver spoon in his mouth and this gave him (unlike other rich families who can be considered too money-conscious), a useful detachment when making decisions in business, although he enjoyed a profit as much as anybody. But he was never moved primarily by the idea of the financial gain. His success lay in his instinctive judgment of people, which enabled him to gather around him a team of men into whom he could instil, by example, his own ideas of how to run a firm for the good of the shareholders, the partners and the staff, and at the same time to do a wholesome and useful job. His chief interest has always been in human beings, and how he could help them. His camp, the Isle of Thorns, which he created in Ashdown Forest, is a fine memorial to this side of his character. Thousands of boys and young men have enjoyed relaxation and fresh air there, many of them probably unaware of the identity of their benefactor, who provided comfortable huts, a swimming pool, a huge playing field, an aviary, and even a nine-hole golf course for their pleasure.

Alfred Wagg was always considering the staff – they all regarded him as their *père de famille* – with the result that at times of pressure any request for further efforts was immediately responded to. He set the tone for our thinking in these matters. It was he who inaugurated a week's winter holiday for the staff, plus three weeks in the summer and four for certain seniors and ladies who had passed the age of forty. He firmly believed that 'all work and no play makes Jack a dull boy'. He bought Wimbledon vouchers and became a member of the M.C.C. so that the staff could watch the tennis and cricket, never going himself.

The result was that we had what I can only call a sweetness of atmosphere and outlook in the firm which is surely unsurpassed. And it was a sweetness too, *not* a softness, as the results and the progress will testify. The staff felt the partners were their friends, were interested in their well-being and that of their families. They appreciated encouragement, but never resented being carpeted. I learnt early that there are very few people who do not respond to a word of encouragement. As time passed and I was destined to meet more illustrious personages, it became even more clear to me that leaders are lonely. There was an *esprit de corps* in the office which was extraordinary in its strength, and this was fostered in manifold ways: golf matches, tennis matches, annual dinners, a garden party each summer for present and old staff at the Isle of Thorns, a house magazine which after starting on roneoed paper eventually reached the dizzy height of appearing in print under the title of *The Wagtail* – and even bridge competitions.

I confess the last named were not undiluted pleasure. Well do I remember the anxiety of playing against the Prudential Assurance team, headed by the famous Mr Crump, the Joint Secretary, who took his game very seriously. But Mr Crump was too friendly a person to hurt, so we kept up those bridge contests until something of a providential nature turned up to release us. I want to record the high personal regard in which Mr Crump was held by us all. He had the most Cockney voice I have ever heard and a most direct and cutting manner too and was completely without sentiment or partiality in business. He always saw a fly in the ointment, even if there wasn't one, but considering that he rose to eminence in the investment world in the 1930s when choosing the right holdings was probably fraught with more difficulty than ever before, his shrewd judgment served the Prudential very well, I am sure.

There was a spirit in H.W. which made a solid base for progress and I am certain was responsible to a large extent for any success the firm achieved. What applied to the staff applied equally to the partners. Obviously there were at times differences of opinion on business and in methods of approach – anything else would be a little too idyllic to envisage as they were men of such varying outlooks. But under Alfred Wagg's chairmanship, the ship stayed on her course, under full sail, only bending to the wind when essential. Apart from the original partners whom I will discuss later, all subsequent ones graduated to their appointments from the staff, with the exception, I think, of one who joined us for a special purpose and soon became assimilated. They were all executive, and on duty every day, except normal holidays; no odd days off to hunt, shoot or fish, or to poodle-fake at a race meeting or such like; no dilettante approach. All energy was directed towards the benefit and development of the firm. There was an alertness, a tautness, which kept us at our desks whenever it was necessary for the good of the business. When a client wrote to us, or telephoned, we were there, and there was always a longstop in case of absence, for all of us shared our problems together. Yet there was a camaraderie and underlying happiness which were our encouragement and our incentive.

When I first joined the firm in 1921 there were few women, but as business grew, it naturally became necessary to employ more. They were ruled over by Mr Washington, known to all of course as 'George'. How he kept his head passes understanding but amidst all the natural exhibitions of temperament, his calm and serenity remain an example to me to this day. Some of the male old-stagers objected strongly to the influx of ladies into the office and one of our particularly sad and gloomy ones began to dislike going out to lunch because he could not bear 'the damn flappers swarming all over the pavements like hordes of locusts'. What he would say today, I dare not guess.

Rules regarding dress for the ladies were very strict. Sleeves to the wrist always, and too much make-up was frowned upon. Smoking for the male staff was totally prohibited on the ground floor in banking hours and the ladies were not allowed to smoke anywhere at any time. I recall the hullabaloo there was when one of our ladies who occupied her own room insisted on having a cigarette when she wanted. Of course she had her way. Married women were not allowed on the staff. One however used her maiden name to gain employment and caused great consternation when her daughter turned up at the office one Saturday morning. A special concession was made only when two members of the staff got married, but even that was for a limited time only. As love affairs grew, however, the directors were forced to relax the rule. There was much more formality then than is the case today. Christian names were seldom used. It was always 'Miss this' or 'Mr that' though nick-names were acquired, mostly derived from the surname. Thus it was almost inevitable that my sweet secretary at that time, Miss Hoffmeister, long since married to a member of the staff, Claud Metcalf, was always known as 'Hoffy'. And Robert Lunt who cared so tenderly and so willingly for the private accounts and financial affairs of the Directors, was affectionately called 'Lunty'.

But I have deviated from telling my readers more about Alfred Wagg, although perhaps I have already said too much to avoid being dressed down by him, and not for the first time. But whether he likes it or not, I pay him the highest tribute I possibly can and I hereby express my gratitude to him for all he has done for me and my family. In the broadest sense I undoubtedly owe most in my life to three people: to my mother, my wife and to Alfred Wagg, as the head for so long of the firm for which I worked since my early youth.

I must just recount a typical act of kindness on Alfred's part which I remember vividly. It concerned my election to the livery of the Worshipful Company of Fishmongers in 1927. Unknown to me, he had put me up and I was surprised but elated to receive a letter from the Clerk informing me of my election and asking for the remittance of £145, I think it was, to cover the fees. I was a bit anxious, I confess, for this was a comparatively big sum for me to fork out. But I need not have worried, for down came a cheque from Alfred for the amount, with a note, typically expressed in his own handwriting, 'I fancy this will be more useful to you than it is to me at this particular moment.' This was only one of scores of similar acts of generosity and thoughtfulness.

I am afraid I have not been a good member of my Livery, the Fishmongers – inasmuch as it has never really held me. It is one of the twelve great Livery Companies of The City and has been in existence for more than seven hundred years. I am well aware too that the Company utilizes a large proportion of its resources in education and charity, besides administering many charitable and other trusts – all this, apart from being responsible for the purity of all fish entering the Port of London and concerning itself with the fishing industry. It has as liverymen and as members of its Court some of the leading figures in their various ways in the country: its standing is beyond discussion, and its purpose irreproachable. It possesses a hall on London Bridge of exceptional beauty which was destroyed completely in the Great Fire of London in 1666 and was severely damaged in the Second War, only to be rebuilt in more stately form. It has gold plate of priceless value and it owns the portrait of H.M. the Queen by Annigoni which I consider to be a superb painting. The Fishmongers' Company has everything, yet this poor member of the Livery is bored by it. Although I shall go on endeavouring to see the light of day I attribute my lack of interest entirely to my own defects. I do not enjoy ceremony, the loving cup and all that, these things pass me by, and I hope my fellow Fishmongers will not be shocked by what I say.

I do not deny that my nature is incompatible with ceremonial affairs. This was why my heart was never in the parades of my Boy Scout troop before and after the First War. The boys enjoyed marching behind the trumpets and cymbals so I fell in with their wishes. It was the reason which prompted me to forgo the honour of becoming Mayor of Chelsea in the early 1950s when the suggestion was tentatively made to me. I could not visualize myself in robes with a fur collar and a chain round my neck although, goodness knows, I appreciate the wonderful and self-sacrificing work done by Lord Mayors and Mayors all over the country. I honour them, I admire them, and I wish I could resemble them.

I think it was this instinctive feeling in me which prevented me from enjoying being a freemason when I joined the Brotherhood soon after the end of the First War. It was all too matey, too forced. The ritual failed to appeal to me, and shutting oneself up in a tightly closed room for hours on end whilst the same old ceremonial was droned out, all dressed up in evening clothes at three o'clock in the afternoon with a little apron on, was too much for me. I know the masonic movement performs wonders in charitable acts, and in their schools and hospitals. But I am afraid I became desperately impatient of the insincerity and adolescent behaviour of some of the brethren, especially after the dinners which followed the proceedings in the afternoon when they toasted one another to such an extent that the speeches became little more than incoherent and platitudinous drivel. A freemason cannot resign but years ago I let the thing lapse. It is not that I am conceited enough to think that all the thousands and thousands of admirable freemasons in this country – men of the highest standing – are wrong and I am right. All I say is that I regret I cannot share their enthusiasm for the social side, the excessive toasting and ceremonial which appear to be such an integral part of what I have no doubt is otherwise a highly laudable movement. I don't see the point of it. I don't like regimentation.

When the Institute of Directors was re-formed fairly soon after the last war, I was persuaded to become a fellow. But I soon realized I had made a mistake, from my own point of view, and after one or two sallies, offered my resignation. It seems to me to be quite unnecessary to have this colossus of a Directors' trade union – a caucus of right-wing business men – for the protection of directors as a class. If you are a member of a board of directors you should be able to look after yourself, even if the company is a small family business in the provinces. Surely directors do not need the Institute of Directors to nurse them, to stand by them in face of the Inland Revenue for instance, to show them how to avoid a heart attack or how to conduct themselves in their relations with their employees. I know the working man has his trade union, and quite rightly so, for he has had to fight for his present satisfactory position. But why do directors require a trade union? To protect them from what? They should be leaders.

Members of the Council of the Institute have flatteringly suggested I might rejoin, but most ungraciously I have replied that I would only do that in order to resign again, so underlining my distaste for this organization. Perhaps I am unreasonable and anyhow I realize I have something of a blind spot about the Institute, which presumably meets somebody's needs. But their gigantic annual meetings, the swank and pomposity of these jamborees, bring only the worst out of me. Again, I was at a loss to comprehend their rush to intervene in the political sphere in December 1962 at the time of Dean Acheson's criticism of Great Britain's role in world affairs. This self-appointed guardianship of our country's greatness by the Institute, as somebody said, seemed to me precipitate and inappropriate.

The original Helbert Wagg partners were hand-picked by Alfred Wagg. Next in seniority to him came Nigel Campbell, afterwards Sir Nigel Campbell. He was quite inarticulate, distrait, with a tousled mop of white hair and ever absent-minded. I often saw him light a new cigarette immediately after putting a half-smoked one on an ashtray in front of him: at times he would emphasize a point with a cigarette in each hand, all unconsciously. He seemed strangely uneducated, although he frequently wore his Old Etonian tie. I believe he started life as a lumberjack in the forests of Canada and finding his way down to New York, became a bond salesman for William A. Read & Co. I am told he actually used to hump the bonds in his satchel, selling door to door, mostly in the susceptible Middle West.

He was as shrewd and as kind as is possible to imagine, yet given to outbursts of temper which subsided almost before they had erupted. Nigel Campbell was an 'ideas' man, but others had to implement them. He could see through brick walls, and was perpetually in motion, planning, working out schemes for the benefit of the firm. In close association with Mr Montagu Norman, Governor of the Bank of England, he devoted much thought and energy to the reconstruction of industry in the post-war years, especially after the great slump of 1929–31. He was chairman of the Nuffield Fund for the Distressed Areas. For a period he was Joint Master of the Old Berkeley Hunt, but we always thought only from a sense of duty at a difficult time for the pack. He was at his best with his charming wife, Harriette, who was totally deaf, and his three beautiful daughters. Many a happy week-end I spent in this delightfully family atmosphere.

Then came Bernard Barrington, known universally as 'Bernie'. A peach of a man if ever there was one. The perfect example of an English gentleman, fine shot, fisherman, ornithologist and a highly knowledge-able gardener. Bernie was one of the first solicitors to become a partner in a banking firm, a precedent which has been frequently followed since. He always said his main job was to keep us out of the Old Bailey, and certainly nobody knew his company law more thoroughly. Tall, erect, immaculately be-spatted, one of his peculiarities was that he could never go through a door without slamming it after him. We always knew when he had arrived from the resounding crash which followed as he stalked into the partners' room each morning. He was hardly adven-turous – indeed he perhaps erred on the cautious side; but having pointed out possible flaws, he would leave his partners to take the decision and seemed to relish being in a minority of one. His proudest appointment was the Chairmanship of the Legal and General Assurance Society to which, after a long period on the Board, he succeeded at the age of sixty-nine in 1945. It was during his tenure of the office which he held until he became the first President of the Society a year before his death in 1959 that 'the Legal' made such tremendous strides. Bernie invited me to the Legal and General annual dinner one year; in referring to me, the proposer of the toast of 'Our Guests' called me 'The Chairman's Chair-man'. He added that he could imagine no greater honour – for me, and he was right.

Bernie was at Charterhouse at the same time as Sir Patrick Hastings, the famous advocate who never minced his words. The latter and I were fellow members of the Garrick and I occasionally played bridge with him. I found him scathing and derogatory until one day he discovered I was a partner of Bernie's. That changed everything and it became crystal clear that that was the highest recommendation I could have in his eyes. The following extract from Sir Patrick's autobiography describes exactly what we all thought about Bernie. He was the same in manhood as when a boy at Charterhouse. 'During most of the time I was at Charterhouse the head of my house was a boy named W. B. L. Barrington. Beyond the fact that he was a first-class cricketer he did very little and spoke even less: he was merely an outstanding personality. In his presence or indeed within his sphere of influence, nothing mean or dirty could possibly exist. By what means he was able to create the atmosphere in which we lived I have never been quite able to understand, but one thing I do know, if there were more head boys like him, there would be fewer anxious parents. There must be very many fathers who probably never knew his name, and who nevertheless owe him a boundless debt, but I should imagine he would be quite the last person who would wish them to acknowledge it.' What a tribute!

My oldest association in my City life was of course with Max Bonn, afterwards Sir Max Bonn. He showed confidence in me right from the beginning when I joined his firm Bonn & Co. in 1911. At one time, I was apparently his heir. Fortunately I was quite unaware of it until he solemnly disclosed at breakfast to my wife and myself when we were staying with him, that instead of leaving me the bulk of his fortune as had been his intention, he had altered his will and had decided to leave me nothing, adding that he considered I was by then well launched and able to look after myself. My wife and I hardly knew where to look, we were so confused. As a matter of fact, he changed his mind again, as after his death his executors sent me a small cheque.

As he died worth a very considerable sum, I have often contemplated what difference such an inheritance would have brought to my life, just as I often ruminate what would have become of me had I been born rich. I believe I might have been more successful, although probably not so happy. Others tell me any incentive would have been removed. I don't know, and obviously will never know, but I do realize how much I admire the really rich who inherited their wealth and who have still achieved additional status during their lives, and reached greater heights than their forbears. Their approach to problems must be different, their responsibilities are heavier; so much more is expected of them than of ordinary mortals, for right from the start of their lives, they grow up with strings attached to them. This is an aspect which is disregarded by the Socialists when they cry 'Bleed the rich!' Personally I do not know what England would do without her good dukes, peers and other members of the aristocracy, so many of whom perform boring, unheralded but important functions in their respective counties of such a varied character, just as a matter of duty and with little joy attached.

Max Bonn had a most brilliant mind, yet it cannot be said that he had commensurate success, or happiness. Born a German Jew, refined, cultured and hyper-sensitive, son of a well known German banker, he established his banking firm in London in 1910. Before he died in 1943 he had the misfortune to pass through two wars against his native country. He felt both most acutely, and the unhappy personal position he found himself in too, especially in the 1914–18 war. He was awarded a K.B.E. in 1926 for his services on behalf of juvenile labour, a cause which had caught his imagination and to which he devoted much of his life. Nobody deserved a distinction more.

In business he was hopeless on his own, for he found it almost impossible to take a decision. He saw every point of view and his vivid imagination, if allowed a chance, tied him up in inextricable knots. But as a partner, in a team, he was of priceless value, so long as he was not permitted to mesmerize us by his qualms and anxieties. He was a really 'white' man, and a fine host and wonderful raconteur of funny, subtle little Jewish stories. Despite his sensitivities he could always laugh at himself, but we had to be careful not to hurt him. He adored England, its tradition and its pomp. If he is ever born again, I know he would like to be at least an Earl or a Marquis. Max Bonn had exquisite taste, and by association and example he carried on my education, and extended my appreciation of furniture, pictures and music. He lost two minor fortunes, and was on both occasions saved from financial disaster by the opportune death of a rich relation. A man bulging with brain, lovable

September 1915

St Albans, before leaving for France, August 1914:
Pte Wilson, W.L.F., Pte Mackness

in so many ways, showing so much friendship and generosity to a large circle of knowns and unknowns: yet what? Considering his talents, hardly an outstanding success in life by any unbiased assessment? I am afraid so, but he taught me a great deal, for which I shall ever remain indebted to him.

I have mentioned Albert Palache. It is difficult to give a true portrayal of him, for he was utterly unusual and conformed to no pattern at all. He also was a Jew and often told me he had Dutch, Spanish, Portuguese and Turkish blood in him – certainly with a fez on his head, he looked the part. He was an international banker to his finger-tips – nobody could mistake him for any other profession. He spoke the major continental languages with equal ease. He was an artist in business – it was the pure accomplishment of a deal which gave him the real pleasure – not the financial gain. A vain man, yet so naïve in his vanity as to make those of us who knew him well disregard it. Wherever he went, business came to him. People from all over the world sought his advice – business was instinctive in him, morning, noon and night. Extravagant, and generous, he knew every good *maître d'hôtel* in Europe. He adored to be recognized as he entered a restaurant. We always called him 'Imperial Palache'.

I remember one grand holiday in 1935 which my wife and I spent with him and his third wife Adeline as their guests at the Salzburg Festival (when he died three previous wives and his widow were still living). We were staying in the Europe Hotel and every detail was arranged by Albert with perfect precision and taste. There were tickets each night for the Opera and I still recall with warmth and joy the wonderment of Toscanini's conducting and Lotte Lehmann's superb singing in *Fidelio* and *Rosenkavalier*. Her performance was of the highest order in both musical and dramatic reception. Toscanini was idolized at Salzburg where he was always received with vociferous cheers. His conducting made an overwhelming impression on me, and his judgment of relationships in music was quite unerring.

When I say Albert was generous, I do not only mean materially, for he was kind in his thinking too. Just as Max Bonn adored the average Englishman because he was English, so Palache tended to keep aloof from them. He had a few really good friends. He never pretended to be anything but a 'bloody foreigner' and indeed was proud of it. He could

[87]   G

write English better than most of us yet in his talking he seemed to be at pains to stress his foreign accent. There was nobody more scrupulous in his business life, nobody more fair and calm in his judgments. At one time his contribution to the profits of Helbert Wagg was so considerable that I believe his share was as much as $33\frac{1}{3}\%$ of the total. As time passed, we became closer and closer together and out of the office we saw much of one another. Palache was a special article – a giant among arbitrageurs – an international figure, at home as well in a banking parlour as in a casino – we are not likely to see many more like him.

Palache liked the opposite sex and there are endless stories of the ladies in distress at the casino tables whom he assisted. He turned the luck of one of his beneficiaries so effectively on one occasion that the next day she sent him a gold cigarette case in gratitude. When I was made a partner in Helbert Wagg, he presented it to my wife. To this day she uses it as a powder box.

I always regretted that his pioneering work in helping to establish the beet sugar industry in this country went unnoticed by the authorities. Beet sugar production was a major factor in the war period and after, when the import of this commodity was so difficult. He also did yeoman work on the Film Council which passed unrecognized.

I hardly dare to mention the remaining partner, Lawrence E. Jones, now Sir Lawrence Jones Bt, 'Jonah', since he has himself written an entertaining, light-hearted description of Helbert Wagg's doings and of City life as seen through his own eyes during the time he was still a member of the firm. Business and City activities have changed since he retired, fifteen or twenty years ago – perhaps we are more professional or competitive, I don't know. He was always at heart a man of letters rather than a business man. He enlivened us with his wit. A prospectus which he wrote regarding the bonds of a sham 'State of Impecuniosité' was a masterpiece of skit and fun. 'Jonah' has attained eminence as an author since he retired from the firm in 1945, but he still loves to visit No. 41 and go over old times spent together. His decision to resign required courage but there is no doubt that the change brought him more satisfaction, as compared with the hurly-burly, perhaps more exacting, certainly less free, life of a City banker.

Those were the six partners of the firm who were to lay the foundations for this comparatively unknown House and to develop it to the leading position it was destined to hold. They were a well balanced team, a mixed bag, all men of high character and standing, enterprising but sound.

Chapter 9

APART FROM MY OWN foreign exchange department, the growth of the business immediately after the war came by way of international stock arbitrage with Amsterdam, Brussels, Paris and New York. Just as there were big margins in currencies as between the different centres, so these discrepancies existed in securities of the international type, and Albert Palache was quick to take advantage of these lucrative opportunities. Together with some local Stock Exchange business of a desultory nature, our activities were more or less confined to arbitrage in the immediate period after the war. Efforts to enter the new issue business were however to some extent successful in October 1920 when we made an issue of £3 million 8% seven-year notes for Explosive Trades Ltd at 96%. Note how expensive it was. I seem to remember this company later became a part of Imperial Chemical Industries.

The major development, however, started in mid-1921 when the firm broke into the foreign loan market hitherto restricted to bankers with entrenched positions both here and in New York. These latter had to face acute competition from us, with Albert Palache as the prime negotiator for all foreign loans, which were always negotiated in the country of the prospective debtor. Palache's policy was to make loan contracts as short as possible, and this paid off well, for it was in sharp contrast with the policy of most American lenders. Their contracts, because they were as yet unskilled in such matters, were enormously lengthy, and attempted to provide for every possible contingency and development – a virtual impossibility which so often resulted in success for our firm in competition.

The first scoop for Helbert Wagg was the public issue with Higginson & Co. in August 1921 of £500,000 Government of Iceland 7%

thirty-year Sterling Loan at a price of 91. Alfred Wagg had the high Icelandic honour of Order of the Falcon conferred on him, as a mark of the Icelandic Government's appreciation of the firm's efforts.

The year 1922 was a very fruitful one as far as foreign loans were concerned, beginning in February with the greatest coup of all, a £3 million 7% thirty-year loan to the Department of the Seine, the premier Department of France, comprising also the City of Paris, with an equivalent *tranche* issued in New York at the same time by Kuhn, Loeb and Co. I took no part in these operations, being fully occupied with foreign exchange, but I was aware of course of the extreme difficulties encountered and the bitter competition from, I think, no less than seven different banking houses. This achievement was a combined effort of Max Bonn and Palache, but all the partners gave the operation their unrestricted attention, so important was it to establish a foothold in this type of business. From the outset it proved to be an unqualified success.

In May 1922 we handled a small loan to the Magasins du Louvre which had opened a store in Oxford Circus. The loan was all right, but the store never had much success in this country.

Then in June there followed a loan to the City of Greater Prague £1½ million 7½% thirty years at 92½% again with the New York issue handled by our friends, Kuhn Loeb. Prague turned out to be a first class debtor before the Second War, and resumed service of the loan promptly after the war, but for some reason of their own they decided to blot their excellent record by defaulting on the very last repayment instalment in 1952.

Even in those days Helbert Wagg had some 'cloth cap' clients. A fishmonger whose wife had some Prague Bonds called at the office to ask a question about the payment of a coupon. He eventually saw the Manager who asked if the lady was the *legitimate* holder of the Bonds. The word 'legitimate' cast what the fishmonger called 'a naspersion' on his wife, and only the polished brass grille saved the Manager from being punched on the nose.

When the regular period came along for the drawing of bonds for redemption, in accordance with the terms of the prospectus, they were all picked out of a box by hand in the board room, in the presence of notaries and others – so much more thrilling than the present day mechanical machinations of 'Ernie'. In those days it took sometimes as long as two weeks to get the allotments of new issues out to the applicants. This involved writing all their names, addresses, etc. on huge allotment sheets. Now of course by more advanced methods, and even with much bigger issues, it requires sometimes as little as twenty-four hours to complete the whole operation. 'Stags' is the description given to applicants who apply for an issue for the sole purpose of selling their allotment as quickly as possible, with a profit they hope. They are expert judges of whether an issue is likely to go to a premium, and they act in devious and varied ways in order to secure as big a total allotment as they can. This is often done by applying in false names, different names at the same address, block applications and many other devices. In the early 1920s they were not as wily as they have since become, and the great fun then used to be what was called stag-hunting, or stag-spotting, i.e., deleting all the obvious ones before reaching a basis for allotment. All the same, the stag is a useful animal at times and, except in blatant cases, I was always rather protective towards him and did not mind giving him a run for his money, when he had ensured over-subscription of our issues!

August 1922 saw further activity, as, jointly with the British Overseas Bank, we arranged the consolidation of the Government of Roumania Loans into one amount of £14½ million 4% Consolidated Loan, undertaken for the most part by Lawrence Jones. We also issued, to provide Roumania with liquid funds, 4% External Bonds to the value of £1 million.

These operations involved much to-ing and fro-ing between the various countries and were by no means as simple to arrange as I may appear to have indicated. Frequent visits, lengthy cables, enormous legal tangles to ensure the security of the loans, drafting contracts, prospectuses – multifarious items calling for the highest skill in negotiation and knowledge of the business; and endless harangues with mayors and city councillors, utterly ignorant of finance, with political wire-pullers all throwing their stones into the pool. It made 1922 one great panjandrum year of immense activity.

Today an announcement that one was spending one's holiday in Tokyo, for instance, would evoke no particular surprise, but thirty or forty years ago, with air travel in its infancy, a journey to the Continent was an event. So, when Albert Palache went on his business travels in Europe, there was an aura of excitement about it all, almost like olden times when this country sent emissaries to Europe on various ambassadorial missions. He was a traveller *par excellence*, always insisting in all circumstances on packing and unpacking his bags himself, like all seasoned travellers.

To top these efforts, there followed in the late autumn a public issue of £1½ million 6½% 1st Debenture Stock for Marconi Wireless, with valuable conversion rights. This operation took place at the beginning of the home wireless boom and although the issue was not made in this connection it caught the public imagination and demand for prospectuses was so enormous that The City police had to be called in to control the crowds clamouring for them.

So we were well launched as an Issuing House with all these feathers in our cap and although 1923 was much quieter, giving us time to get our breath, it was notable for a big issue for the English Electric Co. Ltd. This year was politically significant, of course, for the occupation of the Ruhr by the French and the wild inflation of the German currency, which gave the Foreign Exchange Department, playing with fire I must admit, rare opportunities for talent. Printing presses were working at full stretch and the mark was tumbling catastrophically. It was not, however, one stone-like drop, as might be thought in retrospect by looking at graphs. Sometimes powerful buying took place, mainly by the great banking firm of Mendelssohn & Company operating from their Amsterdam office (one thought officially on behalf of the German Government). These movements were directed for Mendelssohns by the agile mind of a certain Fritz Manheimer and, when it suited him, he would reverse his tracks from one minute to the next, keeping all foreign exchange dealers in a state of frozen anxiety if they were unfortunate enough to find themselves with open positions. One had to be pretty nippy to avoid being caught in the pincer movement. We all knew this crazy, headlong depreciation of a currency could not continue like that for ever, and must stop some time. But when?

My brother was working in Hamburg at this time and was designated by my firm to send us monthly reports on the German situation. For these articles he was paid £25 per annum in sterling. By skilful exchange of these pounds, he was able to live, feed and keep himself out of this minute sum. He told us that when he went to the bank to change a few pounds, he took a suit-case with him to carry the equivalent mark notes away. The suffering and desolation amongst the rentiers, pensioners, etc. in Germany was cruel. Savings invested in fixed interest bearing securities were completely wiped out and those dependent upon their savings endured awful hardship. Those who owed money benefited. The rush was into tangible objects, machinery, goods, etc. These were instantly snapped up whenever they came on offer. The problem was how to restore confidence in money, for the fall in the value of the currency had been so disastrous that financial operations were being conducted on a barter basis.

The mark was eventually stabilized by the issue of a new rentenmark, worth one million million of the old marks, and the rehabilitation of the economic situation was further advanced in 1924 when the famous Dawes Loan was launched. Thereafter it almost became international policy to concentrate on the reconstruction of Germany and Central Europe and for some years the German Government, as well as private enterprise companies, were enabled to borrow big sums in the foreign money markets. In consequence, with more stable conditions established, economic activity there grew feverishly apace.

As part of this official policy of putting Germany and Europe back on their feet, the firm were instrumental, mainly through Palache's brilliance, in transacting a very large business with Germany and with Continental Europe and Scandinavia generally in the form of privately placed loans to, and investment in the shares of, a very wide range of institutions and industrial companies, including some of the most famous names in Germany, Holland, Sweden, Denmark, Austria and Belgium. Palache was supreme in his handling of these operations, and although in retrospect it can perhaps be said that his judgment was not always infallible (whose is?), there was an insatiable appetite in this country for these investments, especially amongst certain of the bigger institutions. It was absolutely essential to get Europe going again and, as part of this plan, international lending was encouraged and its need fully recognized.

When from 1922 onwards it was decided to help the poorer, and therefore less credit-worthy, borrowers, by means of what were known as League of Nations Reconstruction Loans, spread over several years, to such countries as Bulgaria, Hungary, Greece, and also extended to the Municipality of Danzig, the firm, in association with the British Overseas Bank, secured two issues to Danzig, one for the Municipality for £1½ million 7% Sterling Bonds at 90% in April 1925, and in June 1927 another for the Free City of Danzig Tobacco Monopoly of £1,520,000 6½% twenty-year Sterling Bonds State Loan at 91%. Not a penny has been paid on either loan since the outbreak of war in 1939, even though in each case the Chairman of the Financial Committee of the League of Nations was appointed the Trustee and the loans had the most powerful security it would be possible to imagine; secured up to the hilt, but without much avail!

And so our business went on, and grew. Its base was broadening all the while and was increasingly embracing English domestic business. Activity was intense and the progress and development were encouraging, especially since only a few years previously this firm, old-established as it was but thoroughly rejuvenated, had really only a comparatively trivial business.

A good and loyal staff is the main prop of any business and ours was buckling-to in a magnificent way, becoming more experienced and skilled all the while. It had of necessity to be increased. Palache took as his assistant Denis Scott, a man of high academic attainment at Balliol who rapidly acquired the necessary technique and was able to relieve Palache of much of his routine work. Later he left us for stockbroking for a while, eventually finding his right place as Chairman and Managing Director of an industrial company. Another young man possessing great possibilities who joined us was Jack Frazer, but sadly he was killed whilst skiing soon after he arrived. Douglas Jardine was also recruited and was actually on our staff when he went to Australia as Captain of England on the famous body-line bowling tour of 1932–33. He was popular in the office, but his somewhat inflexible and dogged approach, whilst ensuring our battering the Australians at cricket, did not seem the best ingredient for banking and he took some directorships elsewhere and was very successful.

Around these years in the late 1920s Helbert Wagg became a veritable nursery for the *jeunesse dorée*. Those who did not fit into the scheme of things for one reason or another, transferred to other occupations, always, it seemed, grateful for the efficient training they had received with us. Practically all made excellent niches for themselves, and remain our good friends.

Sunday, 3 May 1926 saw the beginning of the disastrous General Strike which, lasting for ten days, completely dislocated life in Great Britain and had a deleterious and enduring effect on industry. This is a kaleidoscopic subject. It comes into nearly every memoir of the period and everyone claims to have had a decisive effect upon it. It is salutary to remember that the coal miners came out on strike on 1 May 1926 and did not return to work until November 27 of that year.

My humble role was that of a special constable and I performed beat duty from the Police Station near St Mary Abbots Church. It was dull tedious work, mostly in Gloucester Road. Whilst on duty, I remember being met by a friend who greeted me with the remark 'Nice to see you, but you are rather off your beat, aren't you?' Thinking he was accusing me of lack of attention to duty, I replied hotly 'What do you mean? This *is* my beat!' not realizing it was his way of saying I was doing a different job from usual.

In May 1926 new ground was broken by the formation of the British & German Trust whose main object was to finance medium-sized German industrial concerns, by means of mortage loans. Alfred Wagg was the Chairman, with Albert Palache, Lord Ashfield and Sir George May, later Lord May (the last named representing the Prudential Assurance Co. Ltd.) as the Britishers, with four of the leading bankers in Berlin constituting the balance of the Board. The Trust got away to an excellent start and high hopes were entertained of a constantly expanding and remunerative business on the Continent. However, these hopes were dashed by the collapse of the thirties, culminating in the war in 1939. German influence and representation on the Board had necessarily to be eliminated and the Trust was faced with very heavy depreciation and forced to default on its preference shares. Later Albert Palache succeeded Alfred Wagg as Chairman, and had the satisfaction of seeing, under its changed name of Broadstone Investment Trust Ltd, all the losses more than made good, arrears of dividend paid off and the Trust take its place as one of the leaders in its field. On Palache's death at the beginning of 1958 I succeeded him as Chairman and H. E. Netherclift, who had served the Trust as Secretary and Director from its inception, was the Deputy Chairman. I take little credit for its healthy and vigorous condition, which is in the main due to the investment genius of Netherclift, supported by expert colleagues in the persons of Lewis Whyte and Charles Wainman, and formerly by Mackenzie Hay, who died a few months ago after more than twenty-three years as a loyal and inspired Director.

Some time after the end of the war in late 1949 the ordinary stock of the Trust was dealt in on The Stock Exchange at £1 10s. 0d. per £100 of stock, and I do not mean to boast when I say that its approximate equivalent value at the end of 1962, allowing for bonus issues and new issues of capital, has increased nearly twelve hundred times. But readers will please not take this as a tip! If the Board has a secret it is that it is small, it acts quickly but thoughtfully, and tends towards an unorthodox and original line in its investment policy.

In 1927 and 1928 came a spate of investment trusts, and in conjunction with American investment interests, Helbert Wagg started the Transoceanic Investment Trust in August 1928. After a chequered start, it too has emerged most successfully. Transoceanic also incorporates the Trading Investment Company, another trust set up many years ago to invest funds belonging to the Strathcona family. Later there were established the Westpool and the Ashdown Investment Trusts. Being well timed, they had to face no early setback and are now eminently prosperous. Investment trusts form a natural ancillary activity for a banking house and independent directors ensure discrimination in investment. They have become of recent years an extremely popular medium of investment and certainly do, to my mind, secure for the widow and orphan and the investor who has no inclination or time to watch over his holdings regularly, skilled management and a wide spread of investments.

There were many other important operations, amongst them substantial issues in 1926 and later in 1930, for the Gas Light & Coke Co., the Norwegian-controlled Kellner Partington Paper & Pulp Co., and the introduction to the London market of the Ely, Ipswich and King's

Lynn Beet Sugar Companies (known as the Van Rossum Group), which with other companies were later, in 1936, merged into the British Sugar Corporation.

Boom conditions continued throughout 1928 and the first part of 1929. The American market reached dizzy heights and brokers were no longer estimating whether stocks would rise but were prognosticating the rises which would *actually* take place. There was no stemming the optimism and while it lasted it was a paradise for the bulls. There had been a slight shadow over the horizon as a result of the unexplained death from a fall from his private aeroplane in July 1928 of Captain Alfred Loewenstein, the Belgian financier, founder of the Hydro-Electric Securities Corporation and the International Holdings and Investment Co. This calamity had caused great excitement and a spectacular decline in the shares of these companies on the Brussels Bourse. This movement perhaps was an example of the tenseness of the situation, and looking back, might have been construed as an indicative straw in the wind.

We ourselves watched the rise in the stock market with ever growing anxiety. It was like a boil which would never burst, yet which became bigger every day. We were very careful to keep our books square. Prices reached absurd heights and fortunes were being made on paper. It is at such times that nerves are tested for it becomes almost irresistible, when in the midst of the excitement, not to participate. Yet the higher the rise, the bigger the fall, and the more damage done to the burnt finger when the setback comes. However, we resisted and so were unscathed, although we found no joy in the ensuing lack of business. This reminds me that at the time of our leaving the gold standard in 1931 after such a brief period of stability, we thought we might protect our reserves if we invested some part by buying in the forward market some commodities such as metals and rubber. This we proceeded to do believing the prices would rise as the pound fell. But it was an unsuccessful venture because we had not realized that as Great Britain was the biggest buyer of raw materials in the world, she was in a position to call the tune. So, against all economic theories, the prices fell rather than rose, and eventually we had to dispose of our tons and tons of these commodities at a loss.

As 1929 drew on, economic conditions began to look less rosy in the world. In September and October of that year the New York Stock Exchange boom seemed at last to be in danger of bursting. There were wild bouts of selling, huge turnovers, accompanied by rumours of serious distress. Talks of 'banking support' buoyed up hopes, but this proved to be just empty surmise.

Meanwhile in England there was a most untoward event: on 23 September 1929, Clarence Hatry who had enjoyed a romantic rise to fame in the previous years as a financier, with three confederates, was charged with obtaining a very large sum of money by false pretences. This resulted in desperate debts – a figure of £19 million was mentioned but a certain part was secured – mostly to banks and stockbrokers. A feature of the catastrophe was that the outside public and the small investor bore little share of the direct loss – probably the only item on the credit side. Immense anxiety followed and this had its reflection in heavy selling on Continental Bourses and especially in New York, already in a highly sensitive condition.

I need not give a detailed repetition of the offences, but the main subsequent interest lies in the fact that they affected professional City people, whom some said should not have been so easily deceived. I do not know Clarence Hatry, but from all I have heard, he is a brilliant and persuasive personality. It was warming to note the rallying which took place at that time in The City to friends who had sustained losses and to observe the co-operative efforts to get heavily involved stockbrokers and others on to their feet again after their disastrous setbacks.

Later on, in December 1929, there followed still another City sensation of magnitude, which shook confidence further, when difficulties in the Inveresk Paper Group were announced, involving the resignation of Mr William Harrison, the Chairman. I remember that when a year or two later Mr Martin Coles Harman was indicted for fraud and misapplication of funds, The City felt it had suffered enough. And so it certainly had, although severe strains were undoubtedly left on The City image that such mishaps could have gone to the lengths they did without detection.

The slump in New York dragged on and off until the middle of 1932 and it brought to Helbert Wagg a marked diminution in business activity. There was a lack of enterprise in industry, no inducement to take on new commitments, and in these conditions bankers do not thrive. It was a terrible period for everybody and it was not aided by a lamentable fall in all commodity prices. Looking back on this most catastrophic of all slumps in my memory, I sometimes am grateful for the experience. Indeed, you can almost divide The City into those who went through this chastening time and those who didn't, and note the difference.

On top of all this, and perhaps to some extent because of it, there came the suicide in March 1932 of Ivar Kreuger, of Swedish Match fame, and the disclosure of his frauds which brought large numbers of investors to their knees. I do not need to enlarge on its results and after-effects, although for fascinating reading I recommend Robert Shaplen's book *Kreuger, Genius and Swindler*. I also strongly recommend *The Great Crash 1929* by J. K. Galbraith. It is more exciting than most thrillers.

A little before Kreuger's death, Helbert Wagg had been involved in a transaction with him, from which, however, we emerged safe and sound. We became aware that he wished to buy £1 million nominal of Roumania 4% External Bonds, a loan which as I have mentioned we issued in 1922. At the time the price was around 50. We managed to secure the amount required from certain holders and duly offered them to Kreuger at that price. He agreed to purchase, and there was then left the question of payment and delivery. We were not by any means happy about Kreuger's reputation, which was beginning to be smirched. He wanted delivery in Amsterdam to which we consented, but we insisted on a banker's cheque in payment. Kreuger jibbed at this, but finally agreed. Netherclift journeyed to Amsterdam with the bonds and duly delivered them to Kreuger's right-hand man. He had been instructed not to let go of them until he had the cheque! He offered the bonds with his right hand and clutched the cheque at the same time with his left. I heard later that Kreuger put the bonds in his balance sheet at their par value, 100, twice what he paid for them.

For many years Nigel Campbell, who had unique contacts in the United States from his previous connections there, had been developing an American Department, headed by Walter Mann who took as his assistant James O'Brien, my old associate in the foreign exchange department. This involved so many trips across the Atlantic that the Directors considered the volume of business made it desirable to establish a New York office, and in consequence Helbert, Wagg & Co. (New York) Ltd, was incorporated on 13 April 1929. This proved an unfortunate venture, due in main to its timing, and having been crippled soon after birth, it was eventually allowed to lapse, merely the name being retained, but no office. All the same, a substantial business was transacted by us and the American Department made a useful contribution to the general building of the firm.

Chapter 10

IMUST NOW CATCH UP WITH MY OWN PERSONAL DOINGS which I last mentioned when the business of the foreign exchange dept was fading somewhat. On the restoration of the Gold Standard in 1925 comparative stability of the exchanges was established. James O'Brien had gone off to co-operate in the American Department and I was drafted into what we called the Dealing Department, while George Bolton became our chief cashier. Thus began my first close contact with The Stock Exchange and many of its members, for my functions were to keep intimate watch over all movements of prices, to assess trends, to execute orders for clients and to give them advice on stock and share investment. I became entirely absorbed in securities, and in my new capacity it also was my job to render service to those in the firm handling new issues in advising on the price at which to fix a placing or public issue. I was interviewing stockbrokers most of the day, and kept everybody in the firm posted as to what was cooking on The Stock Exchange. Our clientele was growing all the while, so my life was again very active.

In those days, not always successfully I fear, we also operated on our own account. It was not always successful because everybody took a hand, and when all had different views on the outlook, failure and confusion could be anticipated. It is notorious that no so-called experts and economists ever agree on trends – it would be impossible to expect that they should. But Alfred Wagg, George Bolton and I put our heads together and ran a highly remunerative book in the Gilt Edged market. We permitted no interference. I remember after a while George and I thought we would like to celebrate and give Alfred Wagg a little dinner. So I went along to Boulestin and ordered a slap-up meal – I

High Holborn 1910

The new City, 1962

know it included caneton pressé, for I had never tasted it before. It was quite expensive, so I asked the *maître d'hôtel* to let me sign the bill, in order not to embarrass Alfred by indelicately dragging out notes from my pocket. After the dinner I was handed the bill, scanned it apprehensively, put my signature on it and gave it back to the waiter. Whereupon Alfred said, 'What are you doing? Signing the bill! A dangerous habit!' It was the first time I had done such a thing, and I do not think I have ever repeated it over all these years.

My wife and I are not regular frequenters of restaurants, preferring to dine quietly at home by ourselves or with the family, or to entertain friends there. I have a horror of uncomfortable restaurants where you sit on an inadequate chair huddled together with people at adjacent tables listening to your conversation. That is purgatory for me and the reason why, as we have grown older, we have tended to discard the 'cosy' little restaurants in Soho and Chelsea, and we are not anyhow great gourmets.

My work continued more or less on the lines recounted above for some years, unchanged in essence, but with an ever increasing volume of business. The first marketing arrangement I had to handle was for the Prudential Assurance Co. in connection with Marks & Spencer with whom they had an intimate relationship. Marks & Spencer needed money and issued, under our auspices, £1 million in a 6% I Mortgage Debenture Stock at 102% and one million 7% Preference Shares at 21/-. The issues were underwritten by the Prudential. But they had no attraction for the public and were complete flops, so that the Prudential had to take up practically the entire amount. I had to look after the market on their behalf, and strangely enough, although the public issue had been so poorly received, a demand soon arose on The Stock Exchange. By feeding it gently and carefully, the whole of both blocks were sold at a satisfactory profit within a fairly brief space of time, thus fully justifying the confidence of the sponsors. It was a simple operation, looking back on it, but it was my first, and for me, substantial business of its sort.

We were very proud of our early connection with Marks & Spencer. Even in those days, it was obvious to us that this concern had genius behind it. Somebody once called Lord Marks 'the Artist of the Penny Bazaars'. Certainly he has gone very far since we acted for him in his first call for money from the public. It has been a story of dynamic leadership, of remarkable enterprise and a unique flexibility of vision. A success which has been created, extraordinarily enough, without any advertising, the reputation and the quality of Marks & Spencer goods being passed by word of mouth. My wife tells me that one of the secrets of their success is to be found in the willingness to change goods at any branch, or to make a cash refund.

The years 1930, 1931, 1932 and 1933 were indeed lean for us, and nothing worth recording springs to my mind.

As for my private life during these years since the war, I continued to live happily at home with my mother and sister in our small house in Victoria Gardens. My world was widening. I was travelling about the Continent very frequently and was enjoying holidays in places like Biarritz and Ostend. Social life was also opening up, and I found myself on hostesses' lists for dance invitations. In 1924 I had bought my first car, a two-seater Standard, with a big dickey in which I used to pile the family for jaunts around the countryside. I was, and remain, utterly unmechanical, and my friends were not surprised early in my motoring career to hear that, when the car over-heated, I had poured cold water into the petrol tank, whose nozzle was adjacent.

My income during the juicy foreign exchange days was big indeed. I spent it all, designedly, although anyhow I am not a saver by nature. I was bent on acquiring my own 'old school tie' and I tasted, with some satisfaction, the joys of the social life. It was of course of a fairly restricted nature. It involved hunt balls, week-end parties in small country houses, golf and general friendly, but simple gaiety. There was wine, mostly champagne, there were women too, and if theatres, concerts and an occasional night club can be called song, there was also song. The intensity and demands of my work required relaxation, and after all, I was young, gullible, and innocent too, I fear, in a new wonder world, into which at that time I did not bother to probe too much. I was merely caught up in its swing and I enjoyed it considerably.

I was undoubtedly susceptible to the charms of the fair sex and I had numerous girl friends. I was always being accused by mothers of leading their daughters up the garden path and then scaring off. If that was true, it was quite unconscious. I suppose I took my girl friends too much for granted, not realizing then, as I do now, that the main object of most girls is to hook a man as quickly as they can. One young lady, when I was packed off with her by her mother to be shown round the garden, made quite sure I knew where she stood when she said to me, 'please don't ask me to marry you, will you?' I didn't tell her the thought had never entered my head, nor that at that minute I felt she was one of the most conceited, unattractive girls I had ever met.

I was very comfortably attended to, indeed horribly spoilt I expect, at home by my mother. She never interfered with my freedom to come and go as I liked and never cross-questioned me about my doings. Thinking back, I am amazed at her self-restraint and tolerance. On one of her birthdays I gave a dinner in a small back room in a favourite little Italian restaurant in Frith Street, Soho. Chianti flowed, and in my excitement I smashed the chandelier. My mother never reproached me, indeed she never mentioned the matter.

But early in 1930 something stirred. I was invited just before Whitsun to dine by Mr and Mrs George Henderson at their house in Cadogan Place, where I had frequently enjoyed hospitality at dinners and family dances. It was a big party – George and his wife were splendid hosts – and I had the good fortune to sit next to a beautiful woman called Mrs Hugh Reeves. After dinner we played bridge and I was partnered against Mrs Reeves and her husband. The occasion was a success, and the impression produced was apparently favourable for I was invited to join their house party the following week-end at their country house at Honingham, near Norwich. It later transpired that Mrs Reeves could not be there owing to indisposition, and I found, on arrival, that her daughter by her first marriage, Cynthia Walter, was acting as hostess. We sat next to one another at dinner, and at once there was mutual sympathy. Almost immediately she went back to Germany to continue her studies, during which there was much cementing correspondence, and eventually on 14 April 1931 we were married at Brompton Parish Church.

But it was not all beer and skittles to obtain the approval of my wife's stepfather, Hugh Reeves, to our marriage. He was a wealthy solicitor, who with his brother Herbert, had inherited a small family business from their father. They soon became aware that there was no money in advising on making wills, arranging marriage settlements and such like.

They therefore branched out into property deals, eventually accumulating for their own respective families a very considerable fortune, which was only realized after the death of the two brothers. Hugh Reeves was a great character and had many facets, generous benefactor to his old school, Cheltenham, famous rowing man, dabbling in politics and farming, and a supporter of lost causes. He was the finest judge of port I ever met, and could tell the shipper and the year from a quick sniff at the decanter. This may not be so unusual, but at the time it seemed amazing to me. Whilst I had been welcomed as a week-end guest in his country house, it was a different matter when this unknown person was asking for the hand of his stepdaughter. He summoned me to his presence. Who was I? What were my prospects? Where had I been to school? Knowing there was no easy answer to any of his questions, which I found rather galling, I referred him to Max Bonn, whom he had met a few times. The latter gave me a good report, it appeared, as thereafter all hesitation was removed and I was accepted by 'Pop' Reeves and the family in a warm-hearted fashion.

Married life cannot be analysed. For each individual it is different. Before I married, I could imagine nothing which appealed to me less, particularly the restrictions, and what I thought was the bondage. I had enjoyed too long a period of bachelordom, or at least I thought I was enjoying it. I was thirty-five, she was twenty, and it has been a wonderful partnership. As we grow older it becomes ever firmer and happier. The marvel is how she tolerates me. I count myself unduly cherished to have had two such exceptional women in my life to support and help me. My mother who so lovingly assisted my early development, and my wife who since then has taken over the wheel and sustained and encouraged me without ever faltering or showing any desire to give up the task, as she certainly has had good reason to do all too often. Happily, my mother and my wife saw eye to eye on most points. Here again my mother displayed her natural breadth of outlook, by never feeling an atom of jealousy towards this inexperienced young woman who had come into my life to take pride of place. How I bless that dinner at the Hendersons' in early 1930!

I could write pages about our married life, the fun and joy of being with my wife, and what I owe to her. But characteristically, she has begged me to confine myself only to what is necessary. 'Say the least you can about me.' These have been her instructions. Although I feel with her that these matters are personal, I hesitate to obey her fully, for she has outstanding qualities and such a clear outlook. She has been an ideal mother and wife – the centrepiece of the family. We all lean on her.

Over these last thirty-two years my wife's and my tastes have grown alike, in reading, in the theatre, the opera, and in films, and in painting we have similar views almost invariably. She knows exactly what I like and vice versa. My main interest in life has been business, which provides for me all the fun, stimulation and interest I can wish. It embraces so much, such diversity of people and situations; never narrow and enclosed, always left wondering what the morrow will bring forth. My wife is completely unmathematical and unaware of the ways of the business world, and admits to total ignorance of stocks and shares. Nevertheless, she shows pride in exhibiting a print of one of her ancestors on her mother's side, Sir Thomas Bury, who was 'Lord Chief Baron of His Majesty's Court of Exchequer' from 1716 to 1722. I tell her the financial blood has thinned out a bit since then! We share our friends, of all types, nationalities and creeds, but we rarely entertain for purely business reasons, and I have never permitted business to encroach unduly upon our family life. Perhaps I have been lucky that it has not been necessary, but anyhow it has prevented impatience and frustration.

We spent our honeymoon in a tiny rented cottage at Trebetherick, on St Enodoc Golf Course, North Cornwall. I don't recommend honeymoons as a general rule: discovering how the girl looks cleaning her teeth or before she has made herself up in the morning are chastening considerations! Ours passed off happily, my wife having her first golf and bridge lessons during the fortnight. Sadly, however, the time was dominated by material factors. We were in the very heart of a ghastly slump. Conditions in The City had been appalling for over a year – business was at a minimum, there were no profits at all, and the gay carefree days of the twenties were over. It was a very sad affair, and I had nothing to fall back upon, having 'invested' any possible surplus of the previous years in living up to the hilt and learning, by experiences and travel, what was going on in the world. So when it had come to buying an engagement ring, things were very tight and a small second-hand eternity ring had to suffice. Not that my fiancée remonstrated – such things don't matter to her. The wedding was a small affair, since my wife declined to sponge on her stepfather, who would have been only too delighted to have been responsible for a big fashionable wedding. But it was not in keeping, either with our thinking, or with the restrictive period in which the wedding took place. But there was to be a choir in the church and there were some lovely flowers – these were insisted upon, and it was the bridegroom's responsibility to pay for them. When I drew the cheques, I wondered whether my bank would be benign, I must say. They were. But worse was to come. When in the commodity market rubber had fallen to 1/- per pound from a high of some 8/- after the war, I was persuaded to 'have a go'. I bought fifty tons for six months' forward delivery. It fell to 2¾d. per pound during the fortnight of our honeymoon. I shuddered as each morning I searched the newspapers in Cornwall, and saw only further slices being knocked off the price. What had I done in marrying this charming girl, I, a worthless speculator, a man of straw, who might go bankrupt if made to pay the difference on the bargain when settlement day came? The beastly stuff couldn't drop any further, could it? Fortunately it didn't, and although I was not able to wait to get my money back, the eventual loss was supportable and seemed almost like a profit by comparison with its worst.

We took a small furnished flat in Beaufort Gardens, Brompton Road, to get to know one another's taste in furniture and decoration. We had seventy stairs to mount to reach it but that number was beaten by five at our next flat in Elvaston Place.

Our first child, Janet Mary, was born there in July 1933. We did not mind whether it was a boy or a girl – we never did when the two boys were born later, Nicholas Andrew in March 1935 and Robert Hugh in August 1937. Had it not been for Hitler and approaching war clouds, we should certainly have had a larger family, for we know of no greater joy or interest. Before our elder son was born, Elvaston Place had already burst its seams and we had taken a house in Chelsea Park Gardens. This proved to be too noisy and closed in, so once again we uprooted ourselves and in mid-1937 moved to 67 Cadogan Place, where we stayed for nineteen years.

Neither my wife nor I ever attempted to 'possess' our children. We guided them, as parents should, and obviously we responded immediately to calls for advice and support, but we saw early that their lives were their own. We stood behind them with all our weight, when necessary, but as soon as we felt they were responsible, we left them to go their ways.

I shall never forget an occasion when we had been on a longish visit abroad and had arranged for our daughter to live with some of her friends during our absence, rather than leave her in our house alone. We were in the car, with her in the rear, when suddenly she asked, so very apologetically and tentatively, whether my wife and I thought there was the remote possibility of her being able to share a small flat with a friend on their own. I could see her eyes, so anxious and yet so keen, reflected in the driving mirror. She was about nineteen at the time. Without any hesitation, I expressed approval, and was at once supported by my wife who I knew instinctively, because our thinking is so attuned, would agree. The eyes in the mirror filled with joy, relief and gratitude, and my wife and I realized that the fact that we had so spontaneously refrained from putting up barriers, was something which would draw our daughter closer to us than anything else. So it proved. On her part she wanted to be free, and on our part, we knew she was responsible enough for freedom. It was, however, a significant event in our family life.

The slump had blown itself out by the end of 1932 and the economic outlook was distinctly more promising. During 1933 and 1934 things picked up for the firm very well. In February 1933 we had pulled off the biggest single operation so far undertaken by us, the issue, with the National Provincial Bank, of £5 million Gaumont British 4½% I Mortage Stock at 98. Money was comparatively cheap and more and more concerns were coming to us to replenish their funds, after the disastrous years which had just passed. Some of the fruits of past work were coming home to roost, although of course foreign business on the Continent was at a standstill with the growing menace of Hitler, which was monthly becoming more clearly established. Not particularly profitably, we nevertheless undertook some attractive business at home and the American department was also coming into its own at that time.

On 1 January 1934, Gordon Munro and I were appointed Directors of the firm. It was an unforgettable day. I was one of the bosses, but except for the title, nothing much was changed. My remuneration was slightly higher, but my work was the same. I attended the partners' 'Mothers' Meetings', as we called them, each Thursday morning at 11 a.m. and was drawn in rather more closely on the inner policy. I also used the partners' lavatory. The others started to call me by my christian name, but it took a long time before I could accustom myself to addressing Alfred Wagg as Alfred, Sir Max Bonn as Max, and Lawrence Jones as Jonah! But this happy event was what I had been subconsciously waiting for, although when it was actually announced, I remember I was rather surprised that my new colleagues had taken the step so soon, even though I was then thirty-nine. Many obvious competitors had fallen by the wayside during the last few years, which probably made the decision easier for them.

Gordon Munro, the other new boy in the partnership, had served with the firm for about ten years, having been through all the departments. We were close friends. He had been a professional soldier in the cavalry, 'Swarthy Gordie of the 4th D.G.s,' as I used irreverently to call him; there was no more typical soldier in the best sense. He was badly wounded at the battle of Mons and so had to retire from the Army when a captain. Had he remained, he would surely have been C.I.G.S. He came to the firm through Alfred Wagg, by way of an introduction from a mutual friend, and never looked back. He had valuable contacts, apart from his own personal ability. Early in the Second War, he was appointed Treasury representative in Ottawa, having many friends there, and later on followed Lord Brand as Treasury representative with the rank of Minister at Washington. He was awarded a K.C.M.G. Eventually in April 1946, after interesting appointments in Southern Rhodesia, he felt it right to sever his connection with the firm. This was to everybody's regret, but it was obvious he was the sort of man destined to do public service. As this attracted him, there was nothing to be done but to applaud and smile.

The year 1935 started well for us, for we issued a 4¼% Preference Share for International Tea Company's Stores at 21/- in conjunction with the Lonsdale Investment Trust. This was an overwhelming success. I remember it for many reasons, but principally because of the impressive personality of Mr Colin Cooper, then the Vice-Chairman and Managing Director of that Company. Also, as a result of this operation, Mr Leopold Lonsdale, who had brought it to us, became a good friend, and indeed a very large shareholder in our firm. He had sold George Mason & Co. Ltd, a subsidiary company of his firm, to International Tea and had been introduced to Alfred Wagg by Mr Owen Smith (one of the great Smith family, so powerful and dominating in City affairs). Leo Lonsdale wanted 'to go into The City', and felt it desirable to link himself, whilst maintaining his own separate identity, with a banking firm. He chose us, and after buying his interest, became a director of Helbert Wagg Holdings, which was a non-executive company established on 15 April 1935 for the express purpose of holding the capital of Helbert, Wagg & Co. Ltd. This proved to be a most happy and friendly arrangement. We all enjoyed Leo Lonsdale and his associates, and we grew fond of him personally. He achieved his desire, and I know our feelings were reciprocated by him. However, some years later in March 1948, wishing to become more active in banking and to take a closer part in business than was feasible in our set-up, he joined forces with Robert Bensons and so they automatically became one of our shareholders. But only for a few days. An amicable arrangement was quickly reached, and in one afternoon I was successful in finding homes for one third of our capital with institutional and other friends, based entirely on the standing and goodwill of the firm and its partners. It was one of the easiest selling jobs I ever had to do, and it was an appropriate outcome for all sides of what had been a most pleasant association with Leo Lonsdale.

During 1936 business prospered, and 1937, apart from one public issue for Horlicks, saw a fair accumulation of 'placings', i.e. direct sales of securities to clients with no offer to the public. Horlicks attracted widespread support and interest from the public for whom this was their first opportunity to participate in a company whose products were so well known and so skilfully advertised. 'Night starvation' had made its mark, and again the queues of people seeking prospectuses were almost frightening in their determination. Some were paying a premium for application forms. Issues by successful and well-known companies whose capital has hitherto been privately owned, are ideal for issuing houses.

They do their own advertising and the public usually like to get on the band wagon of such companies.

1938 was a flat year. With shadows lengthening and war clouds gathering, we made not one single public issue but there was a plethora of placings. 1939 saw our first big issue in conjunction with Morgan Grenfell for John Summers & Co. Ltd the well-known iron and steel founders, but there was nothing much else. This state of stagnation continued pretty well, except for a few isolated transactions here and there, until the end of the war.

I must confess that I was not made any jollier, when staying with Max Bonn at his delightful country place, Upper Ifold, Dunsfold, for the Whit week of 1939, with Lord Tyrrell, formerly Permanent Secretary of the Foreign Office, as one of the fellow guests, to note the anxious whispering and long faces when he was in conversation with Sir Horace Wilson, who had come down for lunch to meet him. Nothing was disclosed, but after the latter's departure, black, black gloom prevailed for the rest of the week-end. When Max Bonn did an air shot on the first tee next morning, he exclaimed, 'Damn and blast Hitler, he ruins my game of golf too.'

Albert Palache held the fort, almost single-handed, throughout the five years of war, and manfully and brilliantly he worked too. He vacated his house in Hampstead and stayed at the Ritz, for easier accessibility. Unperturbed by events, he showed himself at his best, and deep was the gratitude of all partners and staff to him for his self-sacrifice.

I shall devote the following chapter to a description of my own official doings during the war whilst serving in the Treasury, but will interject here some passing details of family and personal happenings.

We all listened with sinking hearts to the Prime Minister's address to the nation that our country was once again at war. I can hear Mr Neville Chamberlain's serious, doleful, thin voice now. In August 1914 I was just nineteen. In 1940 I was a mature man with a wife and three young children. Things were different. Life had been good to me. I had much to do and I wanted to do it. I was, like everybody else, extremely apprehensive, and filled with anxious forebodings, especially about destruction by bombing. I listened to the announcement of war at the Chelsea Town Hall where, with many others, I was learning air-raid precaution duties.

Then came that first whining air-raid alert. It desecrated the lovely autumn day. Were we to be destroyed straightaway? Hideous thoughts entered my mind. What was to stop the desolation of London against the overwhelming air superiority of the Germans? We rushed to our posts outwardly calm (I hope) but inwardly with beating hearts. Then the All Clear sounded. No aeroplane had been heard. It was a false alarm and we were still alive. But it was with low spirits that I went back home, cursing the Germans and Hitler. I felt sure it would be a long-drawn-out bloody struggle. At that overpowering moment of shock on the declaration of war it took me a little while before I could recover that sense of calm and assurance of God's protection, without which the outlook inevitably appeared black and hopeless.

I shall not describe in any detail life for my family and myself during the war; those who were stuck in London throughout the period, as I was, all had much the same type of experiences. Apart from the glorious, overriding and underlying relief and confidence that we were being led by one of the greatest men in history, Winston Churchill, we were all emotionally affected by the swings in our national fortunes, by the bombing which brought misery and discomfort to so many of our friends, by the impenetrability of the blackout and by so many other unaccustomed happenings. Life was a dull laborious affair on the whole and extremely restricted. Apart from work, which fortunately for me was almost all-absorbing, excessive attention had perforce to be paid to petty, but vitally important details; how to eke out one's food and clothing rations, for instance, or how to manage to visit the children.

Funny how trivial things stick in one's memory, but I remember thinking I would give the children an enormous treat by taking them during one of the holidays to the Pastoria Restaurant, off Leicester Square, which seemed able to offer specialities and rarities unobtainable elsewhere. I triumphantly ordered profiterolles, but much to my disappointment their noses went up at the first taste. They had never come across such rich food before, and so automatically disliked it. They had to be persuaded to appreciate bananas later on!

I was conscious the whole war that each one of us was helping to make history and often I felt overwhelmed by the responsibility falling on the British people. But it was a complete and united effort. Just as in the First

War, except at the front, I was spared any special evidence of the disgustingness of war, so in the Second War I was fortunate enough not to witness, or participate in, any major or hideous disaster. Like everybody else, I had narrow misses, especially during fire guard duty, but I was never called upon to be heroic.

We were deluged with offers from thoughtful friends in the United States to send the children over there, most of the cables reading 'When can we expect arrival Janet, Nicholas and Robert?' This was very touching but my wife and I quickly decided not to avail ourselves of these generous offers. We felt that if this was to be a war to end all wars, our children, if they survived, would be thankful to us for not depriving them of sharing the experience. We also saw the danger of estrangement and a change of habits and outlook, especially for children of such impressionable ages. So, we expressed our extreme gratitude and instead of the United States, we moved the children out of London to Sussex to stay with my mother-in-law. There they remained until the guns of Dunkirk could be heard and the south-eastern areas were frequently thrilled by the contests in the air which ended in the fantastic defeat of the German Air Force in the Battle of Britain. My wife then decided to take the family to what was a safer area in Shropshire. So in June 1940 she made off with the three children to Shrewsbury where she not only attended to their needs but did local war work in the W.V.S. getting around, until petrol rationing, in an Austin Seven bought for £20, practically tied together with string. For the previous months she had been tireless in A.R.P. duties, in which I also took part as far as my Treasury work permitted. Meanwhile we continued to live in Cadogan Place, with one loyal old body to help to keep the place clean. My wife and I maintained our rooms on the third floor, never having resort to dug-outs and similar refuges, except when on duty as wardens. We both felt that it was not what you were experiencing that mattered, but what you were thinking. We kept the 91st Psalm prominently in our minds throughout the whole war, and especially later on when V1 doodle-bugs and V2s menaced us so terribly. After nearly two years of absence in Shrewsbury, during which my visits there grew fewer and fewer for work reasons, my wife rejoiced when I telephoned her one morning in March 1942 suggesting she return to London with the children. We resolved that we would no longer permit Hitler, or anybody else, to prolong this miserable family separation. I think she arrived the next day – she says it was on April Fool's Day, but it was a happy day, restoration of family unity.

Functioning schools in London were very scarce at that time, but we had the good fortune, as a makeshift, to have all three children accepted into the Kensington High School for Girls in Campden Hill. The elder boy, Nicholas, then aged seven, stuck this undignified situation for a term, when we were able to secure him a place in a school at Hampstead. For two terms he found his way there and back each day, the winter and spring terms, by one of the few omnibus routes running. Thinking he was wasting too much time travelling like that and waiting about in the dark, we secured a place for him at a prep school, Fan Court, near Chertsey in Surrey. Robert was also detached from the Girls' School and we sent him to a pre-prep school in early 1943, Wagner's near South Kensington.

I have a vivid memory of Nicholas returning home from the Hampstead School one afternoon in a fog. It was a real pea-souper. Such buses as there were had long ceased to run. It was still day-time, but the fog was dense. He had left the school, we ascertained that, but how could this little boy find his way home? However, he did. We discovered that the bus had dropped him off at Marble Arch refusing to go any farther, and he had literally felt his way back from there. He arrived home quite unconcerned as if it was the most natural performance, but greatly to his mother's relief.

We always encouraged the children to express their individuality, but never to be precocious. One incident which occurred when our younger son aged eight had gone to his prep school was almost too much even for us. My wife was suddenly telephoned by the anxious headmaster requesting her to come down at once, as our son was having an upsetting influence on the other boys. My wife hurried down to Chertsey as best she could, to find that the boy had been preaching Communism with such effect that the other pupils were being tainted. Armed with Willie Gallacher's pocket edition *The Case for Communism*, he was calling for the downfall of capitalism in eloquent terms. He had started his own pamphlet *Communism v. Capitalism*. It contained such phrases as:

'The noose tightens round the capitalist's neck' and 'Capitalists have nothing to offer but further security to the upper classes'. My wife, calm and sensible as ever, talked to the boy and showed him how fallacious were his arguments. He willingly gave her possession of the book and that was the end of that little affair. Needless to say, there has been no recurrence of this leaning to the extreme left!

When the children were young, they had all the usual pets, dogs, cats, budgerigars which never would talk, canaries which never would sing, and white mice, which always escaped. I recall our daughter's horror one morning when one of her two white mice was missing, this time with obvious evidence of cannibalism! In those days we had dachshunds. Now we have a coal-black little poodle, Mouche by name, as spoilt by us all as any beautiful young lady should be. Somebody once said to me: 'Poodles are not dogs; they are poodles.' Poodle owners will understand.

Chapter 11

I NAIVELY THOUGHT at the beginning of the Second War that I would be able to serve in some sort of military capacity. Having somewhat ingloriously finished my army activities rather early in the First War, I was anxious to try again. I bothered the War Office and all other contacts, but without the slightest success. I did not interest the army. What was I to do? I must do something. I thought of asking my old friends of Room 40 of the 1914–18 war if they wanted me, but all that had changed since my time. Most of my friends in The City had either been allocated jobs in the Ministry of Economic Warfare or recalled to their regiments. I was left out in the cold.

I therefore had recourse to Mr Montagu Norman, Governor of the Bank of England. He was unique amongst Bank Governors – in appearance, in personality, charm, persuasiveness, wisdom and perception, yet with a determination which never faltered, and a rock-like loyalty to those he liked or appreciated. This picturesque, Rubens-like figure – so artistic in appearance – was the very antithesis of the common idea of a Bank Governor. He was always most gracious to me and I revered him. For a short time before the war I had taken over the control of his investments – he had little time to spare for his own personal matters – and as my former partner Gordon Munro, was unavailable, it fell to my lot to watch over his fortune. This brought me close to him and I took immense pride in talking with him. Since his death he has been much reviled for many reasons, but mainly for his influence in putting us back on the Gold Standard in 1925. Indeed, he did not lack for detractors during his life. But be that as it may – he was a commanding, courageous leader. He worked on flair and instinct, and relied upon his own personal judgment of people and situations, but he took pains to know which button to press, and when, always realizing what he wanted. He was the undisputed leader of The City. There was an automatic quickening of heartbeat, and one's steps on the way to see 'the Governor' were light and expectant – usually! A request from him was in effect a command. Nobody has ever exerted such influence over City people and affairs as Mr Norman did, and although perhaps in present times his reign could not have been so unchallenged, memory of him will never fade. He gave his life to the Bank of England.

It so happened just before I had called on the Governor that he had been requested by the Treasury for help in what was known as the O.F. Division (Overseas Finance) and he suggested I might go along to see Mr S. D. Waley the chief of O.F. This I did with alacrity, and was promptly asked, after the interview on a Friday afternoon, towards the end of October 1939, to report for duty on the following Monday morning. So here again I found a second war offering a challenge to me, this time in The Treasury, His Majesty's Treasury, the Holy of Holies. I believe I was the first outsider to be called upon, certainly the first from The City, and I was naturally proud of my fortune. I was received warmly by Waley on arrival and as time passed, I was to find in him a kindly, brilliant and at the same time most modest and delightful boss. He was a wizard at international finance, trade and commercial inter-Governmental agreements and all the technical details of the financing of overseas trade. These involved mechanisms were child's play to him. The speed with which he worked was bewildering and few could keep pace with his quicksilver brain, certainly not me, at any rate in those early days. He was so quick to take decisions that sometimes insufficient consideration compelled him to revise them, and as I grew to know and understand him, I never took his original 'no' for an answer. So often, with his deliciously quizzical little smile, he would look up and say 'Yes, I was wrong'. Waley was always affectionately known to his friends as 'Sigi', an abbreviation of his first name, Sigismund. When he was created a K.C.M.G. we tried to persuade him to call himself 'Sir Sigi Waley', but he preferred to masquerade as 'Sir David Waley', on condition we all continued to address him as 'Sigi'. None of us could bring ourselves to do anything else!

Almost apologetically, as if I were important, Waley conducted me

C.E.F. as Air Raid Warden 1939

on arrival to the tiniest garret in the Treasury, Whitehall, uncarpeted and freezing – a table, a chair, an inkpot, a telephone and the proverbial In and Out trays. A lesson in humility for me after the somewhat grander surroundings I had been used to! There was a fireplace, but no coal. When this was procured and a match applied, smoke filled the room and the messenger later confessed to me that a fire had never been lit in that room to his knowledge and he had been there for thirty years. However, these little things did not matter. I was actually installed in the Treasury, in a room to myself, inaccessible and remote it was true, but I was there and I would do my best.

This was of course in the original venerable Treasury Chambers in Whitehall. When this building was bombed later on, compelling many of the officials to move to the soulless building in Great George Street, which remains Treasury H.Q. today, I was destined, until I followed them, to occupy for a time the beautiful office of the Permanent Secretary, a room of fine proportions, with unsurpassed views over the Horse Guards' Parade and St James's Park. That was certainly an inspiring place in which to work and I could not help smiling when I thought of some of the eminent previous occupants, Horace Wilson, Warren Fisher, Bradbury and others, and the world-shaking decisions which had been reached there.

Very soon the messenger brought some files in, marked 'For Mr Fraser's attention and action'. One seemed to concern our Payments Agreement with Turkey and another dealt with the purchase of tobacco from Bulgaria. Complete Double Dutch to me, and nobody appeared to think it was necessary to explain anything about past history or such like, and probably they were too busy anyhow. I had not yet cottoned on to the Civil Service assumption that the files speak for themselves; they constitute a complete record and it is an unwritten law that civil servants of the same rank should be interchangeable, and each thus becomes the authority on his subject the moment he takes over.

So I dug into the back files, answered the questions to the best of my ability and sent the results down to Waley. This went on for about three weeks, during which time, in addition to Turkey and Bulgaria, I had been given Roumania to look after. The last-named territory was beginning to assume considerable political importance because of its oil-wells; furthermore, the acquisition of barges on the Danube, in order to prevent their falling into enemy hands, was also being urgently discussed. But somehow I could not get any real grip on the affairs of these countries. Important as it no doubt was to those concerned, I was not really interested in the negotiation of purchases of sultanas and tobacco, for instance, in the Balkan countries. I had not pictured working in the Treasury would be like that, as I had been expecting to be occupied with home economic affairs which I then thought had a more human content than, for example, a highly complicated Payments Agreement with Turkey. Anyhow I was not at all certain I was not making rather a hash of the work. So I sailed in to see Waley and said I thought I did not fit into the scheme of things, I was not happy and ought I not to leave? He took one of his rapid decisions and agreed we did not quite seem to click. I went home that night low in spirits, wondering how I would ever dare disclose to the Governor of the Bank of England that his protégé had resigned from the Treasury after only three weeks. In the morning, however, I ran into Waley as we entered the precincts together. 'We took a hasty decision last night, didn't we?' he remarked. 'Yes, perhaps,' I replied and we went off to our separate rooms. Nothing more was said but we both understood from that brief exchange that we had agreed to ignore our conversation of the previous night. I therefore continued working at Turkish and Balkan problems, later taking over the affairs of Greece and Yugoslavia. I was never particularly at ease, but was learning the technique, the necessary tricks of the trade, and with probably increasing understanding and success. Meanwhile I was getting to know the inner workings of the Treasury and was able to appreciate the extremely high mental qualities of those employed there.

That mutual reversal of decision by Waley and myself proved fortunate for me, for some time later Sir Horace Wilson, the Head of the Civil Service and the Treasury, whom I had met before the war, sent for me. He announced that it was proposed to create a new Division to be called 'The Allies Division'. Would I like to be put in charge, with the rank of Principal Assistant Secretary? He explained that my functions would be to supervise the whole range of H.M.G.'s financial relations with those Governments domiciled in Great Britain whilst their countries were occupied by the enemy. These comprised the Belgians, the

Czechs, Dutch, Free French, Greeks, Norwegians, Poles and the Yugo-slavs. This was work after my own heart – it had an exceptional human appeal – and I accepted enthusiastically, and thanked Sir Horace Wilson for the honour he was doing me, as well as for the opportunity. From that moment until the end of the war I was extremely busy. The job was very onerous and my mental processes were fully stretched. But the duties had many attractions for me, affording not only work of unusual interest but bringing me into close association with distinguished men who represented their countries in Great Britain, ministers, officials and others, so many of whom became my personal friends. I had always had a special penchant for foreigners and had particular sympathy for these exiled people.

My sponsor at the Bank of England, Mr Montagu Norman, was also delighted and, in celebration, invited me to lunch at the Bank. When I declined alcohol during the meal, he expressed surprise and regret, saying that in his experience solutions to problems could often be more happily reached over a whisky and soda and that if I could not establish friendly relations with my new friends in this way, something would be lacking. He feared I might be at a disadvantage and appear unsympathetic, if I did not share a drink with them. I said I hoped I could overcome this difficulty somehow in my own way. When it came to the end of the meal, I was offered a cigar or cigarette and again declined. Mr Norman was horrified. 'What! How unsociable! You don't smoke either?' I, by now almost ashamed, confessed that was so. Whereupon, lighting up his own cigarette, some smoke caught in his throat and he collapsed into a paroxysm of coughing. All conversation ceased whilst he was slapped on the back, then looking out from weeping eyes he squeezed out: 'Fifteen all'!

To digress a little here from my story, I venture to assure those who are fearful of being teetotallers or non-smokers that, as far as I know, no handicap has resulted to me from abstaining. I have never found it necessary to get myself into a state of extra conviviality in order to com-plete a deal or consummate an agreement. Formerly I indulged in both habits, but about thirty years ago lost all desire or taste for them and have had no regrets. The last thing in the world I want to be is self-righteous about this abstention. I never bring the subject up. I take no pride in it and feel only gratitude for freedom from an addiction which had me in bondage. Unfortunately, one effect has been that a smoky atmosphere has now become almost an obsession with me, such as is to be found, for instance, at men's dinners after the loyal toast, especially if the air conditioning is not working well. If one has, at the same time, to listen to speeches through the haze, such occasions have less and less attraction for me, and I am afraid I tend to avoid most of the dull ones whenever possible. Smoking has so little to recommend it and it does not bear analysis, although millions enjoy it. It is odd how insensitive smokers are to polluting the atmosphere for others, frequently causing distress. I was just as unconscious of this myself before I gave up the habit, and I shudder when I reflect how noisome my morning cheroot must have been to many, as I puffed it on my way to The City at a certain period in my life. I was once severely taken aback when staying in a country house to be snapped at by my hostess, a maiden lady, begging me, if I *had* to smoke, to use Turkish cigarettes, as 'those filthy Virginia cigarettes literally poison me'! This was my first surprised realization of how obnoxious smoking can seem to others. Yet the habit persists, in cinemas, some theatres and public places. Although I hope it will not be regarded as smug, I decline to apologize for my enjoyment of the letter from the late Lord Samuel to *The Times* in March 1962. It is short and I reproduce it in its entirety: 'People are asking what they should do in order to stop smoking. The answer is very simple: don't smoke. I did that one day in August 1904, at the age of 33, and haven't smoked anything since. Now, at 91, I am still feeling the benefit.' I have not yet had such a long period of abstinence as Lord Samuel had, but just now I feel exactly as he did!

It was typical of Mr Norman's kindness that each time he paid his regular weekly visit to the Chancellor of the Exchequer, he never failed to seek me out in my little rabbit hutch and inquire how I was getting along. This delightful touch gave me added prestige with the messengers; and with some of my Treasury colleagues who might at that stage have been inclined to look askance at this unknown intruder from The City. Later they became accustomed to new faces.

When I eventually joined my colleagues in Great George Street I was moved into quite a spacious room, commensurate with my higher ranking, vastly better than my original hovel in Whitehall, but not approaching the magnificence of the Permanent Secretary's room where I had been given refuge for a period. It was fully carpeted but dingy, and I hung a few of my own pictures up to hide the filthy walls. I was also given my own personal secretary, a luxury I had grievously missed, as previously I had had to share in a pool. However, the Treasury had its rules and must stick to them, and although in agreement with my partners at Helbert Wagg, I was able to work without remuneration, I of course had to conform. I was very fortunate in the lady allocated to me, Mrs Betty Kenington. She worked with me until the end of the war and I shall remain indebted to her for her devoted help, and especially for her cheerful approach to all our problems. Her smile was a tonic. She was an ardent firewatcher and I remember her telling me that after a particularly vicious air raid she went up to the canteen in Great George Street to get some food, and on switching on the lights she found the entire table covered with cockroaches. She ran!

All the Finance Ministers of 'my' various Governments, and their entourages, came to regard me as their special friend and in a sort of way, their guardian angel. I had to be careful to keep a balance between their demands and our own resources. Naturally this resulted sometimes in strong, divergent pulls, and my sense of what was strictly in the best interests of the war effort was often severely tested.

There was one occasion I shall never forget which brought me into conflict with the great Lord Keynes who by then was, as in the First War, exerting an extremely potent influence on the Treasury and on financial thought. He was indeed omnipotent. Keynes's exact position in the Treasury was never defined; it was unnecessary, he was Maynard Keynes – which endowed him with all the authority he needed, to handle any problem or to challenge anybody's view. The Western Allies were thrilled by the resistance put up by the Greeks in successfully staving off the attacks of the Italians. If I remember correctly they were the first, and indeed the only, nation to show any effective military resistance, and very soon they applied to H.M.G. for sterling credits with which to purchase arms and other necessities as they feared new attacks, this time from the Germans. There was a great discussion in the Treasury as to the desirability of granting these credits. Should we provide them or should we not? I was strongly in favour, but Keynes demurred. As the matter pressed, and required higher authority, being of political significance, we sought a decision from the Chancellor of the Exchequer. At the time it was Sir Kingsley Wood, an astute politician, a tiny Pickwickian figure, with buttoned-up boots and heavy glasses behind which shone a pair of shrewd Cockney eyes. He had no real knowledge of finance, but his political sense was especially keen: he knew just how far he could go in the House of Commons. His ear was near to the ground and he was assisted in this by his Parliamentary Private Secretary, Sir Edward Campbell, who kept him closely posted about how Members of Parliament were thinking and the general political atmosphere. Whenever he was asked a difficult question in the corridors of the House of Commons or elsewhere, for which he was unprepared, Kingsley Wood would invariably reply: 'I'll ask my people and let you know.' He would never get himself more involved than that. He was very kind to me.

My work in the Treasury taught me to appreciate the beauty of Green Park, and St James's Park too, for I used, whenever possible, to exercise myself by walking across them to the office each morning. I often used to meet Sir Kingsley and he would ply me with ceaseless questions in his high-pitched voice. He was a good Chancellor and always dealt expeditiously and decisively with matters when the case was presented clearly to him. On this occasion, as we went into his room, there he was at the head of the huge table, blinking away. Lord Keynes went on one side, and I sat on the Chancellor's left. He asked Keynes to state his case. As usual this was done brilliantly, his power of exposition and persuasion being masterly and his command of the English language complete. When I was requested to expound my arguments, I feared it was a foregone conclusion that the Chancellor's decision would go in favour of Keynes. However, at the end, Sir Kingsley Wood just said: 'I think we should go ahead as proposed by Mr Fraser,' and that was that. Quick and to the point.

It was the first of many wrangles between Keynes and myself, and I must admit it was, as far as I can recall, the only difference which ended wholly in my favour. He reserved some of his most effective vituperative scorn and sarcasm for me and nobody could be more devastating; so much so that even some of the permanent civil servants who were in dreadful awe of Keynes would pluck up their courage now and again and rise to oppose him on my behalf, when he would be most graceful. But his reputation is legendary and rightly so and his influence will live long. I will surely be pounced upon by his special admirers but somehow deep down in me I always felt anxiety at some of his rapid decisions and often equally rapid reversals. Nobody was cleverer than he, nor had a more creative mind. He shared our awareness of that. Keynes was a crusader, splendidly arrogant. He had an extraordinary gift for economics, and at the same time, a deep love of the arts and literature, a simplicity of outlook, acuteness and sensitivity. The financial policies propounded by Keynes affected literally every man, woman and child in the country and Keynesian monetary theories will continue to be discussed whenever these matters arise. His power was immense and he carried a terrifying burden.

Next to him at the Treasury in a communicating room sat Lord Catto, later to become Governor of the Bank of England at the time of its nationalization in 1946. 'Doggo and Catto' they were inevitably and irreverently designated. There was ample evidence that Catto, diminutive, wise and vastly experienced in business and commerce all over the world, gave a sense of balance to some of the less realistic flights of fancy which poured ceaselessly out of Keynes's imagination. Keynes surely sacrificed his life for his country and when his sudden death was announced I had the acute feeling of a frightful national calamity at a time when we were facing what seemed like complete financial disaster, and when his services could have been vital for our recovery. A whole library of books has been written about the Keynesian monetary theory, which in essence is that Governments should compensate against the downswing in business by artificially creating purchasing power by deficit financing. There was much more to it than that of course, but like most great teachers and prophets, Keynes would certainly not have agreed with all, or most, of what his disciples have since preached.

In our Treasury contacts neither Keynes nor I ever referred to the Independent Investment Trust, which though dominated by him and another great economist, Falk, fell on such evil times that the Trust had recourse to the services of Helbert Wagg to restore confidence in its future. In 1932 Bernie Barrington became a Director and had an anxious time keeping Keynes and Falk from each other's throats at Board meetings, before a more orthodox and less ingenious handling of the investment portfolio put the Trust back on its feet, and indeed brought it again to prosperity.

Another difference of opinion I was to have with a great man – this time the greatest of them all – also took place during my period at the Treasury. It was late on a Friday afternoon, when suddenly Mr Churchill called for the Chancellor of the Exchequer – at that time Sir John Anderson, later to become Lord Waverley. It so happened that he had left, and so had those civil servants senior to myself. It therefore fell to me to rush to No. 10 Downing Street to wait on the Prime Minister, as he was impatient and wanted to pinpoint the matter. Not without anxiety and apprehension, I was shown into the Cabinet Room. He was alone, except for Duff Cooper, later Lord Norwich. I was bidden to sit opposite him and was then asked to explain a certain point regarding the Free French financial arrangements – a domestic affair of their own, as a matter of fact. Fortunately the reply presented me with no difficulty, but it was clear that the Prime Minister was hotly opposed to the opinion I had given. However, I felt so strongly on the subject that I reiterated my point. I wanted Mr Churchill to have confidence in the attitude of the Free French in this matter, but he was having none of it. I had, and still have, a high opinion of General de Gaulle. I considered he would be extremely affronted if the P.M.'s line of thinking were persisted in, and said so. 'I totally disagree with you,' said Mr Churchill, and getting up he bustled off to the door on his way to Chequers for the week-end, adding courteously but in measured terms, 'I am sorry we have so completely disagreed on all scores at our first meeting. I hope we shall do better next time.' There has never been a next time, but the Treasury point of view was not changed. No doubt there were more crucial matters to be dealt with. This awe-inspiring incident however, brought me closer to Duff Cooper, whom I liked very much. He later told me he fully shared my views and was secretly cheered by my stand against 'the old man'.

Life in The City had not called for concentrated efforts during the years preceding the war due to the general business malaise. By comparison work in the Treasury meant long and exacting hours. There was no 9.30 to 5.00 any more. Seven p.m. was the earliest hour of departure, and this lasted almost throughout the war, often seven days a week, with only short holidays. Yes, it was an exhausting job, but the interest kept me going. I am not certain that some Civil Servants do not rather revel in work, too much work, and tend to make an idol of it. But perhaps it is their overwhelming sense of service and loyalty to their duties which has this effect on them. The country must be grateful for this devotion on the part of a civil service which is without question the finest in the world.

I should say the two most efficiently administered Ministries during the war were the Treasury and the Ministry of Food. As far as the former was concerned it could never truthfully be said that an appeal failed for lack of funds if it could be shown as essential for the pursuit of the war. But the case naturally had to be well supported to pass muster, and as my contact with Treasury officials grew closer, so my admiration for their ability and their utterly objective approach to all problems, increased. The Treasury was often regarded as sticky and difficult, but being an outsider who had got inside and therefore possibly holding a more dispassionate view, I invariably found them most helpful, and willing to do their best on all occasions, never negative just for the sake of being negative, but of course inquiring and persistent to a degree in their examination of demands. That is how it should be, and it still obtains today.

It might be thought that with such colossal sums being bandied about, a miscalculation or error could easily be hidden and not brought to light. On the contrary, there is a very active Public Accounts Committee, consisting of Members of Parliament whose function it is to delve into and to cross-question on any matter of expenditure of public funds. So effectively do they perform their duties, and with such verve, that the Permanent Secretaries who appear before them on behalf of their Departments always rejoice when the ordeal is over.

There is also the Comptroller and Auditor-General, Exchequer and Audit Department. This office is at present held by Sir Edmund Compton, a war-time friend, who has a brilliant, incisive mind, and says devastating things with a disarming and beguiling smile. When I first knew him, he had come from the Ministry of Aircraft Production and was supposed to be one of the few Civil Servants there upon whom Lord Beaverbrook looked with any favour. This gave him a certain aura and prestige amongst us. The appointment he now holds is not made by the Treasury but by Letters Patent under the Great Seal and he is only removable upon an address from the two Houses of Parliament. His main functions are to give effect to payments from the Exchequer provided he is satisfied they have been authorized by Parliament. He watches carefully that these funds have been used as instructed, and he surveys all other public accounts, including the accounts of Government stores and trading services. His reports on these matters are made direct to the House of Commons. The work of this Department, which is not entangled in any way with the Civil Service, acts as a powerful brake on unauthorized Government expenditure and no hesitation is shown in making highly critical comments where these seem necessary.

Along the corridor from me there was installed in a big, bedraggled room full of files and papers, the Treasury Accountant, a certain Mr Chadwick, now Sir Thomas Chadwick. He was a cheerful character, devoid of any pose or pomposity. We became good friends, often engaging in talks of a more philosophical nature than might have been expected in such surroundings. My rank empowered me to sign cheques on the Exchequer Account and sometimes I would look up and spy Chadwick's happy face peeping round the door of my room. 'Sign, please,' he would say and would put in front of me a draft for some fantastic sum like £300,000,000 which I imagine was approximately a weekly ration of Government expenditure. I have wondered since what he would have said if I had asked for verification, but he inspired such confidence I never thought of it at the time. Perhaps Chadwick felt I was easy and undemanding, or perhaps he knew what a thrill it gave me to put my signature to cheques for such astronomical figures.

Very often the Treasury was blamed for being 'hard-faced' or miserly, but so often the case had not been adequately put to them. Certainly as individuals in their relations with me, they could not have been more charming, thoughtful or kind. They treated me as one of them, and I am proud to have kept their friendship over the years since. It might seem paradoxical but the regular civil servants would, I believe, be the first to admit that the leavening of thought by the introduction into the higher administrative ranks of outsiders – 'bloody temporaries' as we were described – was of vast benefit to the Civil Service. Each side indeed gained a lot from the other, and if I had to criticize the Service it would probably be that its members were inclined to be too in-bred in their thinking, and that few, if any, have had the advantage of working to a Profit and Loss Account as in private industry. The war dispersed many mutual doubts as to one another, and it is to be hoped that as time passes, the lessons learnt then are not being forgotten.

The power and responsibilities of a civil servant even when young are enormous. In private industry, except in rare cases, a young man has to wait much longer before he obtains similar authority or position. That I imagine is one of the attractions of the Service, and even the pay of the lower administrative ranks compares favourably with other callings. The same cannot be said of the salaries of the higher ranks of the Civil Service which, although better than they were formerly, compare poorly with private industry or commerce, with a resulting temptation to defect. The rates of pay have lately been improved, so that an annual emolument of £7,000 can be obtained at the top, plus a good pension and suitable appearances in the Honours Lists. All the same, the exodus from the Civil Service to private industry has been very marked since the war, and many a Chairmanship has been most successfully filled by these brilliant men, most of whom take happily to the new life. I only know of one case where a high Civil Servant, having seceded, later yearned for Government routine and returned. As a rule, they enjoy their freedom from red-tape and the political influence of their Ministers, although it must be said that others appreciate the power, the status and being 'in the know'. The power attached to the person of, for instance, a Head of a Department, is almost without limit in his own sphere of influence. Even lower down the ranks it is very considerable, as I know only too well. But I never saw any sign of abuse or any undue self-inflation. The burdens and the problems were taken as a matter of course, intelligently and objectively. Of course many wonder whether the authority of the bureaucrats is not unduly weighted by comparison with that of Ministers, but that varies according to the strength of character and ability of the particular minister.

'Precedent' is a word frequently on the lips of civil servants – 'creating a precedent'. It is an awful anxiety for them and in some ways I understand their predicament, as the Civil Service and machinery of Government are vast, intermingled, organizations. However, when I used to say 'to blazes with precedent, let's do it', the response was always, if sometimes timorously, favourable. But that was war-time.

Other ministries have from time immemorial cursed the Treasury for its well-known predilection to say 'no', and I have not much doubt that before the war, this clammy hand too frequently slapped down proposals which, whilst untenable on grounds of pure finance, would have been of advantage for the nation politically. Whether we could have gained valuable friends, I mean friends who would have remained firm, is questionable I suppose, but money talks. I have the impression that had we been a bit more generous before the war in the Balkans, buying for instance more of the local tobacco, despite the opposition of the vested interests in this country, such an act might have stood us in good stead at our time of need. As it was, Britain, with her world-wide trade interests, had devoted but little attention to the Balkans, where her economic influence was entirely subordinate to that of Germany.

Even during the war, long before nationalization of the Bank of England was ever contemplated, the liaison between the Treasury and Bank was very intimate. It seemed to me at that time that the influence of the Bank was very powerful. The technical skill of the Bank officials was irresistible – they knew their job thoroughly and their judgment was almost infallible. This strengthening of the higher direction of the Bank of England was set on foot by Lord Norman and it certainly proved itself during the war when the contact with the Treasury was incessant and intimate. Bank of England officials were able to participate in interdepartmental discussions as if the Bank was a Government Department itself. Their freshness and practical approach, reinforced by the vast City machine and fount of financial knowledge and experience, often swayed decisions, or accelerated them.

Although I always understood Sir Horace Wilson was most anxious to continue to leave his experience and knowledge at the disposal of the Government, his resignation, it will be remembered, was accepted by the Prime Minister the moment it was formally offered when he reached the age of sixty. He was a dedicated public servant of the highest order.

I always thought he was badly treated, but with his Munich 'taint', it was probable that anything else but an acceptance of his resignation was unthinkable. I was one of those who applauded Mr Chamberlain's visit to Hitler but it must have been painful to Sir Horace Wilson to be ousted at the height of the war by someone two years older than himself, Sir Richard Hopkins, even though the latter was a remarkable administrator and of course a fine character. Under him there was a galaxy of talent – regular civil servants, university dons, professors and economists, from which it can be appreciated that problems, and they were legion, were very thoroughly thrashed out before their solution was decided. I was undoubtedly amongst the élite. If I listed the names of some of my colleagues, it would be apparent that since those days many have graduated to high posts in the Civil Service, industry, commerce, foreign affairs and in the fields of economics and letters. I still wonder how I kept up with them: if I did.

Some of us used to meet each afternoon for a cup of tea in Waley's room. This was a valuable custom as it gave us a forum, and many a stimulating argument took place. Despite my knowledge that a civil servant must have no political allegiances except at the ballot box, which may cause us to regard him as a trifle thin-blooded and inhuman, I was breath-taken one day at a tea party soon after Dunkirk to hear one of our colleagues propounding the inevitability of a German victory. Fur flew! He was basically a patriotic person, but he could not refrain from being coldly analytical. Hence his prognostications. He was impressed by the material superiority of the Germans, in men and machines; they were at that moment menacing us across the Channel and an attack on our shores seemed imminent. My dear colleague could only see this, and weighing everything in the balance, he calculated that the scales came down heavily in favour of a quick surrender by the British. Indeed he would have asked for terms there and then! But like Hitler, he had underestimated the British character. Our relationship was thereafter always clouded, and I am afraid I never placed much confidence in his judgment. All the same, I met other leading characters who felt that our ultimate defeat was a foregone conclusion, and many lost friendships resulted. There is a prevailing, rather smug belief nowadays, that at the time of Dunkirk and after, no Englishman ever doubted our eventual victory. The cases I have quoted are salutary reminders that this was not so.

Amongst the Allied Governments there were also to be found men well trained in financial matters. Perhaps the Belgians were the most spectacular – certainly the most forthright and dogged. Their team consisted mainly of M. Camille Gutt, M. Hubert Ansiaux and Baron Boel – all three destined to play telling roles in their country after the war. M. Gutt became the eminent head of the International Monetary Fund and is now a private banker in Brussels: Hubert Ansiaux is now the Governor of the National Bank of Belgium, an entirely charming and most able friend: René Boel ('B.B.B.' as I used to call him affectionately, the Bold Bad Baron!) is probably the leading industrialist in Belgium today. I once heard him make a speech in English which for finesse, eloquence and wit was the envy of all his British listeners. The Dutch had a brilliant Finance Minister in William Beyen, lately their ambassador in Paris. He had been the youngest Chairman of the Bank for International Settlements in Basle. This apart, he was a dilettante, and a lover of music. He was kind enough to refer in flattering terms to my part with the Allied Governments during the war in an excellent book published by him a few years ago entitled *Money in a Maelstrom*. His joy was debunking Keynes, or anybody else for that matter. The Greeks were represented by a Professor of Economics, Mr Varvaressos, a huge man, most un-Greek, with a gift for rather long-winded exposition, and Mr Mantzavinos, the Governor of the Central Bank of Greece. The Free French had M. René Pleven, afterwards one of their Prime Ministers in the post-war cascade of Governments. With M. Camille Gutt, he spent the evening of 5 June 1944, his last in London before leaving for North Africa, dining in our basement at No. 67 Cadogan Place. He sent us a little book on Paris, inscribed charmingly 'Je vous remercie du fond du cœur de la sympathie que vous nous avez temoigné, et de l'appui que vous m'avez toujours donné. Je ne pourrai jamais l'oublier'. Pleven, a Breton, knew England very well, having been associated with the banking firm of Blair & Co. at the time when M. Jean Monnet was a partner. We had a happy contact, even if he was exacting and impatient at times – perhaps naturally – when his demands were not fully granted. Sometimes also M. Couve de Murville, ice-cold and uncompromising, now their Secretary of State for Foreign Affairs, and M. Guillaume Guindey, head of the Bank for International Settlements in Basle: both, inevitably, Inspecteurs des Finances, that class of experts from which so many leading figures in France are drawn. Guindey became an intimate friend of our family.

The Polish representatives were Dr Leon Baranski, a shaven-headed, white-faced, intense but delightful man, sonorous and intelligent: and Count Mohl, 'Mohl the Pole', whose English was a drawback in explaining his requests for funds. The Czechs were represented by Dr Feierabend; the Norwegians by Mr Christian Brinch, a lover of English literature who could quote freely from *The Shropshire Lad* and other works; the Yugoslavs by Dimovic, a clever economist who would take up anybody's challenge on international finance, now domiciled in this country.

With most of these I tussled during the war when things were never easy for them, nor indeed for us. They were constantly, and quite obviously, thinking how best they could serve their people in occupation, and prepare for the time when their countries would be freed, but they appreciated the over-all view it was essential for us in the Treasury to take. Some of the Governments were self-supporting – others made big financial demands on us, and being without resources of their own, were often unfavourably placed.

There was a great spirit of co-operation, not only between the various Allied Governments themselves for their own purposes, but in the establishment of many committees to plan and work for an improved and better world after the war. It was a stimulating time, and any seeming, temporary setback in our fortunes only acted as a spur for further determined efforts in the study of the probable post-war financial and economic situation, and the needs for reconstruction and development. The war was a unifying instrument, for we all had that one single aim – to defeat the enemy. As one cynic said: 'The trials will come later, when the unity of purpose is lacking.' Personally I felt that a real basis of co-operation and friendship between the Allied Governments was being established and fostered in London during the war; it became a habit to exchange views and opinions and on the whole the results have been better than the pessimists forecast. At the least some good seed was sown for international co-operation on financial and economic subjects.

I used to hear it whispered that my approach towards my Allied friends was inclined to be too benign at times. I can only say that all their demands were coldly weighed in the balance. Like everybody else, I wanted to see the war ended as speedily as possible, and I had no difficulty in acceding to any request which seemed to me likely to help to achieve that universal aim. The Allied Governments were, so to speak, our guests. They could only plead, most of them. I disliked making them sit up and beg. They had their dignity to think of, and in such circumstances these considerations must be taken into account. I think I was tough, but I hope not ruthless, and never sentimental. Even in the material atmosphere of the Treasury, where money is regarded as something very real, I was unable to look upon it as anything but a means to an end, something to be made subservient to our purposes and not to govern us or to be our master.

Between us we established a relationship of complete mutual confidence, and there was very little jockeying for position on their part. Their propositions for expenditure of money had naturally to go through our Treasury sieve, but it would be giving a false impression if it were thought that it was all 'take' on their side. For instance, the gold from the Belgian Congo and the millions of tons of merchant shipping placed at our disposal by the Norwegians were vital factors, whereas the gallantry of the Polish Air Pilots and others is renowned. I was only superficially in touch with all the underground work being planned in the Allied Countries by their citizens domiciled here, but doubtless it exercised a tremendous effect on the result of the war, especially on the landing in Europe, and afterwards.

It was a rewarding, if at times complicated and delicate, duty for me. One saw many different types of man, but none were overly grasping in their requests. Although the Free French were of course without funds of their own, it was to General de Gaulle's credit that he declined to accept from our Government a penny for his own personal expenses or for his *entourage*, these being provided from money donated for the purpose by Frenchmen from all over the world.

As I have said above, I admired the General enormously. He was not

(*Above*) Drawing of 41 Threadneedle Street.

(*Right*) First of a series of cartoons in the *Evening Standard*, August 1957 – 'Mr Lionel Fraser, head of Helbert Wagg, The City bankers, has taken a country house for an away-from-it-all holiday. There is a big garden and a high wall. But it still has a telephone.'

one of my heroes – I don't think of him that way – but I liked his single-ness of purpose. Frenchmen who remained in France during the occupation will never know how much they owe him for his stand for the dignity of France during the war. Of course he was intransigent and difficult, often absurdly so, but he was determined to uphold the honour and greatness of his country to the utmost of his ability. This attitude led to crises, oft repeated, especially sometimes when the General resolutely refused to respond to the crack of the whip. He has little sense of humour, but I regard him as one of the finest orators of the day. Once when I met him after a typically eloquent speech delivered at the Albert Hall, I told him after the first few pleasantries that I thought he was the third best speechmaker of the war leaders. Without much of a smile, he asked, 'Whom do you put before me?' and when I replied, 'Winston Churchill first, then Roosevelt,' he burst out laughing, 'I thought so!' We then went on to talk about children and the war, and he displayed great humanity and warmth of heart. I often think of this talk when I see flashes of him on television from time to time, being greeted so warmly by the crowds who surround him on his tours in the French provinces, and his equally affectionate response. In April 1962 I was in France on holiday and had the opportunity to hear the addresses on television of the representatives of the various French political parties regarding the Algerian referendum, whether to vote 'Oui' or 'Non'. Every one of them read their speeches, except the General. He delivered his two discourses, eight minutes a time, without hesitation of any sort, exhorting, demanding, cajoling – always with a serious unsmiling expression and with a slight touch of arrogance, but immensely inspiring and word-perfect.

In the middle of November 1944, I was sent to Paris as Head of a Mission ostensibly to discuss economic and financial questions of interest to the two countries, but particularly to try and settle for cash the amount of the Free French indebtedness to us for all our disbursements on their behalf during the war. I had to support me George Bolton and John Lithiby of the Bank of England, Brigadier Rabino late of the Westminster Foreign Bank in Paris and a popular figure with the French, and John Penton who had worked hard and effectively at the Treasury during the war, notably on French and Belgian financial matters. We were installed at the Hotel Castiglione in the Faubourg St Honoré which had been requisitioned for official purposes. We were doomed to failure from the beginning. I think Sir John Anderson expected it, for when I was about to leave London, he sent for me to give final instructions and added 'Try all you can but I know you will have no success. However, good luck.' Discouraging I thought, but realistic.

We were in Paris about ten days, during which we were in tight negotiation at the Ministry of Finance. The French insisted that the discussions should be conducted in French, as is their usual custom. Their leader was M. Jacques Brunet aided by Guillaume Guindey. The former is now Governor of the Banque de France, and even back in 1945 was a formidable figure. We found, between our two missions, no point of contact, perhaps because we were too impatient in attempting a settlement so soon. An unpropitious moment. Feelings on both sides were high. We had won the war, despite the French, and still somewhat resented what we considered was a rather too rapid surrender in 1940. On their side, the French made it clear that they thought we were unsympathetic, and did not understand the misery, humiliation and distress they had endured during the occupation. They felt we owed it to them to be benign and generous. We expected to receive all the financial assistance we could get by way of repayment of indebtedness, in order to enable us to sustain our own crippling post-war burden. It was an entirely friendly and courteous deadlock, but it was nonetheless deadlock. Sir John Anderson did not say on our return, 'I told you so', but as I was reporting to him I thought it stole out of his solemn expression. My successor at the Treasury told me that years afterwards when the heat was off, a settlement was reached, but on a very much lower basis, as a part, I imagine, of a general financial arrangement between France and ourselves.

On return from Paris I contributed an article in *The Daily Telegraph* from 'A recent visitor to Paris' entitled: 'Britain could play a stalwart part in France's revival – her people, shaken and self-pitying, need our understanding friendship'. I portrayed the sadness of Paris and the total lack of understanding of other people's hardships – just as great as their own, but different. Those whom I met in France had no conception of the extent to which British production and manpower had been mobilized for the war effort, nor of the devastation and the physical exhaustion in our country. They thought we had plenty of food, whereas they were struggling to obtain the bare minimum for existence. But many of our poorer classes had been very hungry indeed and were certainly undernourished. The French thought we had plenty of heat whereas their houses were fiendishly cold and the occupants always kept their coats and mufflers on, and even their hats.

There is no doubt they suffered, most of them, profound mental and spiritual anguish during the occupation. The vast majority found it intolerable, and the consequence of the Vichy and German propaganda was to set one Frenchman against another. Resort to the *marché noir* was second nature to most Parisians.

The French people at that moment were dazed and stunned, with probably 2,500,000 of their nationals, men and women, in Germany, prisoners of war or deportees. There was scent in abundance, but no bottles, and most women wore wooden soles to their shoes. But the worst feature was the lack of a unified or coherent thought, no national newspapers, no communication or transport, and a total ignorance of events taking place either in their own country or abroad.

If ever a nation was past sentimentality and in need of infinite patience, understanding and sympathy, it was the French. They screamed for true encouragement to help them regain their self-confidence. Their admiration for us was very deep, almost embarrassing, and Churchill was their hero. One man said to me, 'Churchill, c'est le bon Dieu pour moi.' I pleaded that we should grasp the hand of friendship extended to us. I was confident they would come out of their state of vagueness, incoherence, sadness, and even at times feebleness, and that they would emerge not as the old France, but as a nation invigorated by a new spirit of sacrifice and a determination to build on higher standards. It will be clear that even in those days I was a Francophile.

An interesting additional feature of my Treasury work was watching over our financial arrangements with the U.S.S.R. At a certain moment they were demanding vast quantities of supplies from this country, particularly power stations, transformers and machine tools. We always believed in the Treasury that gold production from within the U.S.S.R. was maintained during the war, and indeed was given priority over other production. Anyhow the Russians were always rigidly prompt in their deliveries of gold in part payment of our supplies, even though this meant running the blockade from Murmansk. The bills were invariably met precisely on the due date, often at great sacrifice in lives.

My wife and I became very friendly with the then head of the Soviet Trade Delegation and his delightful little wife – this was in the early part of 1944 – and we often entertained them at home, discussing many matters of mutual interest, their regime, ours, religion and such like. We felt we had established a happy association which would endure, when suddenly, blank! They became incommunicado and eventually disappeared back to Moscow without a sign and we never heard another word of them. We were sure it was not their personal desire to be so offhand with us and I believe this breach coincided with a general order from Stalin at the time of Yalta, when it will be remembered the attitude of the Russians towards us became so icy.

I cannot claim my work was of such a vital and pressing nature that I was frequently in touch with the Chancellor of the Exchequer. Indeed such meetings were rare – and he was a remote figure. But I came into close contact with the Financial Secretaries of the Treasury and the two who impressed me most were Captain Cruickshank, later Lord Cruick-shank, and Ralph Assheton, now Lord Clitheroe. They were utterly different personalities, but both able and tenacious politicians.

Sir John Anderson was a superb Chancellor, blessed with a fantastic memory and possessed of vast experience. A serious, apparently pompous, exterior tended to make one think he was a cold, unapproachable man. Certainly he was imperturbable. He gave confidence by his steadiness and the deep thought he obviously bestowed on a problem before he came forth with a decision. He was one of our greatest public servants.

With the war against Germany victoriously ended, my Allied Government friends arranged to return to their various countries, and to have their performances judged by their countrymen whose lives had been passed in such completely different circumstances. In some cases the reception was cordial and friendly – in others there was a lack of interest, perhaps too much introspection and jealousy. But my own particular work was drawing to its natural conclusion and I felt it was time to close the book. Although the Treasury were kind enough to express their anxiety for me to remain, I was restive and wanted to get back to the building of a career in The City. Because I had been so fully occupied I had had of necessity to neglect most of my contacts, although I must admit that by comparison with the enthralling duties at the Treasury, investment banking, as I knew it at the beginning of the war, was dull. But, always remembering my private motto – to retire from a position when those around me wished me to continue, provided the duties were finished to my satisfaction – I took my stand and pressed Waley to release me. Finally a date was agreed upon and on 3 January 1945 I bade farewell to my colleagues and went back to The City.

This ended for me something over five years of work in the inner circle of H.M. Treasury. Most of it was highly absorbing, if at times unduly strenuous. Without a doubt the experience broadened my outlook considerably. It sharpened my intellect, and increased my capacity for concentrated work by teaching me the habit because I was able to follow the example set me by my established Civil Service colleagues. So it is no wonder that I feel indebted to all those new friends I made at the Treasury, and in other Departments, to say nothing of those in the Allied Governments domiciled here, whose patience and fortitude I admired so much. Those were five priceless years. To have the curtain lifted, so dramatically and so interestingly, on an entirely different life: to be at the very heart of Government during the greatest struggle in history: these things are unforgettable and cannot fail to leave an indelible mark in the fashioning of one's future career.

In the 1945 New Year's Honours List the C.M.G. (Commander of the Most Honourable Order of St Michael and St George) was conferred on me. When Sir John Anderson congratulated me, he said it was a pretty little ribbon, and so it is.

Chapter 12

ONE OF MY EXTRA DUTIES AT THE TREASURY – outside my ordinary work – but delegated to me, I suppose, because I had had previous commercial and industrial experience, was to keep a special eye from the Treasury angle on a new company which had been formed in April 1940 called the United Kingdom Commercial Corporation Ltd, known as the U.K.C.C. It was entirely financed by public money and I was the Treasury official primarily responsible for its expenditure.

The U.K.C.C. was to become a most valuable instrument in the war effort. *The Times* described it as 'A National Enterprise'. In its early stages the U.K.C.C. was mainly what might be called a pre-emptive purchasing organization, brought into being to meet the pressing need, hitherto unfulfilled, of countering German economic penetration in the Balkans and south-east Europe. Its original chief function was to buy up in neutral countries anything which, in the opinion of its Board of Directors and of the Ministry of Economic Warfare under whose auspices it was created, could assist the enemy in their conduct of the war. This involved the purchase in such spheres as Turkey, the Middle East, Spain and Portugal of certain commodities: oil seeds, rags, valuable metals such as wolfram and chrome – anything to keep these materials out of the hands of the enemy. To all intents and purposes, the prices paid were of minor importance, but as the enemy was often competing strongly in these neutral markets, it can easily be imagined that the cost was exorbitant and uneconomic. That did not matter: the prime object was to deprive the enemy of these vital goods, and success was measured by the quantity acquired, not the price.

Later its functions were extended, as it was found that in order to make pre-emptive purchasing successful the U.K.C.C. had to be prepared to sell those countries things they wanted: otherwise they were reluctant to let us, rather than the enemy, have the goods, even if our price was higher. The U.K.C.C. therefore organized sales from this country, as well as purchases by this country.

The U.K.C.C. was especially active in its operations in the Middle East. Its task was to make the Middle East countries as far as possible self-supporting and thus reduce the need for merchant shipping in the dangerous waters of the Mediterranean. From headquarters in Cairo, under the policy directions of the Middle East Supply Centre, cereals, sugar and other commodities were brought from 'surplus' and supplied to 'deficiency' countries in the area. In association with the Army, distribution arrangements were also set up and operated in areas liberated from the enemy as far south as Eritrea, Jibuti and Abyssinia. Final deficiencies were made good by shipments from Australia, all completed without loss of ship or man. The U.K.C.C. was also used as the medium for all the British non-military supplies to Russia, whether by the northern route or by the Persian route, and did extremely valuable work in this connection. I believe it was responsible for the delivery of supplies to the U.S.S.R. totalling £150 million, besides transporting more than 100,000 refugee Polish soldiers in lorries returning from the Caspian.

The first Chairman was Lord Swinton and under his very able leadership, the Company, starting from tiny beginnings, became an integral and important organization of economic warfare disbursing vast sums in their purchases. Their turnover in their peak year exceeded £150 million. I recall that at its debut it was essential to have ministerial approval to spend even £250,000, involving prolonged inter-departmental committee meetings, but as their activities expanded, it was left to me to give final approval to even their major operations.

Very wisely the Government decided to leave the handling and carrying out of the U.K.C.C.'s operations entirely in the hands of experts, not civil servants, men highly experienced in such matters. To Lord Swinton fell the task of collecting around him a suitable Board of Directors. This was by no means easy, as such men would be expected to possess highly specialized qualifications and to have an original approach – not to conserve but to spend! The Board in their turn had to choose, as best they could from men too old or unfit for the Services, skilled representatives to work in the offices at home, and to set up abroad active organizations in the various neutral countries where convenient centres could be established. Later, as the importance of the work of the U.K.C.C. became better appreciated, I believe their personnel problems were assisted by the readiness of the Army, especially in the Middle East, to release men with the requisite experience and knowledge.

Much of the work was of a secret nature and those who undertook it have kept their counsel. In the event some odd things happened. Industrial diamonds and precision instruments were bought and later arrived in Russia without visible means of transport. They did not pass by sea convoy to Archangel, or over the land lorry service through Persia. Thousands of tons of vital cargo were delivered inside South Russia by motor transport over all the miles from the Persian Gulf, with no payment except the supply of tyres, which were at one time selling at the equivalent of £800 per set of four. The wolfram market in Spain was broken late in the war involving the German agents in years of fruitless litigation trying to get rid of land concessions from which they had hoped to dig fortunes. There were many similar transactions.

That Lord Swinton did his selection with discrimination and judgment is proved by the names of those who composed the Board. They numbered amongst them Sir Leonard Paton, just recently retired from the Chairmanship of Harrisons & Crosfield, a very shrewd Scotsman with a vast experience of trade all over the world; Mr Jack Hambro, a Managing Director of Hambros Bank, whom I once heard described in 1945 by an eminent City authority as 'one of the best young bankers in The City'; Sir Percy Lister, Chairman of R. A. Lister & Sons, a clever industrialist of high order; Sir Frank Nixon, formerly head of the Export Credits Guarantee Department and I believe its creator, a unique phenomenon, a civil servant who knows as much about industry as of the Government machine, and Sir Alfred Chester Beatty who had supreme knowledge of commodity dealing. There were also Captain Leighton, a wonderful old ex-sea captain; Mr Angus Campbell and Mr E. J. Shearer, both distinguished in their special interests; Mr G. A. McEwen of the Co-operative Wholesale Society, and last but not least Mr E. H. Lever, now Sir Ernest Lever, former Secretary of the Prudential Assurance Co and later Chairman of Richard Thomas

& Baldwins Ltd – a man of formidable capacity. When Lord Swinton returned to politics and became Minister of State for West Africa, Sir Francis Joseph assumed the Chairmanship. Coming from most humble origin, he had already achieved distinction, being a Baronet, K.B.E., a Director of the Midland Bank, and having many other interests. He devoted all his skill to ensuring that the U.K.C.C. did its job effectively. A quite extraordinary man, whom I liked very much.

The results achieved by the U.K.C.C. were difficult to assess, as much of its work was of such an intangible nature. We won the war, and of all the many contributory factors, the U.K.C.C. must have been a significant one in its way – of that I am certain. The dedicated work of its Board of Directors was a great example to me and I had wonderful personal relations with them all. In a strictly analytical sense I cannot say that all their pre-emptive schemes were successful. I dare even say they were induced sometimes to pay exorbitant prices, but this was inevitable, as I have pointed out above. Some of their proposals seemed curiously harebrained, but who was I to disregard a powerful case stated by highly responsible men of standing, so well qualified in their handling of such matters? Indeed, when their expenditure reached such dimensions that it had to come under the scrutiny of the Public Accounts Committee, their operations received complete approval.

As I have shown, their function, as the war proceeded, was more and more to act on behalf of the civil and military authorities in various areas, as suppliers and carriers of goods, using all normal trading channels for the purpose. I never heard what the final total of their expenditure was, but the figure was huge. I rather fancy they took losses on their pre-emptive purchases of something under £20 million and that this was squared by their other earnings. There can be no doubt that the U.K.C.C. played a considerable part in the blockade of the enemy. The organization, gathering pace and skill all the while, was at a high pitch of efficiency at the end of the war.

It was an entirely novel conception. The task which the corporation was set, demanding secrecy, speed and an all too frequent but clearly necessary disregard of normal business methods, was itself quite exceptional and it called for original tactics which were sometimes difficult to comprehend and which equally often evoked surprise and criticism. In this short summary I can only mention their activities in broad outline, but my brief judgment would be that under Lord Swinton, and later Sir Francis Joseph, they did brilliantly successful work. I was their supporter, often their critic, but always their understanding and proud friend.

Chapter 13

THE PREVIOUSLY MENTIONED negotiations in Paris at the end of 1944, without tangible results as they were, brought me very close to the French and I was therefore more than pleased when early in 1945, the Foreign Office through the Bank of England, invited me to succeed Sir Charles Addis, as British Censor of the State Bank of Morocco. I never had the pleasure of meeting Sir Charles, as he was too ill at the time, and died soon after his resignation. This sounds an unusual appointment, and indeed so it proved to be. As a matter of fact, it was regarded as almost a joke in this country and the job was rarely referred to by the knowing ones without a smile. It is a typically French institution and all their big Banks have 'Censeurs', which positions, may I humbly say, are invariably held by men of standing and experience. It is impossible to translate correctly the word into English as there is no counterpart here of the function. Our official work was to ensure that the Board of Directors conformed strictly to the statutes of the Bank, notably as regards cover for the note circulation in Morocco, for as its name implies, the Bank was the Bank of Issue. Unofficially, I frequently played a part in the higher policy of the Bank, for as those in authority grew to know me better, I was called into consultation wherever my experience could be useful.

Sir Charles had held the position for thirty-nine years, ever since the formation of the Bank under the Act of Algeciras of 1906 and I was therefore the second holder and, as it later transpired, destined to be the last. In truth, it was one of those positions which are simple and in perfect order until something goes wrong. The Bank had as original shareholders the French, British, German, Italian, Spanish, Dutch, Belgian and Portuguese Governments as well as the Moroccans themselves, but in 1937 the British decided, rather unwisely as it turned out, to sell their participation, and the Germans and Italians also fell out after the First War. But we kept some status by retaining our right to appoint a British Censor. There were also during my time a French and a Spanish Censor. The Censors were entitled to attend all the Board or Committee Meetings of the Bank, but were excluded from taking part in the actual discussions unless, in their opinion, the statutes were contravened. The meetings were usually held in Paris, and statutes laid down that the Censors must meet at least once every two years in Tangier, then an International Zone. These conditions appertaining to our duties made my association an extremely pleasant one, as can well be imagined. I always think the French appreciate better than most other nationalities how much men like to share their journeys abroad with their wives so that they may participate in all the new friendships made whilst *en voyage*. I was not surprised therefore when the Directors of the Bank insisted that my wife should accompany me as their guest on my visits to Paris and Morocco and I was not reluctant to accept this gracious hospitality on behalf of my wife.

In England the tax authorities look undisguisedly askance at such joint journeys. This is right to an extent, for there are those who take advantage of any privilege. However, I am sure that a husband, with a wife in consort, does a vastly better job than if he is left alone since together they can form a 'home team'. There are always exceptions, but I know that when visiting Mexico by myself a few years ago, I felt at a heavy disadvantage through the absence of companionship and the inability to exchange views with my wife on the new situations arising.

The Censors were expected to deliver at the Annual General Meeting in Paris a report on the economic situation of Morocco and to give an assurance to the stockholders of due fulfilment by the Board of Directors of the statutes of the Bank. This was usually carried out by my French colleague, but in his absence on two occasions, it fell to my lot to read the report to the handful of stockholders present. They were invariably a dull, rather seedy-looking lot, never asked a question and understandably showed little animation at the rather boring proceedings. However, I noted a flicker of interest out of the corner of my eye when I did my exacting and tongue-twisting act. Having to announce in French such sums as Frs. 1,208,437,654.20 is no mean task for an Englishman, un-accustomed to talking in public in French. As involved figures were repeated many times during the statement, I was not sorry when the time came for me to sit down.

Altogether I could not claim that in itself the function of British Censor of the Bank was one calling for much mental effort on my part. But it was for me of immense interest, inasmuch as it kept my finger right on the pulse of the French and Moroccan political and economic situations and brought me into contact with some of the leading per-sonalities in the post-war French financial sphere.

The Directeur Général of the Bank was M. Edmond Spitzer, a sound and progressive banker. He and his wife, Renée, a beautiful woman of exceptional intellectual quality, have become amongst our most intimate friends and indeed I started to write this book at their charming villa at Cap d'Antibes where my wife and I have frequently found rest and relaxation. Their insight into the character and bearing of so many of the foremost French political personages is always illuminating and they never fail to provide a dispassionate impression of the current situation. The Spitzers left many friends in Morocco, including the King and the Royal Family. Their personal influence for good could have been vital at the moment of independence, as their awareness of all the difficulties and political complications made them obvious figures to help in the delicate situation resulting from the transference of power in Morocco. But it was not to be, and it was much to be regretted that at the time the Bank was being sold to the Moroccan Government in 1960, Edmond Spitzer was undergoing a serious operation, putting him *hors de combat* for a critical period. He is now Censor of the Banque de Paris et des Pays Bas, amongst other duties, but I think he is still happiest when recalling his years in Morocco, which, although demanding, throbbed with decision and interest.

My French colleague as Censor was Henry de Bletterie, formerly First Deputy Governor of the Banque de France, and now, in retire-ment, Gouverneur Honoraire of the Bank, amongst other important posts. He it was who was detailed to stay behind in Paris and meet the Germans when they occupied the City. The story of his dignity and restraint when the keys of the Banque de France were handed over has often been recounted and I can well imagine it. We grew to know him very well indeed and the more we saw of him, the more we appreciated him. Alert and amusing, he can paraphrase a whole series of events in one apt sentence. We toured Morocco together by car on three or four occasions and these journeys were always made more lively by his dry French wit. He was succeeded as Censor by the newly appointed First Deputy Governor of the Banque de France, whose 'perk' it always was to assume the censorship of the Banque d'Etat du Maroc. This was Jean Saltes – an altogether different character; younger, vivid, of the 'Midi', and with an amazingly penetrating mind and an ability to cut right through a problem. Curiously enough, like de Bletterie, he speaks no English. Saltes is now President of the Crédit National, one of the plum jobs in the hierarchy of the celebrated Inspecteurs des Finances and usually one from which future Governors of the Banque de France are recruited. I likewise value his friendship highly, seeing in him staunch integrity and loyalty.

The Board of the Banque d'Etat du Maroc always had as its Chairman a nominee of the Banque de Paris et des Pays Bas, the Bank which in effect controlled it. The other Banks who owned shares were also represented on the Board. There were representatives of the Bank of Spain, Madrid; the Bank of Portugal, Lisbon; the Banque de la Société Générale de Belgique, Brussels; the Amsterdamsche Bank, Amsterdam; and the Stockholms Enskilda Bank, Stockholm. Surely overweighted in talent and knowledge as was the Board, I rarely heard the Directors pass any controversial or potent comments, except at luncheon after the Board Meetings. The President held the field and the rest were, as a body, unfailingly submissive.

Apart from my particular friends amongst members of the Board, the Banque de France invariably gives me a warm welcome on my visits to Paris. The first post-war Governor was M. Emmanuel Monick, who knew London well, having served here as the French Government financial representative before the war. I shall never forget the dinner which was given in his honour in mid-December 1944 at the Bank of England. It was a memorable, even sentimental occasion, and was the first time Central Bank representatives from any of the occupied countries had been received at the Bank since the war. M. Monick on his retirement from the Governorship of the Banque de France in 1949 assumed the Chairmanship of the Banque de Paris et des Pays Bas and also became a Director and a Vice-President of the Banque d'Etat du Maroc. His successor as Governor, M. W. Baumgartner, afterwards Minister of Finance, also extended a hand of friendship to me on all occasions and many is the happy and absorbing lunch I have had at the Bank with him and his colleagues. Possessed of infinite charm and an acute memory, he has exerted a powerful influence on the French financial scene during recent years. I am sure that now he has left public life, he feels more carefree; but whatever direction he pursues, he will certainly have success, so fine are his intellect and perspicacity. M. Baumgartner was followed by M. Jacques Brunet whom I have already mentioned. I cannot claim to know him well, although he too was at one time a director of the Banque d'Etat du Maroc. He is universally described as a most competent Governor. I do know also how much his colleagues are drawn to him which says a great deal in his favour. His first Deputy Governor is Pierre Calvet, a youthful, rosy-cheeked boy of a man who probably understands more of European and British finance than most. With a smile he can debunk arguments with lightning speed, as well in English as in his native language. Calvet is a Trustee of the Musée du Louvre and a hungry reader of contemporary English novels.

But to return to the Banque d'Etat du Maroc, the Censors had to assemble at least once every two years in Tangier, as I said above. Thus, since I occupied the position until the sale of the Bank in 1960, I paid official visits to Morocco on six occasions. Apart from the formal initial meeting at Tangier, those visits involved inspecting branches of the Bank far and wide all over Morocco. In these circumstances we saw much of Morocco, staying at Fez, Meknès and Marrakech and on one trip we travelled down by motor-car over the Atlas Mountains.

My wife and I paid our first visit in March 1947. We left London snowbound. I remember hearing that someone at that time found skiing easier than walking in Eaton Square! It was the winter of the fuel shortage and we were all shivering, which made it an exciting prospect to fly to Morocco. Except for my brief mission to Paris, it was the first journey abroad for either of us since before the war. This in itself was an event, but the thought of Morocco was indeed exotic in contrast with our grey and icy London. In those days the flight took two days with a night in Lisbon *en route*. The balmy air of Lisbon acted as an appetizer for all that was to follow; the sunshine and sight of geraniums everywhere seemed miraculous after the grim winter at home and the even grimmer six years of war. We had time for a trip round the city in a taxi, the driver, I remember, reserving the most praise for the football stadium!

Leaving Lisbon some time after midnight, we reached the brassy, modern city of Casablanca in the extremely early morning, which was the nearest point by aeroplane to our destination, Rabat. On arrival at Casablanca we were at once taken to the private apartment of the Banque d'Etat where we were served a delectable breakfast by the Bank's *chaouch*, consisting of fresh orange juice, croissants, coffee and limitless butter and apricot jam. Nothing unduly luxurious today but to rationed Britons it seemed like an abundant fairyland, and so it has remained in memory. The figure of the *chaouch*, the Bank's messenger, became thereafter a familiar and friendly sight to us at each Branch we visited, for he would act as our friend and guide, and sometimes as our protector as well as interpreter when bargaining in the souks (native markets) for he was always a French-speaking Moroccan. He wore a uniform of bright blue cloth with the initials B.E.M. on the lapel of his jacket, long baggy Moroccan trousers, and a red fez on his head. Refreshed by breakfast, we were motored to Rabat, the capital city, the main residence of the Sultan, the domicile of the Corps Diplomatique and of course the headquarters of the Banque d'Etat du Maroc. There we were to meet the Directeur Général and Madame Spitzer for the first time in their beautiful villa. I shall never forget this drive, as it was our introduction to the Moroccan scene, its countryside, its spaciousness, its carpets of wild flowers, its soft rolling hills, its primitive inhabitants cultivating their patches of fields in biblical fashion, straggling clusters of them walking or riding or leading their donkeys along the road – the latter often almost invisible beneath burdens of charcoal, grass or firewood. The Muslim women, who do more than their share of burden-carrying, struggle along with even heavier loads, whilst the male more frequently than not sits happily swinging his legs on a donkey.

I was disappointed and surprised at the colourless clothing worn by Moroccans and depressed by the primitive huts and hovels they lived in, though on another occasion, we were to find Europeans occupying much the same type of dwelling in southern Spain. We were attracted by Rabat, the profusion and beauty of flowers everywhere, and the elegance and ceremony of the French-Muslim life which was in distinct contrast to the England which we had left.

We were soon to become immensely attached to Morocco. It is special and individual in its charm and character, a country of natural beauty and historical interest all its own. Until the end of May, the climate is reasonably temperate, a dry heat and clear atmosphere, but thereafter until the autumn the heat inland can be intense and the French who work there always spend the summer months on the coast or in France whenever possible. We became conscious of all that the French had achieved, and we learnt to respect the memory of Marshal Lyautey. He had been responsible not only for the pacification of Morocco but for the subsequent organization and administration of the entire country – a stupendous feat. As France's first Resident General in 1922, he was much beloved by its inhabitants. Over the whole of the country there rests the unfading memory of that great Frenchman who by his vision, his sense of justice, and his sympathy for the native population, laid the foundations upon which the Protectorate was built.

Although poor and illiterate, the natives were everywhere friendly at this time, which was before the upsurge of political unrest. A European could go anywhere unarmed, and we ourselves frequently walked alone in the medinas, or native quarters. We even were lost for a while in the Atlas Mountains on one occasion when owing to floods we were diverted from the main road and neither our Spanish driver nor our map could help us back again. Eventually, as dusk was falling we found ourselves motoring along little more than a track and we were getting anxious. We were just climbing a steep and rough section when our engine failed. We barely concealed the inner sense of anxiety this gave us and dearly wished we could communicate more freely with our Spanish-speaking chauffeur. At this very moment of confusion, however, a Moroccan magnificent in his native garb – a cream-coloured djellabah – flashing eyes and white teeth, loomed up from nowhere, and in faulty French offered us food and shelter for the night in his nearby casbah – a sort of citadel. We accepted only water for the car and not the night's

L

shelter. His invitation tendered with such a mixture of suavity and firmness made us a little apprehensive, and after a glance at his ramshackle casbah we decided in all the circumstances we infinitely preferred the directions given us back to the main road. I confess we were relieved when our chauffeur got the car going again. We shall never know what the Moroccan really had in his mind, probably warmth and friendliness only, typical of the spirit of the country.

There are two distinct native races, the Berbers who are the original inhabitants, a sturdy energetic people, mostly living in the hills, and the Arabs, more numerous, comprising all classes, lackadaisical and easy-going but intelligent. There are also the Jews who form a certain part of the urban population. Women remain heavily veiled and are treated as second-class citizens by their menfolk. Muslims are permitted by law to have up to four wives, but economic reasons and modern conditions often preclude advantage being taken of this privilege. The rich women lead useless, monotonous lives, in the harems, and the poor ones are little better than slaves. Nevertheless, there is no doubt that during the last five years there has been an immense evolution in feminine circles. Except for those living in the cities, who have naturally become more sophisticated, the majority of the natives are simple, uneducated, friendly souls, anxious to be led, quite content to conduct their lives on lines exactly similar to those of their forefathers. Many are still very ill-clad, often in grimy rags or pieces of sacking, but nevertheless they are reasonably happy as their religion does little to encourage progress and the country people are devout Muslims. They help one another generously, are hospitable and are markedly fond of children.

When one is banqueted, which occurred for us on several occasions, by a 'Pasha' (chief of a district), or a 'Caid' (chief of a tribe), one is received in a lavish and splendiferous fashion. This entails squatting on cushions and using only the thumb and first two fingers of the right hand in place of knives and forks. These feasts, or diffas as they are called, consist of an endless stream of dishes, starting usually with pastry stuffed with minced pigeon – the pastry was always light and flaky and excellent. This would be followed by the proverbial couscous, a mixture of semolina and pieces of mutton. Entire sheep and chickens are then laid before the guests, and it is no mean feat to pluck morsels off these carcasses, freshly cooked, steaming hot. For this somewhat messy performance, one has a napkin tied round one's neck; before arriving at the 'pudding' stage, a huge finger-bowl of rose water is passed around. It is quite a ceremony – almost a bath!

The feasts of the ancient and famous Pasha of Marrakech, El Glaoui, were celebrated. He remained silent and impassive throughout the meal: this is a general, rather disconcerting custom, for the host prefers not to push himself forward in any way, but to leave his guests full freedom to please themselves. The Glaoui did not partake himself, but often made a gesture to indicate a particularly tasty morsel hidden in the gravy.

Over the years we visited all the larger towns of Morocco where there was an established branch of the Banque d'Etat. I always think how little Tangier represents Morocco; it is a typically pleasant Mediterranean port, but its inhabitants are untypical of the real Morocco for they are a thoroughly mixed lot. In the European part of the town the patisserie named Maison Porte – still flourishing – makes the best cakes I have ever eaten.

Then there is Meknès, made famous in the seventeenth century by the ruthless tyrant, Moulay Ismail. It is an important city and is the centre of the rich agricultural region. And Fez, the intellectual and cultural centre, has one of the oldest existing universities in the Islamic world, named Karaouin, with a library containing amongst other things priceless articles and books, as well as some precious old manuscripts. This ancient city was formerly the capital and Holy City, and possesses exceptional charm: its medina is the usual labyrinth of narrow streets, alley ways and teeming crowds. The alley ways seem even narrower than elsewhere, all flowing down into a maze cupped at the bottom of the medina. Walking there one stumbles on exquisite examples of architecture and carving of the twelfth and thirteenth centuries. Schools, universities and countless mosques, to say nothing of the endless souks, are all crowded and packed within the city walls. Actually the souks at Fez are the most famous in Morocco for fine leather work and other handcrafts which continue to be practised with an unbelievable skill often by children as well as the aged. They are true artisans. In the machine age one is amazed at their patience and wonders for how many more decades these methods – beautiful in their way – will continue in

[153]

Morocco. A purchase has always to be spread over as long as possible to allow time for bargaining, a process I always thoroughly enjoyed! It was not just beating the merchant down in price: it was testing the market and getting down to a basis. He stated his asking price which was much too high – you ridiculed, and countered with yours, which was much too low. The fun was in ascertaining how far down you could persuade him to come towards you, without showing any keenness. Completion sometimes took several days and yet I always had the sneaking feeling I had been outdone! But it didn't matter, and we have one or two lovely rugs acquired in the souks.

Marrakech, the largest town of the south, is built within a crumbling wall of pink-red earth, and has as its back-cloth the snow-capped Atlas mountains. It seems to capture all the romance of Africa, with its palms, gorgeous sunsets, orange and lemon groves, gardens and exotic birds, and particularly its famous Place Djemaa-El-Fna, a large expanse in the centre of the town where the population from far and wide gather all day and all night long, as if it were the rendezvous of the whole southern region. In the morning a market is held, merchandise of every sort is on sale, and letter-writers, doctors, barbers and dentists are available. In the afternoon it is principally turned over to amusement – dancing, story-telling, and music, made on strange instruments by even stranger-looking people from the south. On our first visit there were also snake charmers but since the day a tourist was bitten, they have been banned. The whole area is hot and dusty and in perpetual motion and noise. It is the hub where north meets south. Marrakech has a distinct flavour of 'Black Africa' and the Sahara, with so many people of negroid appearance jostling in the crowds. The locals speak with infinite pride of their famous and distinguished visitor, Sir Winston Churchill. It was not difficult to understand his liking for Marrakech.

It is in the south that one gets the real feel and remoteness of Morocco, and when we traversed the Atlas mountains we saw native villages emerging like citadels out of the very mountain face. At Tafraout, our most southerly point, there are breathtaking rock formations, presenting the most amazing surrealistic landscape I have ever seen. These red rocks rise up on either side of the road in extraordinary shapes, silhouetted against the deep blue sky. We spent a night at Ouarzazate, an outpost strongly reminiscent of *Beau Geste*. We dined with the commandant and slept in the *gîte* – a sort of barracks, with one dormitory for men, another for women. My wife had a spahi guard posted outside her door, sleeping on the floor. Now, I believe, there is a hotel and everything arranged for tourists.

From there we reached Taroudant, with its alluring souk, fantastic casbahs of the local *seigneurs*, fields of wild orchids and goats climbing in the aloe trees. After the usual haggling, I bought a silver-mounted dagger in the souk which I still regard nostalgically, though it has no value or particular beauty.

And so on to Agadir with its inviting Atlantic rollers and to one of the loveliest of sandy beaches, utterly unfrequented. It has also an up-to-date port, mainly for the handling of fish. Sardines are there in profusion. Agadir was a charming, simple resort, the main European population being French officials and their families on holiday, boasting at that time only one good hotel, an unpretentious *plage*, a tennis club and a romantic old casbah high up on the ramparts with a restaurant from which one could watch the sunset whilst drinking mint tea. Poor Agadir, its destruction by the earthquake of 1959 caused us the deepest concern, knowing it as intimately as we did after such happy visits. Once we had to battle our way there from Mogador through a plague of locusts, an unpleasant experience. Hundreds lodged in the car's radiator and thereabouts. We had to keep stopping to scrape them off with a shovel, and were forced to travel even in the great heat with all the windows shut tight. I realized at first hand the utter desolation these plagues cause, totally stripping the countryside of everything edible.

Our last visit to Morocco was in spring 1960. With independence, changes had taken place not only in the administration but throughout the country. The departing French Army was leaving a vacuum. With it had disappeared many of the French shop owners and settlers, also the more recent arrivals – the American Air Force. Morocco was in fact being left to the Moroccans and although independence is sweet, it is famous for bringing its problems. The stupendous tasks to be undertaken were only too apparent. Money and trade were vanishing overnight and without the French, standards were everywhere lowering. One of the most vital questions is that of education, as only one in ten of the inhabitants can read or write. The old time schools merely taught the repetition of the Koran and children are reared in the remotest areas devoid of transport. But since independence, educational instruction has much improved, and the French Government have drafted many professors and teachers to the country.

Work on such a vast scale is required to bring Morocco anything like up to date, that the administration must feel overwhelmed by such a backward country's needs in housing, medical care, education, agriculture, and in the augmentation of the supply of electricity. An intensive irrigation scheme is essential to render the land more fruitful and the harvests less dependent on the weather.

Nevertheless, it cannot be questioned that the French have reason to be proud of their achievements in Morocco. Law and order had been established, and in spite of their poverty the natives assuredly enjoyed to some degree a state of peace and satisfaction. The present young King is held in high esteem, and as he also has great authority, there is reason to hope that his influence and leadership will be welding and will contribute to the development of this vital country.

Although some of the glamour and mystery which we first encountered have evaporated as the country has become better known, and the Coca Cola signs so numerous, I strongly recommend a visit. For me there was always an endless attraction in mixing in the medinas with these shrewd, kindly, primitive folk, a sort of relaxation derived from observing a world and a people whose civilization is in such complete contrast to one's own.

Chapter 14

MY FIRST OUTSIDE DIRECTORSHIP was with Spicers Limited, the well-known paper company to which I was appointed in 1940. Due to an old friendship between Sir Dykes Spicer and Alfred Wagg, they approached Helbert, Wagg & Co. for an independent Director, one who was not *parti pris*, to join the Board to keep the balance between the two branches of the family who could not always agree. Spicers, as we knew, was an amalgamation of two proud family concerns, and the mainspring of the difficulty may have been that one family made paper while the other used paper as its raw material for manufacturing paper products. Different interests may have caused different outlooks, and possibly some jealousy. The old Chairman, one of the paper manufacturing family, always seemed aloof and lonely – probably from choice. I think they wanted one of our more senior directors, but finally Alfred Wagg persuaded them to accept me, at the bottom of the list.

This Directorship was not a particularly enviable duty although as a matter of fact I had the authority of a final referee when disputes arose. It often called for the exercise of a delicately balanced mixture of tact and firmness if I were to retain the goodwill of the contending parties, without which I could not function. I was 'on loan' to the Treasury at the time, but I soon discovered that a period of training in the Diplomatic Service would have been more helpful!

It was impossible for me to attend the frequent Board meetings and it was arranged that my old friend and colleague, James O'Brien should act as my alternate to keep an eye on current problems for me, and as it happened, most of the heat and burden of the day fell on him. I turned up at as many Board Meetings as I could, and when delicate or contentious points arose, I endeavoured to the best of my ability to get a compromise between the contestants before they had to face each other for a decision. This state of affairs is not unknown in many old established family businesses. I remember that the Board Meetings always opened with prayers, but this did not prevent the fur from flying at times.

I remained on the Board for ten years – perched sometimes precariously and thanklessly on the middle of the see-saw. When James Spicer returned from war service and settled down to work in perfect harmony with his cousin Lancelot Spicer, they lost little time in making it clear that they would prefer, from then on, to be free to paddle their own canoe. The results show how successful they have been. For our part, I cannot say we were sorry to retire. Yet it had been an interesting, if telling experience, and was a further advance of some sort for me.

A merchant banking firm is constantly approached by industrial companies, insurance companies, banks and others to supply directors to go on their Boards. Some of us have had innumerable such approaches which had to be declined for the general good of the business, but often with infinite regret. Obviously many factors have to be weighed before action is taken, and frequently awkward decisions are involved. If we accepted all the invitations we received, partners would be fully occupied in outside directorships alone and would never be in the office to attend to the business of the day, which must have priority. Again there are personal considerations, arising from family connections where a sense of obligation is uppermost. Then there is the location of the Board Meetings, the time required. Everything must be judged on its merits. We had to be very selective. A popular and suitable character could secure so many directorships that he would rapidly become independent of his 'home' firm, and although this could not happen in a well-knit, understanding and loyal partnership, such as our own always was, it is something to be pondered.

Sometimes a particular directorship precisely fills the bill, or it brings grist to the mill, or the pressure is irresistible. And there is always the call of the national interest. There are all sorts of reasons for and against, but happy is the firm which can apportion these plums, ripe or not so ripe, to the mutual satisfaction of all concerned.

This question of filling of board appointments is certain to constitute a major problem over the years – and it will become more and more acute in the nationalized industries. The average fee for an outside director is, I suppose, £1,000 per annum, which is little enough when one considers the responsibility, the concentrated attention, the reading and study which have to be undertaken and the constant telephoning and inquiries between Board Meetings. There is great *cachet*, even honour, to be obtained from election to certain Boards. One can learn much, and usually finds contact with interesting people who can broaden and extend one's own horizon.

Chapter 15

MY SECOND DIRECTORSHIP was Thomas Tilling Limited, to which Board I was appointed in July 1942. Like so many other happenings in my life, it almost appeared predestined. Alfred Wagg had been a Tillings Director for some years and, making his influence felt in many ways, had effected some important changes in the company. At that time it was almost exclusively a bus company, owning buses and garages all over the country, and its Chairman was Mr J. Frederick Heaton, later to become Sir Frederick. I hardly knew him, but one day during the war I was chasing back in the rain on foot to Treasury Chambers when I was hailed by Alfred Wagg and offered a lift. He was accompanied by Heaton in the taxi, and we exchanged a few pleasantries of a light-hearted nature. The next day, to my amazement, the latter wrote asking me to join the Board of Tillings, saying he was also intending to approach Lord Brabazon. We always made it a practice in H.W., if it could be avoided, not to have two directors on the same Board, and here were the Chairman and the most junior Partner invited to sit together. I naturally pointed this out to Heaton, after consulting Alfred Wagg, but the former was adamant. 'I don't mind about partnership rules,' he said, typically, 'and I like the idea of the top and the bottom.' So it happened, and with the noble Lord Brabazon, surely one of the most talented and versatile human beings, I joined the Board of Thomas Tilling Limited. Perhaps the following brief history of Tillings may be interesting, as forming a romantic business success story.

Thomas Tilling was born on 3 February 1825 into a successful farming family. In 1845 he went into business on his own account when he purchased a dairy at Walworth, and soon afterwards a grey mare and carriage. A few years later he moved to Peckham, where stables were taken, and the omnibus branch of his business gradually developed. The first regular journey was between Peckham and Oxford Circus, and on this route Thomas Tilling initiated the system of a fixed schedule. But Tillings also supplied horses and carriages for private hire – for the Metropolitan Police, night-mail services, fire brigades, weddings, and all the most important events in the London area. Ten years after his modest start Thomas Tilling owned seventy horses, and on his death in 1893 the number had risen to two thousand five hundred. He was succeeded as head of the business by his elder son Richard, and in 1897 a public limited company was formed.

In 1904 Tillings became the first of the established public transportation companies to adopt the motor-bus, when a Milnes-Daimler double-deck motor-bus was placed in service. The seven thousand horses were gradually replaced by motor vehicles and the five hundred stables gave way to garages. By 1913 Tillings owned some three hundred motor vehicles, besides more than four thousand horses.

An agreement with the London General Omnibus Company in 1913 restricted Tillings' London bus operations, but a new agreement in 1923 enabled Tillings to participate in the growth and development of London's traffic. Ten years later, however, an Act of Parliament established a comprehensive body for London's transport, and Tilling London buses were transferred to the London Passenger Transport Board. For some years Tillings and other bus operators had been opening up or acquiring omnibus businesses throughout the country, and between them they operated four to five thousand omnibuses and coaches – probably more than any other similar undertaking in the world. In the 1930s Tillings progressed further under the Chairmanship of Mr J. F. Heaton.

In November 1937, the company established its headquarters in Crewe House, Curzon Street, London, the freehold being bought from the Crewe family. The house was originally built about 1730 by Edward Shepherd who gave his name to the market he built nearby in 1735. I consider Crewe House to have one of the most beautiful and distinguished façades of any house in London and apart from its giving us pleasure we seemingly afford pleasure to many thousands of passers-by and to those who enjoy its flood-lit splendour every night after dark.

Heaton proved to be a very tough Yorkshireman. It was soon obvious that his voice and his alone would prevail at the Board Meetings. He had every detail of the company, and every detail of every subsidiary company, at his fingertips. He knew everything. He made the appointments, he awarded the salaries and the promotions. Being a person who 'likes to know', I had many a struggle with him. Alfred Wagg, feeling the awkwardness which we had both anticipated, decided to retire fairly soon from the Board, which was a pity and a sadness for his colleagues, including myself. He had been, as would be expected, a calming and softening influence on the Chairman. The latter was one of the most efficient 'machines' I have ever encountered, and probably because of that, was almost without intimate friends. He slaved for Tillings; no effort was too much. He was daring too, but always completely confident of his own powers to succeed. He built up Tillings, literally and absolutely, aided by some very able colleagues, notably the brothers Tom and Walter Wolsey, grandsons of the founder of the business, of whom the latter is still living happily in well-deserved retirement; a splendid old fellow; and Cardwell and Kennedy, both of whom were experts in the 'bus' game and later did fine service with the British Transport Commission.

I recall one testing moment at a Board Meeting when, without providing any supporting facts or figures, the Chairman asked us to confirm a purchase involving capital expenditure of well over £1 million. I ventured to ask a few questions before I would fall into line, and probing a bit deeper, I got a rasping reply from Heaton: 'I hope that will do now. What can you possibly know about it? Anyhow your opinion would not be worth having!' Even coming from Heaton, this was too much to stomach, and I protested hotly. In the ensuing consternation he apologized handsomely, saying that what he meant was that his knowledge of the position was infinitely greater than mine. That was obvious and I admitted it straightaway. But it is a position in which many 'outside' directors must find themselves, and never should they desist from asking the awkward question for that reason. It is one of their main functions, even though the result can be unpalatable to the Chairman. Thereafter Heaton and I appreciated one another much more, and indeed it was not long before he asked his colleagues to agree to my appointment as Deputy Chairman of the Parent Company.

Heaton always took the line that it was ridiculous for buses to compete with railways. He was rabid on the point and worked hard for unification of the systems. He felt this so strongly that rather than hold out against the London Transport Board, he asked our authority to start negotiations with Lord Ashfield, the then Chairman, for the sale of our bus and garage interests all over the country to the Transport Commission. It is sometimes thought that Tillings was nationalized, but it is untrue. The operation was a freely negotiated sale on our part and it was finally settled on the basis of seven years' purchase, calculated on the profits for the previous year which were the highest in the Group's history. The figure worked out at just under £25 million, and with satisfaction Heaton reported this admirable bargain to the Board.

Almost immediately after this successful conclusion, Heaton fell sick and I realized I should have the task, as the newly appointed and very inexperienced Deputy Chairman, of taking the Chair at the Extraordinary General Meeting of Shareholders which was held to confirm the sale. During the preceding weeks I spent long hours at Heaton's bedside, when he would recount to me all his hopes and aspirations for the Group. I valued that period deeply, and with his public mask down, I was privileged to see inside the mind of this remarkably dedicated man. The following tribute which I sent to *The Times* of 5 May 1949 represents my feelings about him:

'Although Sir Frederick Heaton had a comparatively small circle of intimate friends, his achievements were admired by very many people, while a still larger number of the general travelling public, who had never heard his name, had reason to be grateful to him for his efforts on their behalf. Those who got through his natural reserve had affection for him, and were stirred by the grit he displayed during the closing weeks of his life. All his Yorkshire shrewdness, farsightedness, and immense administrative ability were put into the development of the Tilling Group of bus and haulage companies. He devoted his life to this work and it is a matter of infinite regret that at this particular time his deep knowledge of road transport is lost to the country.'

When negotiations with the Transport Commission began, Tilling shares stood at about 51/- per £1 share. When they were completed, the same shares were quoted on the Stock Exchange at 30/- per share, but in the meanwhile shareholders had received in capital dividend Transport 3% Stock equal in value to about £5 per share. This was a tremendous personal tribute to Heaton and as a Board we decided to invite the shareholders to offer him the sum of £25,000 as a mark of appreciation. I did not expect any opposition, but to my surprise an objection was raised by one shareholder at the special meeting. I scornfully beat him off, saying that if I had had my own way, I would have been proposing a sum four times higher and that I did not think even that sufficient for the services Heaton had rendered to the company and its shareholders. The proposition was carried but I am ashamed to say with three dissentients. A few weeks later Heaton died. He left a letter suggesting to my colleagues that they should appoint me Chairman, and this they graciously and charmingly did on 8 May 1949. Thus began one of the most adventurous and fruitful episodes in my life. It has continued with gathering interest and pace ever since, and I will try to tell the story.

The first big problem under my chairmanship was what to do with the British Transport 3% Stock 1968–73, which we had been allotted at 101 by the Government in payment for our assets. This gave us much food for thought. Instead of assets, buses, garages and so on, we had a huge block of Transport 3% Stock yielding a return of less than 3%. We could not pay a respectable dividend out of that, so what should we do? We could see little point in holding on. The price had already slid away and had tumbled to 97. We therefore decided to distribute £21 million nominal to our shareholders as capital dividend, as I said earlier, and to sell forthwith the balance of approximately £4 million for account of the company. Looking back, it may have seemed an easy decision, but actually it required a lot of courage. We were in the middle of Doctor Dalton's notorious cheap money period and all the talk was of still lower interest rates. However, we sold, and of course have never regretted the decision. That same stock, at its lowest, fell to 70½ in August 1961.

We thereupon resolved to use our available funds to create what we now call 'a Family of Firms'. We announced to the shareholders that the company was entering upon a new era, that we envisaged for ourselves a positive and active role, using our surplus money in a constructive manner by direct participation in industry and by the development and expansion of the other interests which remained to us after the sale of our buses. At first our efforts were regarded with some suspicion by the financial scribes, but from the outset we had the support and approval of a loyal body of shareholders. In the process of redevelopment we had perforce to exercise special care and discrimination. We had to look before we leaped but we never allowed our actions to be fettered by pessimism. We realized that if we were to be successful we must show sound judgment in our actions, whilst not lacking in courage and enterprise, nor fearing to take reasonable risks.

In retrospect, I will confess that those early days were in fact anxious ones. We were hardly up on our knees and one serious setback or misjudgment could have bowled us over completely. We had to win the confidence of our critics in our policy of diversification. It was a new departure, pioneering work, which had hardly been attempted before, but because it was a novelty conservative British people looked with misgivings on our efforts. How would it be possible, they asked, to supervise, to watch over and keep close contact with so many widely differing interests? We were to some extent feeling our way, but we knew what our target was. Early on we decided to outline in a few short sentences our precise credo and how we envisaged our future. We therefore circulate each year in the annual report what we describe as 'Aims and considerations which direct the policy of the Board'. They run as follows:

1. To play an active and progressive role in British industry.
2. To extend the activities of our member companies.
3. To add to our numbers whenever suitable opportunities present themselves, provided such new concerns are directed by men of high character and proven ability and that continuity of management is assured.
4. To preserve the freedom of the boards of our member companies to manage their businesses in their own way, subject always to our guidance and supervision, particularly on matters of policy and finance.

5. To maintain an energetic, strong and efficient organisation; a varied but well co-ordinated group of companies with an underlying sense of unity.

I do not remember ever having seen such principles set out by any other Board of Directors. Our reason was to try and explain to everyone where we were going and to demonstrate that our ideas were firm and not in any way haphazard.

Our policy is to ensure that our interests are well spread and that above all, we have first-class men of vision and energy to work for us. Those are comforting elements in testing times, and we have certainly realized it in these twelve years of our 'new' existence in Tillings. Our foundations were well constructed. Our companies joined us of their own free will – not one was subject to an enforced take-over, which may well be suitable for certain combinations, but take-overs form no part of our philosophy. Ours are willing partners, who retain their own sense of identity and their freedom to manage their own companies. They are our friends and they enjoy our entire support in all their legitimate endeavours for their development and expansion. We on our part are fully aware of the responsibility this close association entails and we formed a Headquarters Executive Staff at Crewe House, consisting, apart from the Managing Director, Deputy Managing Director and Executive Directors, of engineers, accountants, lawyers, surveyors, marketing experts etc., all highly skilled men in their specialist functions who are constantly available to our companies for advice and guidance. On their wise counsel depend in no small measure the fortunes of the Group.

We constantly seek ways and means of going ahead and of strengthening our business for the building of progress with prosperity. I have often told shareholders we are not interested in negative thinking. So many people spend too much time in gloomy predictions, instead of taking vigorous counter-measures. I cannot enjoy singing the blues – I am against the blues. I am a positive expansionist and natural optimist, confident in the British people and in the efforts of the company. Tillings is constructive but competitive, tough too, but never ruthlessly so. We have always pinned our faith on diversification but we know that diversification is ineffective without inspiration, co-ordination and

Crewe House

A Tilling Omnibus, about 1910

buoyancy. But this must not be a one-way traffic affair. Our companies must feel the benefit of their association with us and be given incentives. They are, I think, aware that we can afford them better opportunities than they would have alone without our elder-brother leadership, whilst they retain under our auspices the family environment which has had such a beneficial influence in the development of British industry.

I am often asked: 'Is diversification a good thing?' Although many have followed our lead, I can only properly speak of our own case, where I say unhesitatingly that having our eggs in many baskets has proved itself to be an excellent thing. This dates back very many years, for let it be said we were an embryonic Family of Firms long before our transport assets were sold in 1949, possessing, as we then did, considerable outside investments.

We cannot expect, in the event of a general setback, to escape its effects altogether, but if we are careful in the selection of our member companies, as well as judicious in our supervision of them, we can surely hope that our future will unfold to our satisfaction.

To grow is natural, but it requires more than just a watchful eye to maintain the rhythm of orderly growth. We study with care the pattern of our spread of companies, industry by industry, and are as determined as ever to participate in new businesses if we feel they would prosper in the enterprising atmosphere of the Group. In Tillings there is ceaseless desire to make any success so far obtained even more successful.

When we started along our new path in 1949, we had 8,750 ordinary shareholders: when in 1959 we reduced the denomination to 4/-, we totalled 9,359 and at the end of 1962 the figure was over 20,000. If to this are added more than 5,000 preference shareholders, it adds up to a substantial family of shareholders. A heavy responsibility. If £100 had been invested in Thomas Tilling Ordinary Shares immediately after the payment of the capital dividend in 1949, the value at the end of 1962 was about £550. Sometimes I have sleepless nights wondering how we can keep up our rate of progress. Shall we let the shareholders down? Is our judgment fallible? Will we suffer in a general economic setback? All sorts of questions of this sort rise constantly in my mind and I have no doubt these anxious moments are shared by all chairmen of companies who have had any success and whose shares enjoy a high rating with investors. Life is a constant battle to defeat the troubles which seem inevitable in industry, and inherent in all human relations. It makes our daily tasks eventful, and never dull. Yes, being chairman of a big concern like Tillings is no childish game but, as I said at the beginning, it is a thoroughly worthwhile undertaking.

From the outset there has rallied around me a body of outstanding men, from my colleagues on the Board right down to the telephone operators (the mirror of any business) and the receptionist who smilingly and gracefully greets all visitors to Crewe House. In our early beginnings we owed much to the first Managing Director, Alec Falconer – a Scot, a chartered accountant of experience and wisdom. In May 1957 he was succeeded by Peter Ryder and in the latter we have a most able Managing Director full of understanding, initiative and farsightedness.

In 1957 Graham G. Thompson came to us with a wealth of financial and industrial experience, and in 1959 was appointed Deputy Managing Director. In the following year Kenneth Chapman – the popular old Harlequin who had been on our staff for ten years and had rendered excellent service – was welcomed to the Board as an Executive Director. There are also of course the outside members of the Board, as well as the Crewe House Executives, all men of standing; they know how much we rely on them to support us.

Executives from our underlying companies regard Crewe House as a centre to which they have access at any desired moment, and on any subject concerning themselves or their businesses. I am not going to pretend that this sort of relationship is always easy. Indeed, it sometimes calls for considerable patience and understanding on both sides. Sometimes circumstances demand strong treatment, a change in the upper management: sometimes an official who has been promoted does not blossom as we would wish or had hoped. Manifold problems arise, as is inevitable in businesses which seek to develop and progress. It all boils down in the end to the human factor – men and women, getting their willing co-operation, ensuring they will give of their best. It is new ideas which fertilize a business, but they have to be worked out before they can hope to become profitable transactions.

The British are notoriously conservative, and management, unless it is kept on its toes, is often apathetic, too willing to adhere to outworn ways on which it can rely for a reasonable living. Labour is equally often anxious about progressive thinking lest quicker and more efficient means might ultimately have the results of reducing the amount of work available. On the whole, I am inclined to lay more blame on management if progress is static and uninspiring. Frequently they remain aloof from their workpeople – the human approach is missing. Men are treated as automatons, and that won't do. They lose interest and all incentive or pleasure, longing only for the end of the day or the week, when they can get to their television sets, their pubs, their football, cricket or bowls as the case may be. Of course it is a desperate problem keeping up the interest of the working man, preventing him from regarding his job simply as a means to an end, i.e. getting money as opposed to earning it. These sentiments are well appreciated by our higher management in the Tilling Group of Companies, for in almost every case there is enlightened and forward thinking.

My excuse for this lengthy discussion of Tillings is that it plays such a leading part in my life that I have felt it appropriate to enlarge somewhat on a conception, in which I can perhaps claim to have taken a prominent line and to which I have devoted so much of my energies.

This leads me on to the question of being a chairman, particularly an 'outside' chairman. The higher management of a company has a heavy responsibility to produce constructive ideas since they run through a business like lightning. A chairman who rubber-stamps his board or takes them for granted is a fool. I would go further and say that members of a board who permit such a state of affairs are worthless. A chairman, especially if he is an executive chairman, obviously has at his fingertips the entire organization and running of the business, but frequently even he does not see the wood for the trees. If he is supported by a body of men on his board, executives as well as outside directors, who are not men of straw, not yes-men, he will value to the full their comments on problems and situations and will be ready, on occasion, to adjust his thinking accordingly.

There are many ways of handling a board. Some chairmen follow the agenda, allow full discussion by the board, and then take a line in accordance with the majority. Personally, rightly or wrongly, I have always considered it more satisfactory to expose the position as I see it or to allow the Managing Director or other executive colleague to do so and then to throw my own views or recommendations in broad principle into the arena to be discussed or amended depending upon the reactions from the other members of the board. Frequently, the end product is quite different from my opening suggestion, but that can be all to the good. It means that all of us have devoted our minds towards the best decision and that is the one which the chairman, if he is wise, will allow to go forward. Where opinion seems evenly balanced, the chairman of course has the casting vote. Never on any board on which I have served as chairman have I put a decision to the vote but have happily always obtained a basis agreed by all parties on which to proceed.

A few words about 'outside chairmen'. These are men who do not devote their entire time to a particular company. They do not have their headquarters there, but give as much time and attention as is necessary to perform their duties, particularly in consultation with the Managing Director and other executives. They ensure that the Board is kept fully informed at Board Meetings of all relevant matters, as well as in the intervals between Boards if necessary. The other type of chairman is an executive chairman who governs the policy of the company and who is often also Managing Director. Which do I favour? On the whole, except in the case of vast concerns such as Imperial Chemical Industries, Shell, and such like, or in those family businesses which, from tiny beginnings, have been developed by one man, I view an outside chairman as preferable. If not, the executive chairman is all-powerful – there is no higher authority than his, no appeal from his decisions, especially on staff and personnel matters, there is nobody to reprove him when necessary; he is all-supreme. On the other hand, an outside chairman, removed from day-to-day affairs, can usually bring abundant experience and detached thinking to the company's problems which is most valuable.

A moment of anxiety for a chairman comes each year, when he has to face his shareholders at the Annual General Meeting, for he is liable to be cross-questioned on any matter concerning the company's affairs. Indeed, he always invites comments and inquiries, but he is obviously relieved if none are addressed to him. It is a fear of the un-expected which causes the nervousness, but except, as I have said, when a company has met adversity, the attendances are usually poor, and those who bother to come are docile. Some chairmen seem to run competitions on the rapidity with which they can dispose of Annual General Meetings, but I don't. Naturally this rush is not appreciated by the shareholder who may have made a special journey from the country to see his Board, and likes to get his money's worth by hearing some exposition of the company's doings and prospects.

Contrary to general belief, Board Meetings of companies provide lively and illuminating discussions, and in my experience I can only remember one Board on which sleep overcame any of my colleagues. The meetings were held immediately after lunch, and for one reason or another, on this one occasion, two members dozed off at the same time. As their heads got lower and lower on their chests, I had a bet with myself which of the two would hit the table first. It was a dead heat, but even this did not disturb the imperturbability of the chairman. He merely coughed, rather loudly, whereupon the dozers jumped to and carried on as if nothing had occurred.

One last word. This is the day of specialists, scientists, accountants, lawyers and the whole gamut. But I wonder sometimes whether the pendulum has not swung too far that way, and whether the man of commonsense and over-all intelligence and experience does not make better stuff from which, for instance, to recruit chairmen and leaders, than the man who has concentrated too much on a particular aspect. It is a debatable subject. I hope I am not prejudiced, just because I am without any specialist skills. But I do know there is a dearth of good and suitable chairmen.

Chapter 16

BACK FROM THE TREASURY EARLY IN 1945 life seemed crushingly dull. The tempo was absurdly slow and, pushed away in a back room in 41 Threadneedle Street as the junior partner, I soon doubted whether I was wise to have accelerated my return to City life. I was a nobody again. I missed the power I had held at the Treasury, the activity and the discussions, the files and the In and Out trays. I had no trays at No. 41 and if I had, no papers or letters would have found their way into them, for there just weren't any. Nobody was interested in me. The City had not got back into rhythm.

My financial position too was very dicky. I had, for me, a substantial overdraft and no capital or prospect of any coming my way. I decided to wipe the slate clean by capitalizing my pension contributions, which just about covered my deficiency. Later, as I was again outrunning the constable, I surrendered my insurance policies, feeling hopefully that pensions and death were both still far off, and that I should let the future look after itself. I thought my present needs more important and I never was security-minded because security damps initiative.

The only out of the ordinary happening as far as I remember was a great luncheon given in my honour by the Chairman, Directors, and principal executives of the United Kingdom Commercial Corporation Ltd on 20 January 1945. This was a festive and hospitable occasion. But it was in itself a farewell and took me back to the past, and the had-beens. Nevertheless, it was a charming touch on their part. Lord Swinton, the Chairman, gave me his photograph, inscribed, 'To my Treasury friend'. That was flattering and well meant, but I am not certain he should not have written 'To my Treasury critic'.

Having rather enjoyed national work during the war, I wondered what I could try which would bring me the same feeling of 'doing something'. In my search, I was invited to stand for Parliament but I rejected this suggestion on more than one score. The chief was that I was not confident I could make a career for myself in banking and at the same time have any hope of success as a parliamentarian. I felt I might be a flop in both, if I so divided my energies. I was also not sure I should make an acceptable Party man, obeying the whip, taking a line which the Party decided was right. I have too independent an outlook to be such a conformist. Nor did the bazaar-opening side etc. have a particular appeal for me. So I left it, as a tentative proposal.

But I thought Borough Council work would have its attractions and give me the outlet I sought. So I lined up at the Conservative Party organization in Chelsea and asked whether there was any possibility of my becoming a candidate at the next municipal elections which were due to take place at the end of 1945. They were hopeful, and eventually I was adopted as one of the Municipal Reform candidates for the Hans Town Ward of Chelsea – one of six. In that district, election was a foregone conclusion, and there was not even any opposition. If there had been, it would only have been feeble, and would have been overwhelmed, more's the pity, perhaps. I found Borough Council work decidedly more political than I had expected. There were 'party' views on most subjects, some of which seemed to me without any apparent political bias whatever. Before every Council Meeting we all gathered in conference under the party leader to decide on our line of action.

The Council members numbered thirty-six, excluding six Aldermen. In 1945 there was a Labour Party minority, consisting of five Councillors, two women and three men. Of these only two could be called cloth cap, one of each sex: of the ladies, one was an established worker in the Labour cause, and the other inclined towards tub-thumping: of the males one was an eloquent, able Old Etonian who seemed strangely out of place but at any rate sincere: another was also an intelligent young man who has since made a fortune for himself in industry and commerce. The third man was given to parade ground shouting to make his points but we all respected him.

The Council is in effect run by committees, devoted to various matters such as Housing, Finance, etc., and is presided over by the Mayor, supported by the Aldermen. Although the Mayor is selected from the majority party, he maintains strict impartiality and does not participate in the debate. Committee Meetings are of course conducted in private, but the Council Meetings are public, the press and any interested parties being admitted into the gallery. The Town Clerk, invariably a lawyer, is the chief administrative officer of the Council. He acts as Secretary to the Council and to all committees. He advises the Mayor on matters of procedure and interprets legal problems, but, like the Mayor, does not take part in the general discussion.

I was soon invited to become Chairman of the Finance and General Purposes Committee, and thus found myself, so to speak, the local Chancellor of the Exchequer. This Committee, advised by the Borough Treasurer (an untiring enthusiast, Mr H. E. Benson) fixes the rate to be paid each year, is responsible for controlling the entire expenditure of the Borough, and has to vet carefully the estimates of all the other committees to ensure that there is no extravagance, and misuse or misappropriation of Council funds. It is the key committee and certainly the most powerful. In Borough Council affairs, as elsewhere, finance dominates.

I do not believe I left any particularly worthwhile mark on the Council in my capacity as Chairman of the Finance Committee. But I did inaugurate a system which still endures, whereby each ratepaper personally receives with his rate claim precise details of all expected expenditure during the coming year, setting out the different items, with the special allocations attributable to each. I thought it wrong that this information should never have been forthcoming in the past.

It was also under my Chairmanship that the Finance Committee suggested the employment of a firm of business consultants to survey the organization and methods of administration of the Borough Council. In this proposal the Council was ahead of other local authorities, and although in Chelsea there were few changes as a result of the report, the example set has since been followed by many other local authorities, both large and small, throughout the country.

I enjoyed my five years on the Council. Perhaps it was comparatively pedestrian stuff but I felt I was doing something useful. There was much enthusiasm on the Council and distinct pride in upholding the old traditions of Chelsea. I regard it as a good Borough in which to live. It has its own special charm and atmosphere. I fully approved the policy of maintenance of the residential character and the resolute refusal to allow business offices to encroach on the big houses in the lovely Chelsea squares, as has been done elsewhere, even though the rates could thereby have been brought down. I like the elegance of the Borough and much regretted having to move out of it a year or so ago after nearly thirty years of residence there.

There was not much liveliness in the Council debates although the tiny opposition did their best to keep their end up in cut and thrust, and sometimes by the obvious 'underdog appeal'. Theirs was not an easy task, but they acquitted themselves well in difficult circumstances, and served a purpose by their perpetual pin-pricking. Only once did the Mayor have to intervene to stop the torrent of wordy abuse poured on our heads by the 'sergeant-major', and discipline was soon restored.

I had taken over the Chairmanship of Cadogan Place Gardens, as there seemed to be nobody else willing to carry out this rather domestic job. As a matter of fact, the gardens are amongst the most beautiful in London and form a real oasis for those occupying the surrounding houses and flats. This duty gave me pleasure and at the same time caused me many headaches. I was fortunate in having a head gardener, H. F. Flangham, of wonderful old-world courtesy, charm, and unusual tact, who had reigned over the gardens for forty-five years when he died in 1956. He knew every shrub, every tree, every flower, almost every blade of grass. He loved the place, and children flocked around him and loved him in return.

During the war the railings were torn down, and dug-outs, allotments and vegetable gardens were established. Flangham and I set about the restoration after the war; we had the beds replanted, the lawns re-sown, the dug-outs demolished, trees lopped and one of the tennis courts which had been uprooted by a direct hit from a small bomb, reconstructed. It was quite a task to induce people to understand that it was right for the gardens again to be fenced and locked, especially those who had roamed freely there during the war. They could not realize that garden squares serve as the communal back or front gardens of the tenants who have no personal gardens of their own as are enjoyed by occupiers of even small houses in the suburbs.

Once back to pre-war perfection, the troubles started – little human troubles which inevitably seem to afflict such centres. They mainly concerned children, dogs and the older people. Parents wanted their offspring to run where they liked, the dog owners saw the gardens as a happy hunting ground for their animals, whereas the older folks wanted peace and quiet away from the annoyance of crying babies, playing children and barking dogs. This was the perpetual wrangle. After the war we had over six hundred members, which probably meant that including their families at least two thousand people were using the gardens at one time or another. Eventually we allocated strict spheres of influence and I issued constant appeals for co-operation. One dealing with perambulators, children, old people and the soiling of lawns by dogs was sent to *The New Yorker* magazine, I suppose by an American member with a sense of humour, and printed verbatim under the title 'There'll always be an English garden'. It was extremely funny in its seriousness, even to me, its author, when read out of context.

During the war many houses in Cadogan Place were requisitioned for American soldiers, some of whom found the gardens and the trenches a convenient love nest. I must say we were somewhat rocked when they daily installed themselves there to practise their jazz band!

Dear old Flangham was a wonderful character with a lovely Wiltshire accent which he never lost. I was blessed to have him around me, but then I have always been fortunate with my associations of this sort. I have had over the last fifteen years at various times three old chauffeurs, one of whom I must admit could not forget, when driving the car, that he had been a Grand National jockey and was liable to regard other cars somewhat as Becher's Brooks: and Mrs Collis, our daily maid, is a wise and devoted woman. And I am grateful too for other good and loyal friends, caddies, hall porters and so on, who in so many small ways have made life more pleasant for me.

Around the end of 1947, there was some anxiety about our children's education. Janet, our daughter, was well placed at Claremont Girl's

School at Esher, in a most stately and beautiful house originally built by Capability Brown for Clive of India between 1768 and 1774 and later bought by Act of Parliament as the home of Princess Charlotte and her husband Prince Leopold of Saxe-Coburg. Janet spent some happy and beneficial years there.

Robert, the younger boy was at Fan Court Prep School with his elder brother Nicholas. The trouble was to decide what public school the latter was to go to. When Robert was born in 1937, because my prospects looked favourable, we had been enterprising enough to put him down for Eton the day after his birth, which gave him a more than average chance of entry. Nicholas, however, who was then nearing three and for whom we had not until that time sought entry for Eton, had only managed to secure what was called a 'Chance Vacancy', effective only if somebody fell out. As we particularly wanted both sons to be together I mustered all guns and with a very favourable letter of recommendation from the boy's prep school headmaster, I sought an interview with the headmaster of Eton. I was received with great courtesy but with no particular optimism about the outcome. At the judicious moment I produced my son's prep school headmaster's letter, which was read approvingly, but in silence, until the words were reached 'He is captain of the school cricket eleven'. 'That will help' said the headmaster and that was his only comment. As I left I could not refrain from asking what my son's chances were of obtaining entry into Eton. The reply came 'I am not a betting man, but I should say about fifty-fifty', which gave me some cheer. Next day a letter came from Francis Cruso, a housemaster, saying that he had a vacancy on his list for the next 'half' (term) and would I confirm straightaway that we would accept it. We were of course delighted, if inwardly surprised.

Now why did I take trouble to get my two sons into Eton, I who lacked the education and social standing of an Etonian? I think I was influenced in the main by the natural wishes of every parent to ensure for his children something at least as good as he himself had, and if possible better. I saw in Eton the best club in the world and I was convinced that if my sons could become members, they would be able to enjoy the advantages of the unequalled traditions of the school. At the same time they would meet on level pegging contemporaries who were likely to become prominent figures in industry, commerce or politics. I confess at once that our first visit was a great shock, especially to my wife who, used to trim little prep schoolboys, thought the Eton boys looked horribly scruffy and uncared for. But we got acclimatized to that and found that as the boys progress up the school, so they become sprucer.

Although Eton is regarded as the supreme example of the 'exclusive' school, I do not think I had any snobbish intentions, nor did I want my sons to become snobs. How often do I hear 'He's a typical Old Etonian and a frightful snob', but I myself no longer say this. I know so many Old Etonians in various professions and business, not all successful, and I have found them to be as diverse a selection of people as any amongst my acquaintances. In my opinion there is no such article as a 'typical Old Etonian' but if there were I must say he would not be typical for his snobbery.

I am inclined to believe that the standard of teaching at Eton is as high as one could desire and I have discussed this with many Old Etonian friends, as well as with other parents. The fact that Old Etonians are frequently at the top of their professions and businesses cannot always be due in these democratic days to the fact that they are Old Etonians. There must be a something 'extra' and I suppose this is what I was seeking for my sons.

If I have any quarrel it is that the compulsion to work is less insistent at Eton than at other schools. The strong spirit of individuality which is encouraged by the Eton system leaves boys to organize their own time without perhaps sufficient supervision from the authorities. 'Come and get it if you want it, but we won't force you', and this availability is not always obvious to the boys. By this 'take it or leave it' attitude, boys often lack awareness of resources of their own and many look back on their years at Eton as having been a period of wasted opportunities. The unambitious or lazy boy can bump along on the bottom, just 'getting by' each term, and not making the best of the educational opportunities offered. It appears to me particularly true of Eton that so much, often too much, depends upon the personality of the housemaster. A weak, badly chosen man can prove disastrous to many of his boys and can have an adverse effect upon their lives and their future outlook in so many respects. His interests and standards react on all his pupils.

The distinguishing factor of Eton in my opinion stems from the emphasis laid on the importance of each individual boy and the absence of the herd spirit. This freedom can work to the great benefit of the brilliant boy who seizes the occasion to absorb what is there in abundance. He can participate in a curriculum of highly diversified proportions and can at the same time acquire a bearing and social accomplishments, which can prove an equipment of enormous usefulness. If, however, he happens to have great academic or athletic success, or he gets into 'Pop', he is deified to such an extent by lesser boys that he will be tested to the extreme by the general adulation. He will indeed be fortunate if he can resist having his head turned or becoming obnoxiously arrogant. Everything that immediately follows in his young life seems but a pallid undertaking by comparison.

On the whole, the general run of boys come out of the melting pot as individuals, not stereotyped, and if to an outsider some of them appear disdainful and superior, my summing up is that the system works somehow. Of course a portion are oaf-like, and I have even encountered Etonians who found difficulty in constructing sentences of more than six words, but such specimens would have been no different whatever school they had attended. That Harold Macmillan and George Orwell are both Old Etonians bears witness to the flexibility and diversity of the school's products.

Yes, I am glad I made the effort to send my sons to Eton, so rich in history, so mellow and, I believe, quite as well geared to modern conditions as other less traditional schools.

On the whole I venture to think Eton passes the test well and that my experiment has been successful, although I speak merely as an observant father of two Etonian sons. I do not anticipate that even in this rapidly changing world, an Old Etonian tie will work to the detriment of the wearer.

Chapter 17

On 30 April 1946 Sir Nigel Campbell expressed his wish to give up the Deputy Chairmanship of the firm, and I was raised from junior partner to succeed him. This came as a great surprise to me, but I naturally accepted the honour with much pride and pleasure. It was a heartening moment.

On 1 May 1946 Alan Russell, whose father had been a notable partner in the firm in its stockbroking days (at one time its name was in fact 'Helbert, Wagg & Russell') became a Director. Alan Russell, who joined straight from school, was destined to play a substantial part in its post-war development along with Michael Verey and Gordon Gunson who became partners on 1 January 1948 and Charles Villiers who was appointed six months later on 1 July 1948. Younger men, Robert Hollond, David Murison and Ashley Ponsonby, who came to us direct from war service, joined the Board on 1 January 1957, thus completing what I proudly say was one of the best combinations in The City.

Nothing would give me greater pleasure than to sing the praises of those partners of mine, whom I know so well and esteem so highly, but I shall refrain lest they might be embarrassed. Where each has contributed so much in his own way it might also be invidious to set out their individual virtues and qualities. I have mentioned them at this stage because I wish to stress the teamwork, and never for one minute do I want my readers to underestimate that aspect in the pages which follow. For me it has been an uplifting experience to work with such men, backed by such a fine staff. They will all know how deeply I appreciate them and how grateful I have been for their support and forbearance. We had Alfred Wagg as our leader until 1 January 1954 when he handed over the Chairmanship to me and I have mentioned in earlier pages what we owe to him.

There are hosts of other friends in this country and all over the world with whom I have worked in close harmony and interest and whom I would have been proud to salute – as well as many others in varied walks of life, but they will realize I am sure that within the confines of a book like this, it would have been quite impossible to do as I would wish.

In the office activity was hotting up following the pent-up demand for new capital after the 'dead' period, between 1939 and 1945. As a result there was a great amount of new issue work to provide funds to re-equip industry with up-to-date machinery and plant. In addition, a large number of private owners of companies were forced, mainly in order to prepare for crushing death duties, to dispose of part of their interests to the public by means of either public issues or private placings on The Stock Exchange. Helbert Wagg, as an Issuing House, were thus experiencing a period of useful work and took part in a wide variety of issues during 1946 and 1947.

Late in 1945 some of the senior merchant and investment bankers decided to form an Issuing Houses Association. This establishment of their own Association was a mighty step in the history of issuing houses. It gave them a better sense of unity and common support, whilst maintaining full competition as in the past. The main objects were to enable them to speak with one voice on all matters of principle affecting the issuing business. The rules made a special point that the Association should not seek to fetter, prescribe or regulate the manner in which its members carry on their respective businesses, but power was given to refuse membership to any firm or company of which it did not approve.

Colonel Bertram Abel Smith was appointed first Chairman of the Association and I was the Deputy Chairman. Sadly, the Chairman became a sick man soon after his appointment and in October 1946 I assumed the Chairmanship and was succeeded as Deputy Chairman by Rufus Smith, now Lord Bicester and head of Morgan Grenfell, a great friend. There were many growing pains; in fact, the Association made a poor start, being criticized in the financial press for not being fully representative, as certain so-called West End Issuing Houses had been excluded from membership in the original conception of a few of the leading bankers who gave birth to the idea. One or two of these West Enders at the time the Association was announced, took umbrage, with some justification, at their omission and were egged on by the agitation in the press. It did not seem to some of us that it mattered where issuing houses plied their trade: so long as their standing was good, and their business was respectable and conformed to normal standards, they could surely suit their own convenience as to their domicile. We went to work accordingly, despite certain new mumblings that we were making membership too easy, but it was either to be an Issuing Houses Association with full representation, or it was destined to disruption amid charges of undemocratic behaviour. Common sense prevailed and soon we had even elected partners in West End houses to the Executive Committee. But launching a new idea so often meets unexpected difficulties. I firmly believe associations such as the Issuing Houses Association, the Accepting Houses Committee, the Association of Investment Trusts and the Insurance Protection Committee of the British Insurance Association, permit views to be expressed and problems to be ironed out, which must be all to the good and helpful, not only for The City but for The City's important client, the public at large. Nothing like a bit of talk, letting off steam, to solve a situation, but don't let the Committees be too unwieldy.

In many earlier pages I have mentioned 'issuing houses, public issues, private placings' and so on – to such an extent that I wonder whether some of my readers less acquainted with such matters would welcome a brief explanation. I will trace the history and origin of issuing houses to tell how they came into being and to say something about their activities, methods, and the preparatory work and effort which go into the making of a public issue of securities.

Issuing houses have a proud history and it is no exaggeration to say that the older ones contributed in large measure towards the development of the British Empire: at the same time they were the cradle of the Americas. It was the capital provided by The City of London which opened up the prairie lands of North America and the pampas of South America and which linked them to their ports by railways; which fertilized the barren lands of the Empire and Egypt, and which constructed a network of communications in India and the Far East. A glance at a list of old prospectuses of issues made in The City of London readily bears this out. They reveal the contribution which these

After-dinner speech

activities made to this small island, when, without any special natural mineral advantages except coal, it succeeded in balancing its own trade, rose to a paramount position in the world, and became the pivot of the British Empire.

So important were the achievements of the old investment bankers and issuing houses that even twenty years after the First War, in 1938, it was estimated that British long-term investments abroad – not counting liquid balances and gold – still amounted to some £4,500 millions. Translated into terms of today's money values, this total would be vastly greater.

Approximately £2,300 millions were invested in British Empire countries, some £1,500 millions in the United States of America and South America and the balance was scattered over Europe and Asia. The income derived from these overseas investments amounted to nearly £200 millions a year and covered the cost of about twenty-five per cent of our imports in 1938.

As with so many other British institutions, the machinery for raising capital was not consciously created. It grew gradually as a natural process, the reason being that Britain was a great commercial nation long before the industrial revolution, and long before she became a great financial nation and the banker of the world.

In the eighteenth century The City of London was the centre for world trade and commerce. The great continental merchant banking houses, some of which are still going strong today, established themselves in The City. These private banks were first and foremost active in promoting commerce; later, however, they made themselves responsible for the raising and issuing of foreign loans and thereby became the first investment bankers or issuing houses. It was not, however, until this century, and really only since the end of the First World War, that the well-known issuing houses in The City began to underwrite the raising of capital for home industrial purposes, as distinct from foreign loans.

The raising of long-term capital in The City for the needs of industry in this country is thus a comparatively recent event. The reason is largely historical. The first industrial units were small and it was possible to finance them on a family basis. As they grew larger and additional resources were required, these were obtained from relatives and friends, profits being ploughed back all the while. It will be understood how comparatively simple it was to do this in those days, when it is realized that as recently as the beginning of this century the highest income group paid only five per cent or so in taxation, whereas today the highest graded taxpayers in Britain, by contrast, pay over ninety per cent of their gross income.

With low taxation and good profits, a section of the population was always seeking opportunities for employing its money to better advantage and at times at considerable risk. Capital could be raised locally and largely through the personal knowledge and standing of the firm concerned; there was no need for the employment of an intermediary organization such as an issuing house.

The approach to the raising of long-term capital in England during the nineteenth century was very different from that on the Continent. Germany, for instance, deliberately set out to create an industrial state. The impetus for expansion came from above rather than from below and the demand for capital could only be met by the banks, there being at that time no public savings of any consequence available for investment. This led to the development of the great German credit banks and to a much closer connection there between the banks and industry. In France a not quite comparable but somewhat similar evolution took place. There the *banques d'affaires* emerged as instruments to finance industry, but it was not a lack of private savings for investment as in Germany, but rather a century-old habit of investing in French and foreign government bonds and other fixed interest bearing securities, which kept the public aloof from industrial securities with their attendant risks.

In this way a close connection grew up on the Continent between the banks and industry, the reverse of what was happening in England where the banks confined themselves to short-term finance and took no deliberate or controlling interest in industry which continued to be financed in the main by the private individual.

Towards the end of the nineteenth century industry everywhere was not only rapidly expanding, but also was more international both in scope and character. Capital issues were becoming more frequent and on a scale not dreamt of fifty years earlier. In addition, foreign governments and municipalities were looking to London not only for short-term commercial loans, but also for long-term finance.

In the home market private finance of a sufficient volume to meet the increasing requirements of industry was more difficult to find, and as a result issuing houses came into their own. They gradually became the recognized arbiter, assessing the justification for a demand for capital and, when satisfied, subsequently presented that demand to the public by means of an issue, pledging their name in support of it.

It was only during the early part of the twentieth century that the rise of issuing houses commenced on a larger scale, but the First World War intervened before the underwriting of home industrial issues was common practice. In the meantime trade and industry were expanding apace, and, as we have already seen, the period after the war of 1914–18 saw an increase in the demand for long-term loans and permanent capital to finance all the reconstruction and new development work which had to be undertaken.

But the capital market for home industry was not really effectively organized in The City at that time, and it is doubtful if there were sufficient issuing houses of standing to deal with the demands for industrial capital. England had led the world till then in other fields of financial activity and it was only natural that she should attempt to do likewise in the raising of capital. Unfortunately, attracted by the opportunities offered, numbers of finance companies with inadequate resources and sketchy connections, appeared on the scene: they were only too eager to profit whilst the public were in an investing mood and generally to make hay while the sun was shining. They were responsible for the marketing of many issues covering projects only too scantily investigated and many investors were bamboozled during that period of speculative fever. The public's loss was indeed very great, and many of the securities concerned had, all too soon, no ascertainable value.

The troubles of this period were thus a sorry commentary on the first post-war effort, and were largely responsible for the aspersions which were cast on everyone engaged in this type of business. The failure to rise to the occasion of some issuing houses, mostly newcomers, and the subsequent default of many of them when their issues found no response, were partly the cause for the setting up by the government of the day of an important committee on finance and industry. This committee, generally known as the Macmillan Committee, made its report in 1931.

In this report the interesting and significant statement appeared that 'it would be an important reform that relations between finance and industry should be so developed that Issuing Institutions of first class strength and repute should vouch to the investor more normally and more fully for the intrinsic soundness of the issues made. . . . In this way the investor would be encouraged to support well-vouched issues and be put on guard against others.'

The truth is that in this period a new investing public had made its appearance – a public which was by no means well informed and which was far too inclined to venture its money in speculative projects, which ultimately, as mentioned before, proved spurious in many cases. At the same time, the collapse of international exchange made the raising of international loans in London impossible, and it followed almost as a matter of course that the acceptance houses, merchant bankers and investment bankers turned more of their attention to the underwriting and raising of home industrial issues. Thus, the decade prior to the outbreak of the Second World War saw another upswing in the volume of this type of business launched under their auspices. During the war industrial issues were only permitted in cases of paramount importance for the war effort.

Since 1945 some new houses have been added to the list, whilst others have been rejuvenated, and in the majority of cases they have upheld the best traditions of the new issue world.

Investors now have many safeguards, which were not in existence when they suffered such heavy losses in the slump which followed the 1928–29 boom period. Since then there have been two major revisions of the Companies Acts – those of 1929 and 1948 – and in addition the rules of The Stock Exchange have been revised and greatly increased in their severity. In the last resort The Stock Exchange have the power to refuse the request of a company which wishes to have its shares quoted, if the information provided is not considered worthy – a powerful weapon with which to protect the investing public from subscribing to undesirable undertakings.

It is unusual for issuing houses to lock up their own funds in investments of a permanent nature since they must keep liquid to meet eventualities and must therefore rely for subscriptions to their issues practically entirely from outside sources: in other words, the general public, the pooled resources of the man in the street, together with the accumulated funds and reserves of financial institutions such as insurance companies, investment trusts and pension funds. This body of potential investors must all be fully informed and satisfied in regard to the propositions put before them: hence, the issuing house, before it makes itself responsible for an issue, must examine the proposals with the utmost care, looking not so much to the short-term prospects (whether an immediate success can be achieved by obtaining an over subscription, although this is very desirable) but to what is vastly more important, whether the investment concerned, if it is an ordinary share, has more than a reasonable possibility of yielding the holder a steady and increasing return on his money over the course of years. Considering the great responsibilities they assume, and the vast amount of work involved in an issue, issuing houses are normally very modest in their charges, and I might stress that contrary to the general trend, the rate is no higher and frequently lower than before the war, although admittedly the amounts involved are bigger.

Although the majority of issues today appear under the auspices of an issuing house, it happens sometimes that stockbrokers who are members of The Stock Exchange undertake the responsibility for new issues. This tendency is usually more noticeable when general conditions are flourishing and the raising of new capital presents few difficulties. However, recent experience teaches that companies needing new finance are coming to realize that issuing houses, whose speciality that business is, offer the best service, possessing as most do highly skilled and well equipped organizations for both pre-natal and after-care attention.

In general, issuing houses work in close harmony and friendship with The Stock Exchange, and one should not underrate the important part stockbrokers play in the preparation and launching of new issues, albeit mainly in an advisory capacity. It is essential that this close co-operation between the two main bodies dealing with investments should continue, but for the reasons stated it would seem that the making of issues is more the function of an issuing house than of a stockbroker. However, the borrowers and the public must be the best judges of this question, on which a measure of controversy exists, but I cannot get away from the thought that possibly a duality of function arises when new issues are sponsored by stockbrokers.

I have merely touched the fringe of a complex subject, but I would like to stress the vital importance of the continuation of the existing efficient arrangements in The City of London for marrying the supply of new savings with the demand for new money on the part of a multitude of borrowers. The issuing houses perform that important role by bringing about these marriages of convenience. As long as they continue to pursue their clearly defined task, maintaining the high standard they have set themselves, there is no doubt that they will remain an all-important link in the development of our economy, and that they can add to their past a still greater future.

H.W., since my early days in the 1920s, has handled hundreds of new issues and placings of one sort or another, and there are very few industries, or countries for that matter, which we have not had to study at various moments. The scope of the industries is too vast to enumerate, from malted milk and the fifty-seven varieties to tipping gears and boilers. Sometimes my role was that of chief negotiator; sometimes latterly I was kept in reserve, 'the heavy artillery' in case of need, when some of my highly skilled partners took the lead. But always I surveyed the over-all scene, and our entire team was invariably called in to express an opinion on every problem. Nobody was ever left out and as a result there was a remarkable sense of unity and an excellent spirit.

I have often been made aware by friends in industry and commerce, especially in the provinces, that feelings akin to terror are struck in their hearts at the thought of penetrating into the parlour of a banking house in The City. Some are not only frightened but also very suspicious. They feel as if they were in the witness box, having to justify themselves and prove their case. Happily, I believe these misgivings are disappearing, if gradually, although some still linger. My partners and I never harboured any sense of superiority in this way, having only respect and admiration for the achievements of our friends in industry, and anxious only to join

[188]

with them to work out a solution of problems, in friendship and under-standing.

Once one of our clients in the early stages of a negotiation put it to us that if he went elsewhere, naming an issuing house of third rate standing, he had been advised he would have as good service but cheaper. I told him he must choose; he was as free as the air, but reminded him the comparison was as between shopping in Bond Street or in Houndsditch. He stayed with us and has remained a most loyal friend.

Chapter 18

ANOTHER PLEASANT STEP in my life was taken in October 1946 when I was elected a Director of the Atlas Assurance Company Ltd. It happened very informally, like this. Colonel Abel Smith with whom I had been working on the Issuing Houses Association invited me to lunch at the National Provincial Bank in Bishopsgate, ostensibly for a friendly chat. However, I found on arrival that he had placed me between himself and Mr Hotblack, another member of the Board of the Bank. The latter, it transpired, was also Chairman of the Atlas and Colonel Abel Smith was Deputy Chairman. Without more ado, he asked me to join the Board. I was flattered and accepted because I knew it was a first-class company, with the highest reputation. I was soon to realize, however, that as an ordinary member of the Board of an Insurance Company, one's main contribution concerns investment and general policy. It is the highly skilled managers who run the insurance side of the business, life, fire, accident, marine, etc.

At each board meeting there was a recital of the diseases which had caused the death of our policy holders and annuitants. I found this altogether nauseating and unnecessary, and after frequent protests, the Chairman yielded to my pleadings, and the details were eliminated, merely the numbers of deaths being stated. I noticed the discussion by my colleagues of their various aches and pains stopped at once thereafter. Later, after the sad deaths of Mr Hotblack and Colonel Abel Smith, my great friend Rudolph de Trafford became Chairman and the Board asked me to be his Deputy. When in 1959 suggestions were made for the Atlas to be absorbed into the Royal Exchange Assurance Group, no merger could have been more mutually acceptable. Consequently, Rudolph de Trafford and I were invited to become members of the Royal Exchange Court, full of highly diversified notabilities.

In January 1948 I was presented with a further challenge in the industrial world when I was invited by Mr (now Sir) Ivan Stedeford, to become a Director of Tube Investments Limited, and to join Sir Greville Maginness as a Deputy Chairman. This was a fine compliment which I much appreciated, for the company is well known as one of the foremost industrial organizations in the country, its shares holding very high, blue-chip status. As I came to know the Group I quickly realized that this reputation was fully deserved, and I was to be impressed by the efficiency shown, and the wide diversification of its interests. Under the brilliant leadership of Sir Ivan, 'T.I.' as it is always known, expanded and developed tremendously and no Chairman ever had a greater grip on a company's affairs than he. During the two years of my office I absorbed much, as I was able to obtain a wide view of industrial Britain, which proved very helpful.

Sir Greville Maginness was a leading industrialist, a much respected figure, especially versed in labour negotiations, whereas I, a banker, was on the Board for my financial knowledge. Not only was there a contrast in the functions and outlook of the two Deputy Chairmen, but this was even more marked in our figures: Sir Greville was short and round as a ball; I, a very different shape, towered twelve or fourteen inches above him. Sir Greville, now sadly passed away, called us 'Mutt and Jeff'. I sometimes wondered whether it was Sir Ivan's sense of fun which prompted him to invite me to join the Board, because he enjoyed seeing his two Deputy Chairmen together. He swears he had other good reasons and when circumstances in my life compelled me to retire from T.I., I received personal letters from the Chairman and from each member of the Board saying flattering things. I was greatly touched by this evidence of their appreciation.

The 'circumstances' resulted from a visit at the end of 1949 by Air Chief Marshal Sir Wilfrid Freeman and Mr (now Sir) Kenneth Hague, Directors of Babcock & Wilcox Limited, the famous boiler makers and constructional engineers, with a world-wide business. I had met Wilfrid Freeman just after the war when he was the technical director and I the financial director nominated by the Government on the Board of the original British European Airways. At that time when Lord Swinton was Minister for Air, it was proposed that the internal airway system should be run in co-operation with the railways, not then nationalized, and the Government. The idea was stifled almost as soon as born but it was very stimulating to me sitting under the Chairmanship of Sir Harold Hartley between that master figure Wilfrid Freeman and a dynamic hero Brigadier Critchley.

Freeman and Hague came to say that their Board, having just had the searing news that their Chairman, Sir John Greenly, was not expected to live long, had decided to invite me to join the Board and succeed him. This seemed almost too flattering, and I had to protest that neither of them knew me well enough to warrant such an invitation. Helbert Wagg had undertaken a big issue eighteen months earlier for Babcock & Wilcox, part of which was in 4% Preference Shares at par – one of the last, if not the last, issues of preference shares to be handled on this low basis. I had done the negotiations and had met Kenneth Hague across the table. Anyhow, I could not induce them to alter their course; they were insistent, and finally I became Chairman of the company on 1 July 1950. Sadly, Sir John Greenly who was dearly loved in the company, died very shortly afterwards and I was only able to have one brief talk with him before I took over. All the same, I never forgot his advice: 'As an outside Chairman, don't ever bore them. Let them get on with their jobs!' With my unfailing desire always to know what was going on, I am not sure I succeeded in the former bit of advice, but I tried.

It did not take me long to discover that I had undertaken a stupendous task if I was to do it well, and it was equally obvious that I was at the head of an organization which was unique, not only in achievement but in the friendliness of the spirit which pervaded the entire group. They say 'B & W spans the world' and so it does. From every corner of the globe, where there were subsidiaries, associated companies, branch offices or licensees, came messages of welcome to me as the new Chairman. This was a setting in which no one but a stony-hearted individual could fail to blossom. I revelled in the atmosphere and set to work enthusiastically to get abreast of the Group's position. Financially it was to some extent at my fingertips following the previously mentioned issue, but there was more than the financial aspect to concern a new Chairman. I was like a new boy at school who next day found himself the Head Prefect. There are about 16,000 to 17,000 people employed directly in the Group and I saw it as helpful to try and establish some sort of personal contact with them and their leaders and executives. So I not only visited the works in various parts of England, but also the main factories in Renfrew, Scotland, which cover some one hundred and sixty acres of land, employing 6,000 men and women. This done, it was desirable to let the overseas companies have a look at me, and more important, for me to fit them into the jigsaw.

So over the course of some years I visited the Continental companies, Canada and the United States several times, and unforgettably exotic Honolulu twice; South Africa twice, enjoying the contact and the climate but detesting the atmosphere of the country; Mexico once, a progressive country of the future; Brazil, never fulfilling its promise, where I was received by the then President, Mr Kubitschek, with a camera man to take our photographs for insertion in the Rio de Janeiro newspapers the next day for propaganda purposes under the heading 'President receives leading British Industrialist'; Argentina, where I gave a rousing address on Great Britain to a large assembly of industrialists and bankers in Buenos Aires; and last but not least Australia, where the warmth of the welcome was almost overwhelming, as evidenced by the number of speeches. I also visited Kenya and the Rhodesias on the way back from South Africa – at that time they seemed havens of peace in comparison with the latter territory.

I remember on our first visit to the Victoria Falls, the flow of water was the highest on record, and the Zambesi had burst its banks in many places. There is what is called 'a Rain Forest' only penetrable at such times in bathing kit, in which the spray from the falls nearby has given growth to the most unusually beautiful tropical plants. It is like a lovely open-air Turkish bath. But in this world of Stanley and Livingstone, I was saddened by the rapid extermination of the wild animals. Civilization constantly encroaches on their preserves. For instance, aeroplanes full of tourists go out at dawn to spot them, and zoom down on the wretched herds, which disperse and scamper away in terror, as they are photographed by these selfish enthusiasts.

On one of my visits to Spain at the end of 1953 I decided I would like to make an assessment of General Franco and in consequence I instituted steps to seek an audience. Our Embassy in Madrid was unenthusiastic, saying that Franco had received no Englishman for years and only on rare occasions saw the Ambassador. All the more reason to persist, I thought, so I approached the matter in my own way through Spanish sources. To my surprise, I'll admit, and certainly to the Embassy's surprise, an audience was fixed for the next morning, 18 November 1953, at El Pardo Palace, about fifteen kilometres outside Madrid which was one of Franco's out-of-town residences. The Ambassador, Sir John Balfour, seemed anxious and wanted to school me, but I preferred to leave the interview to unfold. It was not an official occasion, and I was only going as a private individual. I had nothing to worry about.

An interpreter from the Spanish Foreign Office picked me up at my hotel. He had been educated at an English public school and was very companionable. At the Palace we passed a series of guards, all of whom seemed to have been informed of our approach. We went through many beautiful salons, hung with Spanish pictures and tapestries of notable quality, and were ushered straight in to the Generalissimo. He was in uniform and greeted me warmly with a broad smile.

My impression was of a tiny, nearly podgy man, bald, flat-faced with a not very strong chin, but a most alert pair of eyes, quick to smile: middle class and highly intelligent. He is a teetotaller and non-smoker. I noticed as he sat on his semi-throne armchair that his feet dangled in the air and that he wore short black silk socks with a bit of white leg showing over the top. He had no decorations, except a lovely big sparkling diamond star on the left of his chest. He was alone and, without waiting for a word from me, proceeded to tell me how poisonously the British Press treated him, and that he was happy to receive an Englishman without political prejudices. There followed a homily upon the betterment of conditions for the Spanish people since he had taken charge, and I did not find it difficult to express my own admiration for certain of his economic achievements. Franco then said how shocked he had been to note the disintegration of our 'Empire'. What would happen to Britain if all her friends deserted her? I begged him not to formulate his policy on this theme, and surprised him by a short dissertation on the Commonwealth, as distinct from what he called the British Empire, showing how spontaneously the whole change had taken place.

I stayed with Franco for about half an hour, and in my position I did not need to mince my words. The interpreter, returning me to my hotel, expressed his delight at my frank breaking down of the ivory tower of the Generalissimo. I certainly found him just as ignorant about us as we were about him. When I met my Spanish friends who had arranged my audience, later in the afternoon, I discovered they had remained in prayer throughout the whole morning to ensure all would be well with me! When I showed my passport on leaving Madrid airport next day we were immediately passed through the customs and so avoided the usual turning upside down of one's baggage – one tiny benefit resulting from the audience.

Whilst being shocked by Franco's abysmal lack of knowledge of the British outlook and conditions, and equally regretful of our apparent cold-shouldering of him, I could not fail to be satisfied by meeting him. There was no sign of swagger, dictatorial strutting or raving. On the contrary, he was quiet in his speaking, confident, perhaps over confident, tough, shut up within himself and no doubt cunning as a fox.

It is not for me to teach the Foreign Office its business, and progress may have been made since the above episode occurred in 1953, but if I had anything to do with it, I would encourage British personalities to meet the political leaders in overseas countries as much as possible. These talks could reinforce the duties of the local Ambassador, for he cannot, in the very nature of things, be constantly in contact. Certainly General Franco professed to be pleased to meet me and to hear from my lips how I saw things in the world.

After almost ten years as Chairman of Babcock & Wilcox Limited, I felt I should make way for the Deputy Chairman, Sir Kenneth Hague, who with the Managing Director, Mr Hector McNeil, assisted by their executive colleagues, had done such monumental work for the development of the Group. When I first became Chairman in 1950 conditions were very rosy but increasing competition and decreasing volume brought extremely difficult times. From doing approximately one half of the boiler work commissioned in the world, the Group's position was fiercely contested and the introduction of the unknown quantity, atomic energy, created anxieties. I was distressed to give up the helm at such a time but it was my decision and I knew it to be right. I had had ten years of constructive work, supported by most loyal and able colleagues. In-cluding the inspection visits here and abroad, my functions had certainly occupied at least one third of my working hours. A chairman of a group like B & W cannot rest. He has many chores to do, apart from his general overseeing of the Company and handling of policy matters with the Board. He is called upon to make speeches, to attend conferences, to write messages in staff magazines, to compose his annual report and generally to be at the beck and call of the company's interests. There are over 25,000 ordinary and preference shareholders in B & W and I was at great pains each year so to write my review to them as to be sure they would have the fullest information about their interests. Apart from the figures and other financial facts I composed every word myself, and always shall as a Chairman, even if to the chagrin of the Secretary, some-times having as many as ten drafts before finalization. I once sat next to a chairman of an important company who confessed he had never been responsible for one word of his reviews. 'I leave it to the secretariat,' he said, 'and just put my name at the bottom.' I cannot understand that, believing as I do that a chairman's personality, whatever it may be, should be stamped on his annual statement, which should be a direct communication from him to his shareholders.

On my retirement my colleagues created the post of President and honoured me by appointing me as the first holder of the position. I thus maintain some contact with them, although the function of President is an honorary one and carries no duties or remuneration. The idea has been followed in many places since and surely it is a good one. Decora-tive, perhaps even ineffective, but a President can always be called upon for advice where his intimate past knowledge of the conduct of the company may be useful. Anyhow for me, the parting from colleagues and staff whom I had grown to respect and of whom I became very fond, was made less conclusive in this way. I am confident that the Group's future cannot fail to be favourable with such a wealth of skill and good-will.

Few people realize that the original Mr Babcock and Mr Wilcox were Americans who established the company in the United States in June 1881 in succession to a partnership dating from 1867. The father of the present Chairman of the Babcock & Wilcox Company of America started a branch in Scotland later in 1881. Babcock & Wilcox Limited (the British company) was formed in 1891. At the last Babcock International Conference which we attended in Washington in 1958, as guests of the American company, I nominated the Chairman of the American company, Mr Augustus Pratt (known affectionately as 'Gus') as *'père de famille'* of the whole Babcock family, making it clear that there was no interlocking interest of any sort between the two companies. Gus Pratt, in reply, shyly opened with the following story, as the occasion reminded him of it; I think it is worth repeating:

'It concerns a young lad who was instructed to learn a declamation for presentation at the Lincoln's Birthday exercise at his school. When his time arrived he walked to the platform, head erect and his chest thrown out, and said in a loud voice: "Abraham Lincoln is dead." He could not remember what came next, but he did remember that his teacher had told him that the thing to do in such circumstances was to start again and the words would come to him. So he said, in not quite such a loud voice: "Abraham Lincoln is dead." Again he could not remember what came next, but seeing his teacher glowering at him, he realized that he must make another effort. He took a deep breath and said, again in a still lower voice: "Abraham Lincoln is dead, and I don't feel so good myself. . . ." '

Chapter 19

AFTER THE 1929–31 SLUMP, Wall Street, and bankers in particular, became extremely unpopular in the United States, where their handling of the situation at that time had been the subject of violent criticism. They were baited by both parties, Democratic and Republican, and they replaced mothers-in-law as music hall jokes, except that the jibes were even more direct and cutting. The cry spread to this country, and after the Second War, instead of the just insinuating comment: 'You're a banker, aren't you?' or 'You're in The City', the Labour Party openly poured contumely on The City as a whole and on all capitalists at random.

I well recall when I was Chairman of the Issuing Houses Association being a member of a delegation to the Chancellor of the Exchequer, Dr Dalton, begging him to take a stand and make strong representations to the Japanese to pay the arrears of coupons on their loans, which then stood at absurdly low figures, some of them being quoted at almost nothing, if near arrears of interest were calculated.

He surprised and disgusted us all by saying that he could do nothing to help and went on to express it as his personal opinion that there was not a remote chance of payment, that the Bonds were worthless and that anybody who was stupid enough to lend money to Japan deserved what he got! As a matter of fact, the Japanese later made a handsome settlement of their debts and the price of the Bonds rose to as much as four or five times their value in the late 1940s, not including arrears of interest payment.

This anti-capitalist, anti-City outcry was echoed by many Socialists and others who delivered venomous attacks on those who worked in The City, painting them indiscriminately as selfish, greedy people living in their own world of money and gain, anxious only to keep taxes down,

With Hector McNeil, Managing Director of Babcock and Wilcox, at Gleneagles, 1953

and dividends up, interested in feathering their own nests, to the detriment of their fellow citizens and contrary to the best interests of the nation.

A leader in this line of thinking was Mr Aneurin Bevan, who devoted some of his most effective eloquence to running down The City and all it represented. There was an occasion around the height of the campaign when I was out one Sunday afternoon in the car, with my wife sitting beside me and the three children at the back. As we were emerging from Cadogan Place into Sloane Street, who should we see crossing the road in front of us but Mr Bevan himself. I was pulling up to allow him to pass, when one of my bloodthirsty children cried out from behind: 'There's Aneurin Bevan. Run him down, Daddy, quick, kill him!' I remonstrated that I would not murder even to please one of my children, when the rapid retort came 'Well, he's running you down all the while, isn't he?' When, years later, I happened to sit next to Mr Bevan at a function, I told him this little story which amused him greatly. Despite some of his views, I admired him as a patriot and always felt the country would not have come to harm under him as Prime Minister.

Even if these extreme opinions were not held by the majority of our fellow citizens, a vast number of the British public have no knowledge whatsoever of The City's purpose and of the incalculable services which it has rendered for generations, not only to Britain but to the world at large. It is a popular tag to regard The City and all its works with hesitancy and suspicion and to create a sinister aura of mystery around it which in reality does not exist.

In the middle of 1951 I could bear these attacks no longer without retaliation, and in a letter to *The Times* in August I put forward a strong plea that The City of London should advance a scheme for informing public opinion of the vital part The City plays in the life of the country. I admitted that The City could only blame its own traditional reticence for the public's lack of knowledge of its achievements. The City was renowned for, and even prided itself on, hiding its light under a bushel. Perhaps this was to some extent unconscious, but whatever it was, I regarded it as unnatural and even unhealthy. For far too long City people have preferred to go their unheralded way, but in an age of universal suffrage, silence can no longer necessarily be considered golden. I added that the time called aloud for an active campaign and that a more out-spoken attitude should be adopted to inform the public, and to promote an understanding of that vital cog called The City in our national economic wheel.

I pleaded, I made speeches all over the country to chambers of commerce and other small societies and groups. I am still doing it. But nothing of a concrete nature emerged. The City did not see the point of co-operation for such a purpose. There was practically no response. Perhaps they were right, perhaps it was a tribute to an independent, competitive spirit. However, I cannot see it that way, but I could perceive that thinking was undergoing a change, even if gradually. It is interesting that recently at least two leading merchant banks have engaged public relations officers. This is good in its way, especially if it means that some more of the gross ignorance about The City is dispelled. It should be, and deserves to be, known and appreciated more widely.

It is true that The City of London Society was formed with the Lord Mayor of London as President and Mr Harley Drayton – that robust City personality – as Chairman 'to make known far and wide the business activities of The City of London and that they are vital to the flow of trade throughout the world'. The Society has an impressive Court of Governors and Vice-Presidents, and has made noble efforts in the cause of education about The City. It was good enough to publish a pamphlet of mine, 'The Whole World Needs The City' which was given wide circulation. But well-based as the Society is, it falls short of my original idea for well-spread representation of the different sections of The City under one co-ordinated whole; there is for example no merchant banker, as far as I can see, connected with it.

The Governor of the Bank of England at the time, Mr C. F. Cobbold, now Lord Cobbold, interested himself in this question and deplored the anti-City attacks in a speech at the Mansion House. The Governor is the natural leader of the banking fraternity, and by reason of the authority and responsibility his post carries, exercises a substantial influence in wider City circles.

In general, however, The City retains its own individual way of freedom, but ignorance and secrecy are playing right into the hands of the enemies of capitalism, thereby harming the whole community. The present generation of electors must be taught the value of capital and that it is the life-blood of industry, and also taught how the purchasing power of their very pay packets is directly related to the volume of capital employed: how in the East where there is a dearth of capital, men work in gangs for little pay, whereas in the West where there has always been an abundance of capital, the machine has alleviated in part the work of man and his standard of living is high. One wonders how the working man can ever be imbued with a real understanding of the essential part that capital plays in his personal life, how directly and indirectly it affects his daily employment and how necessary it is for capital and labour to work together in harmony, and not against one another. But the task has to be done and The City must help.

Whilst on the subject of publicity I want to pay a high tribute to that often much-maligned body of professionals, The City Editors, those pundits who earn their living by writing on economic subjects, by offering comment, sometimes approving but frequently devastatingly critical, on financial operations undertaken in The City and elsewhere. In the 1920s a near monopoly of financial reporting seemed to be in the hands of two individuals, at least in personal contacts with City houses: Mr Mill, City Editor of *The Times*, and Mr Kiddy, who represented the *Morning Post*. They blazed the trail. If Mr Mill were invited for a cup of tea, all the partners gathered round him, to collect tit-bits of City news from him, and of course to reciprocate. More or less the same applied to Mr Kiddy. They were stalwart, and they were steady, but mostly their articles were dry reading. Then came Mr S. W. Alexander, late of the Beaverbrook Press, who now has a successful financial newspaper of his own, *The City Press*. His visits became a regular feature. He instituted the personal, lively approach to financial matters. But perhaps the pioneer in this direction was Fred Ellis of the *Daily Express*. Often impish, he never fears to debunk, whether it be friend or foe, if he considers, not always correctly of course, that a rebuke is called for. And he does not hesitate to paint for us a picture of any individual upon whom he is commenting – employing epithets such as 'portly', 'tall', 'handsome', 'distinguished' for chairmen, City people and others. He has many more in his repertoire of a less complimentary nature.

Harold Wincott, in the *Investors' Chronicle* and elsewhere, is a leader of financial thought, explaining in his brilliant articles with simple language and unusual clarity so many complicated financial problems. 'Lex' of the *Financial Times* wields immense power in his daily column; *The Times* maintains anonymity but is very worth-while; Richard Fry in *The Guardian* carries weight; Francis Whitmore in *The Daily Telegraph* is always readable and objective, and I never miss Patrick Sergeant in the *Daily Mail* wherever I am. Of the Sunday papers, I go to Alexander Thomson in the *Sunday Express* for liveliness and shrewdness, to Rees-Mogg in *The Sunday Times* to make me think and to Nigel Lawson in *The Sunday Telegraph* for stimulation. Samuel Brittan in *The Observer* is full of realism. It is also essential to read William Davis in the *Evening Standard*. Whilst I am on the subject I would like also to applaud the *Financial Times*, 'The Pink 'un'. Having achieved a virtual monopoly, in its position as the only daily newspaper devoting itself exclusively to financial and economic reporting, it does not sit back and bask. On the contrary, it is now broadening its scope by giving its readers an excellent coverage on the theatre, ballet, opera, films, art shows and many other outside subjects.

I feel the investor and The City owe these financial editors and many others whom I have not been able to mention, as well as the weeklies, a heavy debt of gratitude. They have enlivened financial reading, so that even the old lady in Surbiton who used to profess to be 'mystified by it all', can now find entertainment in, and some interpretation, often simple and lighthearted, of these complicated matters. And I would like to put it on record that I have never been let down by one of them. They always play the game, although I cannot say this of some of their *confrères* on other pages of newspapers. The financial editors have never disclosed a secret when requested to keep it to themselves and goodness knows, how tempted they must have been on occasion to be ahead of their competitors. They are aware, of course, that their sources of information in the future would soon be jeopardized if they succumbed. I always try to remember when asked for information that they have their livings to earn, and in these circumstances feel it is only natural that they are constantly pressing and prodding to be in 'on the know'. All reporters want to publish a startling piece of news which no other competitor has yet obtained and often something leaks through to the alert ones. To my mind the secrecy which is maintained in practically all big operations is remarkable when one realizes the number of persons who are acquainted with the details, often long ahead of the announcement. There are the parties directly concerned, accountants, lawyers, printers, and many other experts, and human nature being what it is, it is small wonder that occasionally, but very occasionally, mind you, rumours filter through to the financial press. Obviously, they are on to it like a knife and go the rounds for possible confirmation. Even in these cases I have known financial editors willing to defer to a request to withhold publication. Frequently advance publication is most inappropriate, and in consequence all possible attention is given to early disclosure to the press, sometimes in the form of a preliminary notice, just to prevent unnecessary speculation as to what is happening. But as I have said above, the financial editors conduct themselves admirably in all the circumstances.

Publicity is a curious thing. No prominent man of affairs can avoid it in these days or can do without it; indeed I go so far as to say it is essential to him. Yet an excess of it can be a pest and bring endless embarrassment, and, if it is courted, it can have unpleasant reactions. Some newspapers and periodicals enjoy 'plugging' certain characters on all possible occasions, and politicians must have skins of hide, so unmercifully are they dealt with, by writers and cartoonists. The financiers are as a rule treated delicately and handsomely by comparison.

Some believe The City is a headquarters of privilege, but I regard it as a headquarters of experience. There is a much more diversified, more progressive, more competitive and more professional outlook now, compared with my early days. Many a man who began as an office boy and worked up the hard way now occupies a position of influence and responsibility. Very few succeed unless they know their jobs, and there is less and less chance for the privileged fellow, if he does not apply himself as diligently as the man who has had to fight for himself. Of course some do come from influential, or semi-influential families, but whatever their origin, they will have to rely for success in the last analysis on the natural ability with which most men are endowed – to a lesser or greater extent – integrity, flair, persistence and an inner desire to achieve. In sum, I am saying that nepotism, being a duke, a son of Lord

Tomnoddy, or knowing the boss, will not of itself ensure candidature for a City career. England being what she is, a land of snobs, it may help to some extent. It is no use pretending otherwise, for such sentiments dispel themselves slowly. But family tradition is now a much less powerful advantage and testimonial than when I was a youngster, even if it is discernible in certain cases. Just as so many of our old families have found renewed strength through an infusion of peasant blood, so The City must look to its future by opening possibilities to those who have the essential equipment, both as to intelligence and character, whatever their background.

We often hear tell of The City Establishment. People outside The City constantly assert that I am a member. But I confess I do not know precisely what it is nor what it consists of. Is it perhaps an indefinable, nebulous sort of influence, exerted almost unconsciously by certain personalities, which moulds opinion and directs thinking, just by dint of their being in authority, willy-nilly, in various spheres? I am not sure. There is no election to membership. They never meet as a body. I don't know who would call them together anyhow. Yet they all know one another and trust one another, and they indulge in much cross-checking. News of a shabby trick – quite unthinkable – would flash round amongst them almost instantaneously, and so would anything akin to being 'hot' or 'sharp'. The perpetrator would at once be 'out', even though he never knew he was a member. Perhaps I am too simple, perhaps if I had not had to work my passage, perhaps if I had been born the son of a peer or been blessed with a famous name like Rothschild, I should have known better how to describe this curious thing called The City Establishment.

Deep down in me I am opposed to it, because I don't like secret hole-in-the-corner meetings and decisions. I prefer 'clubs' to be all-embracing and I detest reactionaries. This ephemeral society, anonymous as is its membership, will surely melt into its native nothingness as time marches on and The City broadens its scope and extends its areas by the accession of new and energetic constituents free from the old influences.

I am all for letting air into situations and am instinctively against the 'old boy, good family' types if they consider that without much else to support them, they are entitled *automatically* to lead and to take decisions. As I have said elsewhere, they have their place, but not in The

City nor in industry, where those of experience and competence must provide our leaders if we are to hold our own. Happily, I sense that this view is being more and more accepted within the Square Mile.

But what is this City, not the city of Birmingham, Bristol, Cardiff or Glasgow, but THE City, The City of London? Its history and development make a romantic and thrilling story. Practically nothing is manufactured there except possibly paper, but by a very slow process developed over hundreds of years, The City has grown to be the hub of Britain's financial and commercial life. It is situated in a little patch wedged between St Paul's Cathedral and Liverpool Street Station; which is why it is known as the Square Mile, since that is about its size. Within its narrow boundaries are centred the headquarters of most of our Banks, our Commerce, our Insurance and our Shipping Companies, and clustered around are the Bank of England, Lloyd's, The Stock Exchange, the Baltic Exchange, to mention only a few institutions, and the Mansion House where the Lord Mayor lives and works.

In some quarters there is an idea that The City consists only of The Stock Exchange. This is erroneous, important as The Stock Exchange certainly is as a mart for securities, stocks and shares of every description. It is also a fallacy to say that The City and The Stock Exchange are the cause of fluctuations in stock market prices. 'City slumps, City booms' one reads. Those movements take place on The Stock Exchange of course, but they result automatically and almost instantaneously in response to buying or selling orders from the general public – from thousands of different Societies, Charities, Savings Banks, Pension Funds, and such like. The Stock Exchange reflects public reactions to events, forecasts, company balance sheets and so on, and is a barometer of the nation's appreciation of all these factors.

It would be absurd to suggest that there is no gambling on The Stock Exchange. Indeed, it is obvious that mainly owing to the high level of taxation and the mounting cost of living, gambling in some form or other has increased enormously of recent years, whether it be on The Stock Exchange, the pools, on the turf, the dogs, or now at the casino tables established throughout the country.

In some way speculation on The Stock Exchange helps to stabilize markets and there is much to be said for the punter, who prior to the

Capital Gains Tax, dabbled in and out of the market. He takes his risk and is not always right. Although the finger is constantly pointed at him, his offence against society does not seem to me to be any more heinous than any other gambler. Some people enjoy a little fling as a relief from their otherwise restricted existences. Personally I find bingo as dull as ditchwater, but I can well understand its fascination for the maiden lady in the suburbs who does not have a surfeit of thrills.

In status the stockbroking profession has risen enormously over the last twenty or thirty years. Before that I would have been loath to see one of my sons 'on The Stock Exchange' – not that either ever had that ambition – but nowadays I would regard it as an admirable occupation. Gone are the days when a buying or selling order was obtained by a clap on the back, or just on the 'jolly good fellow' principle. It is a highly professional game now, where only experts can flourish. And The Stock Exchange, even if it is of course tantamount to a monopoly and does its best to ensure a continuance of this situation, whilst, I must say, not abusing it, has worked doggedly to make its organization more efficient, and particularly to afford ever more protection for the investor. It would be almost impossible today for the public to be swindled as it was in the 1920s when spurious gramophone companies and others were floated off to an ignorant public, which mostly lost all its money. And we are all familiar with the pushing little stockbroker of former days who would tip any share so long as it brought him an order and some commission. They still exist but are rarer, because business is more widely spread and the public are better versed in these matters.

The Stock Exchange has gone forward apace and has torn down the curtains of secrecy which formerly surrounded it. Whilst the public is not allowed on the floor of the House, and a stranger there is still liable to be debagged, a gallery has been formed, with usherettes to point out the features to the public. The 'opening-up' was put in hand under the chairmanship of Sir John Braithwaite, who early in his stewardship saw the light. He was succeeded in 1959 by Lord Ritchie, who has carried the process considerably farther. There is now even corporate advertising. Lord Ritchie and his Council have done splendid and enlightened work and deserve the thanks and congratulations of The City and the out-side public.

I know many of the present leaders on The Stock Exchange, but where so many are personal friends, it is a little difficult to discuss them. However, I *will* fall to the temptation to refer to Kit Hoare. He has built a magnificent business, and commands much personal loyalty. Indiscreet and puckish as he is, his opinion is widely sought and valued. I have a sketch of him in my drawer, done years ago picturing him as a prima donna in a ballet tutu. I used to bring it out whenever he was particularly 'Kit-ish'. It always did the trick and he enjoyed it as much as anybody. I can hardly resist describing many other members whom I know and so much appreciate, but they will understand why I have selected Kit Hoare.

I always thought the partnership of Claud Serocold and Charles Micklem of Cazenove, Akroyds as it was then, was the ideal one, probably forming the pattern for others who have followed their example. They brought something new to stockbroking. One, shrewd and charming, opened the door, and the other detailed and able, did the work. They laid the foundations of a fine business.

A stockbroker's advice and opinion on new issues is always of particular value to an Issuing House. For the institutional investors the bigger firms cover almost the entire ground, and there is not much to choose between the ten to twelve leading concerns, who come within the bracket of 'issuing brokers', although all Houses have their own favourites. Sometimes one personality is more suitable than another for a particular piece of work, and so on. It is the function of these brokers to sub-underwrite issues on behalf of the bankers or issuing houses and their judgment must be very finely drawn to advise on the price of issue. Some firms have such a following, in fair weather or foul, that they know to a flick exactly what the big investors will take, and who is on the feed for this or that type of security.

With the enormous increase in interest in the stock markets of recent years, small investors have become a potent force. This increase is all to the good and I hope it will continue, for it is desirable that stocks and shares should be more generally distributed and that the smaller capitalist should be included. I am sure the encouragement of a wider spread of share ownership will, as a consequence, promote growth in British industry, and in the economy as a whole. It will enable an increasing number of private individuals, by holding a stake in enterprises of their choice, to have a greater sense of participation in the development and expansion of industry. They will thereby be enabled to share more directly in the rewards and risks of private enterprise.

Hence one notices that many a retired man, or even country spinsters, now turn first of all to the financial pages of their newspapers to see how their investments have fared, and avidly read the comments of their favourite financial editors. At dinner it is soon evident whether a lady neighbour holds investments, for no sooner does she find out that you are 'something in The City' than she plies you with questions such as 'Is it true there will be a Greek Bond settlement?' or 'What do you think of the boot-lace industry?' Sometimes with a flashing smile she adds 'I have got some of your shares, should I keep them?' My invariable reply is 'Chairmen are bad judges of the value of their own shares' and leave it in that unhelpful way. All the same, a large majority of people are baffled by Stock Exchange machinery and find the whole process of investment too mysterious and complicated to follow. That is one of the main reasons why the average small investor shows such reluctance to invest money in shares. May I therefore venture to give my own prescription? It is like everything else, no more than a matter of common sense, once one knows the ropes.

I have not the mentality of a speculator and it is only of recent years that I have possessed any stocks and shares worth talking about. During that period I have been too busy to pay much attention to daily gyrations in the prices on The Stock Exchange and have therefore simply put any available funds into good equities, disregarding the swings. I have had cause to regret succumbing to the temptation to sell first-class shares when they looked too high. Almost always that is the moment to retain them. I first look at the company's record, its management and directors. Then if satisfied I briefly consider its products or services, and if they seem to be what the public will want, I buy, and put the shares away. Timing is vital in investment, and if my conditions are fulfilled, and provided I have the money, I usually try to judge the moment and to go against the general trend if possible. Investors are nearly always sheep-like; they buy when things are going up and when everybody else is buying, and they sell when markets are falling.

I knew a man who a year or so before the American crash of 1929 had not only sold his holdings, but had gone short of stock. This is called 'going a bear', which means selling stock which one does not possess in the hope of buying it back at a lower price before the settlement date, thus becoming square and scooping the cash difference. A dangerous operation. My friend kept his 'bear' position open, on and on, despite the very serious difference against him. Stocks rose fantastically, the bulls, the reverse animals, had the bit between their teeth and nothing could halt their advance. In August 1929 my friend's nerve broke and he bought back his stock and took a ghastly loss. If he had only waited a few weeks longer, he would have made a terrific *coup*, for even in twenty-four hours, the market in some stocks dropped by a third of their value. My poor friend was right in principle, but his timing was badly at fault.

New investors must however realize that in holding ordinary shares there is always an element of risk. This cannot be avoided, but it can to some extent be guarded against. Investment is much more than sticking a pin into a list of shares. The risks must be thoroughly understood and carefully weighed up. Very full information is provided nowadays by public companies and a perusal of the last reports allows a detailed and easily comprehensible assessment to be reached.

Almost all activities in The City revolve around the pound sterling. The Old Lady of Threadneedle Street, as the Bank of England is some-times called, does her job magnificently. Indeed she is no Old Lady, but vigorous, courageous and skilful. It is of supreme importance that sterling should be maintained as an international currency, for the economic and to some extent the political system of hundreds of millions of people within what is known as the Sterling Area depends directly and indirectly on the soundness of sterling.

To take a practical example of the way in which The City is of vital importance in everyday life, let us consider the food on our breakfast table. We give little thought where it has all come from – from places all over the world – the tea from India or China, or coffee from Brazil; the flour from Canada, the butter from Denmark or New Zealand, the sugar from the West Indies, the marmalade from Spanish oranges. Even the eggs may have travelled thousands of miles! The City of London will have had a hand in all this. Merchants will have established the price in the appropriate market, brokers will have arranged the freight, underwriters insured against loss and bankers financed the goods from their original destination to the retailer, and so to our breakfast table.

I could tell of the many and varied insurance policies issued by Lloyd's and the Insurance Companies, and how hardly a ship sails the seas which is not insured in The City against every possible risk. Lloyd's is a national institution. There is also the Baltic Exchange, long famous for shipping freights. If, say, a Japanese wants to buy wheat in Australia, ten to one the freight and shipping will be booked and arranged in London on the Baltic Exchange.

And there is Mincing Lane and its commodity markets. The headquarters of most of the nation's shipping lines are in Fenchurch Street and Leadenhall Street and they are as well known to the sailor as Threadneedle Street and Lombard Street are to the banker.

The commodity markets, insurance, shipping, money and exchange markets, and the international banking system are all linked together in The City, and provide the most efficient service of its kind in the world – a mechanism, a technique, which is one of our priceless and most envied assets. And it is not sustained by mere wealth. If that were so, New York with all its gold and dollars would long ago have out-distanced London, but although I have immense respect and admiration for the American nation, there are doubts whether the United States could take our place even if they had the desire, because their banking and trading methods do not quite seem, as yet, to measure up to ours, based as they are on centuries of experience.

In The City, transactions take place all day and at all levels, often for large sums of money just at the nod of a head. To my mind, the strength of The City lies in its absolute integrity and profound experience. I do not pretend that occasionally we do not find 'wrong'uns' amongst us, as in other walks of life, but they are quickly detected and as quickly eradicated.

Chapter 20

M Y CAMPAIGNING on behalf of The City had encouraged me to burst into print in *The Sunday Times*, for on 22 October 1950 they accepted the first article I had contributed to this newspaper. It was given a pretty hackneyed title, 'The Challenge of Today' and I made a special, rather highbrow appeal for greater individual leadership. It coincided with many strikes and labour disputes and I tried to show that the world was no longer dependent upon new Messiahs. It was what each individual was thinking and doing which was of the utmost importance. I disputed the old adage that human nature cannot be altered. *The Sunday Times* had it reprinted and circulated widely and I was gratified that my first effort had been successful.

My second article on 11 May 1952 was called 'True Values', another unoriginal title. This time I pleaded for a more simple, less intellectual approach to the issues of the day, lest we became confused, befogged and negatived thereby.

The children took a personal, if perhaps reserved interest in these articles, and we rejoiced in their steady progress. We had always encouraged them to meet our friends whenever it was mutually convenient, so that they were well accustomed to grown-ups and to foreigners of all countries and early learnt to appreciate them. In the late 1940s we took to spending our summer holidays together at the Marine Hotel, North Berwick, whose manager, Mr Peter Hiller, coddled us considerably. Three years ago he rescued himself from hotel life and became Secretary of the St James' Club, so that my contact with this excellent man is happily maintained. North Berwick has gorgeous memories for us as a family, the golf lessons for the children, the heart-breaking air shots, the icy bathing, seeing old friends each year, 'old so-

and-so who had got fatter, and hadn't Billy Thomas grown a lot?' Renewing acquaintance with the waiters and the maids, watching the children dancing for the first time so nervously and self-consciously, later graduating to the Scottish reels, the wonderful picnics on the moors, the Edinburgh Tattoo and later the Festival. It was much the same as most families experience in a greater or lesser degree.

In 1950 we experimented and took the children for their first holiday abroad at Concarneau in Brittany. We were cramped like sardines in our small car and had fourteen suitcases of varying sizes on the roof, tied up with cord, with sufficient kit for all five of us for a month. We went across the channel by air ferry to Le Touquet and fortunately encountered benign French customs officials who did not require us to unload. First lunch at Rouen, great excitement, a night en route, all wonderful, new experiences for the children, but for me anxiety as to whether the luggage would skid off if I went fast or had to corner quickly. It was an unqualified success, so much so, that we repeated the holiday again next year.

Our eighteen-year-old daughter, Janet, who had been applauded at her school for a stage performance on Parents' Day, earnestly wanted, like so many young girls, to make acting her career. Her mother and I were never discouraging and she endeavoured to enter a drama school without success. So we suggested that before trying the stage, she might learn something more about life by going to Paris for a bit. After that we could see. She spent a happy year in Paris and we heard no more about a stage career. On her return she embarked enthusiastically on a secretarial course and found her own first job herself in the Conservative Central Office. Later she joined the secretarial staff of *The Times* and at twenty-one was appointed secretary to the editor, Sir William Haley. He was extremely kind to her and she was proud to work for him. After a year or two she had the urge to go to the States for about twelve months and found herself inclining towards literary interests. The newspaper-magazine bug, however, caught hold of her and she returned to London full of determination to make her way in Fleet Street. Finally, after some disappointments, she achieved her desire and joined the staff of the *Daily Mail*. I shall never forget her joy. Then, falling deeply in love with a fine young man, Richard Proby, she became engaged and was to be married on 8 May 1958. But a few weeks before, when driving home one night together from Windsor, they were killed instantaneously in a collision, she twenty-five years of age and he a few years older. It was tragic for the Proby family and for us. They both gave such high promise. Our daughter's ideals and standards had become so strong, yet she maintained a gaiety and purposefulness which radiated throughout the family. She was so full of life. Things were very different for us without her but we shall always be grateful to her for what she gave us. We have consoled ourselves with the thought that the qualities which she displayed in such abundance are still available to be drawn upon and to be enjoyed and that we cannot be deprived of them.

Our elder son Nicholas had duly gone to Eton in 1947, followed in 1950 by Robert. For eight years we made regular visits to the school, consecutive Fourth of Junes, firework displays, cricket matches, the field game, St Andrew's Days, and all the other paraphernalia of Eton life. We used particularly to look forward to the boys' reports, so detailed and tantalizing, which reached us three times a year. For some boys school is like the Elysian fields, for others it is a perpetual trial and a drag. This probably sums up the different sentiments of our two sons. Nicholas went on to King's College Cambridge, whereas Robert, having to do National Service, was posted to the Grenadiers as a guardsman. Finding the Brigade unwilling to adapt itself to his personal idea of discipline, he was commissioned to the King's African Rifles and served a cooling period in Uganda with that first-class African regiment. Both sons are good men. The elder, Nicholas, after some years in Helbert Wagg, where he was doing very well, decided he did not want to follow the rosy path set for him by his father, so he retired and departed to explore possibilities in the States. Our younger son has now established his own picture gallery in London, and leans powerfully towards the most modern in art, an appreciation shared warmly by his parents and brother.

Chapter 21

I WANT TO DEVOTE THIS CHAPTER to three subjects on which I have long wished to express an opinion, but which do not fit chronologically into my story.

Clubs

The first club in London is supposed to have been the Friday Street or Bread Street Club, originated by Sir Walter Ralegh about the end of the sixteenth century, But it was the coffee houses, which came into being in the middle of the seventeenth century, that were the real forerunners of the modern club house. I believe the first coffee house in London was opened in 1652 in St Michael's Alley, Cornhill, called 'At the sign of my own Head'. These coffee houses were 'the meeting places for the wits, and men of fashion, as well as for learned men, merchants and politicians'. Without the telephone or wireless, and mail deliveries few and far between, business men and others would meet to gather the latest news. Soon the coffee houses became so numerous and such a feature of social life, their influence increasing simultaneously, that they took up the entire accommodation of the coffee house or tavern where their meetings were held: thus they became club houses. Some of the clubs, now famous, retained the name of the original keeper, such as White's, Boodles, and Brooks's.

Almost every interest, rank and profession has its club, although nearly all have lost their original characteristics. Clubs are an integral part of English social life and membership can be very pleasant. Entrance and annual fees are really very modest, considering the amenities offered. The entrance fee is usually twenty-five guineas and the annual fee varies as a rule between twenty-five and fifty guineas, very low in comparison

C.E.F.

with clubs in the States, although, especially in the case of the country clubs, the facilities there are considerably more diversified and attractive.

Those clubs will endure in London which open their doors on a favourable basis to eligible young members, and which permit candidates to join who, whilst of course knowing how to conduct themselves, could well be drawn from humbler stock than that which at present fills most of London's West End Clubs. What I am saying is that so-called 'self-made men' should not automatically be frowned upon as members, just because they are self-made. Equally, I am not advocating that all self-made men should be candidates, since obviously it is important to maintain a standard, for if that drops, so the attraction of membership declines. But I do not believe it is such a difficult task as some committees like to make it. Besides, survival in these changing days is not otherwise certain.

I was thirty-four before I became a member of a club – when Alfred Wagg and Claud Serocold suggested I might like to join the Garrick. The idea pleased me greatly, for I felt I might find relaxation there in a change of scenery and association. I would not be likely to encounter too many City people, and having a natural love for the theatre, I hoped I would form new friendships and interests in a club whose motto is 'All the world's a stage'. So my name went forward. It was by no means a certainty that I would pass the scrutiny of the Committee, as I was unknown and could muster only small support from amongst the membership. But I had two excellent and respected sponsors, old members of the Club, and this proved the deciding factor. Afterwards I was told that one or two members of the Committee were suspicious of me, echoing the usual warning that although I might be acceptable myself and probably could be relied on to behave, they were anxious about whom I might bring into the Club, and the quality of my friends. I recently heard of a similar case, and the reservations were conveyed to the notice of the candidate by a well-wisher. The latter immediately wrote to the Chairman giving him an assurance that he would never bring any of his doubtful associates into the Club. Silly man! The ballot box was thick with black balls, needless to say!

There are several types of candidates for membership of a club: 1) like me, at the Garrick, an unknown who is sponsored by two top members and supported by others: he has an excellent chance. 2) A thoroughly good chap, benign and 'clubbable', known to many: he usually waltzes in. 3) A well-known person without any very firm views: he also is welcomed. 4) A well-known personality known to have strong opinions and to express them forcibly: he faces difficulty. 5) A successful self-made man, particularly if he is a Jew, or without background, perhaps a trifle bumptious and over confident: he will also not find entry easy. Personally, I have always thought clubs should have a fair mixture of animated, interesting personalities, for if the limitations are carried too far *ad absurdum* membership would consist of boring nonentities – nice chaps who conform.

To return to the Garrick: I have enjoyed it immensely over the years and especially during the Second War when I was working at the Treasury, and used the Club a great deal. A few days after my election I ventured timidly into the coffee room for dinner. It was early, as I wanted to escape the ordeal of being quizzed by the assembled members. Seeing what appeared to be at first glance a formidable member sitting alone at the big table, I turned tail. However, I was at once hailed and told to come in. Would I like a drink? The formidable one proved to be no other than Sir Harold Gillies – the eminent plastic surgeon, known to everybody as 'Giles'. We spent a delightful evening together, during which he regaled me with many golfing and fishing yarns. Baptism made easy! Later I got to know and enjoy many of the great personalities of the theatre and the legal profession, such as Lord Russell of Killowen, Seymour Hicks, Gerald du Maurier, Allan Aynesworth, Patrick Hastings and Bronnie Albery. The actor members of the Club were very jealous of their membership and would react strongly, even petulantly, when less famous members of their profession sought entry. I remember it took a long time before Leslie Henson and Jack Buchanan were put up because they were only in musical comedy.

The Garrick, started in 1831, is essentially for patrons and supporters of the drama and the other arts, and the building echoes with the memories of its members of long ago, poets, dramatists, musicians, painters, lawyers, authors and publishers – a perfect and varied assortment of talent and character. They numbered amongst them, to mention but a few, Thackeray, Dickens, Trollope, Sir Edward Clarke, Henry Irving,

Millais, Sir Edward Elgar, Lord Carson, Marshall Hall, Sir Charles Wyndham and Sir Herbert Tree. The glory of the Club is its wonderful collection of theatrical pictures, mostly dated from 1760 to 1850, including many by Zoffany, De Wilde and Hayman.

In 1937 I joined the St James' and there was no difficulty on this occasion. I was attracted to the Club by its diplomatic aura and the number of foreign members, to say nothing of its lovely premises situated at 106 Piccadilly. I like its international flavour and find much pleasure in the unusually stimulating and interesting membership, still comprising many foreigners of distinction, even if the character of the Club has changed a little of recent years. But I enjoy it very much.

I became a Trustee in 1954 and in May 1960 was elected to the chairmanship. Although undoubtedly an honour, I am not sure I would recommend the job to my worst enemy, but it is a chore which somebody has to do. To be successful, a chairman of a club should have tact, firmness, a sense of humour, understanding of human relationships and at times a thick skin. If he takes things too seriously he is lost, and certainly destined to be made unhappy. He must be prepared for the most thankless of all tasks, trying to please all members, whose points of view and desires appear as far apart as the two Poles. Men in their clubs are different from men in their homes. They like to feel free and to relax, which I suppose is why they join.

A chairman must be ready to appease disgruntled members and listen patiently to their complaints at all times. Subjects range from the suitability of prospective candidates, to too much water in the Brussels sprouts for yesterday's lunch; why there is a hole in the carpet, to why the strawberries were unripe at dinner last Sunday week. He is tackled whenever it suits the member, on the telephone, in his office or at home, when he is entertaining a guest in the club, or more frequently, for what in the eyes of the member appear to be really important matters, in the cloakroom when he is washing his hands. Being chairman of a club has its compensations, if few, but when he enjoys the wholehearted support of his committee, and the club has a good secretary and chef, a chairman's task is lightened and grumbles are less frequent.

In 1950, Colonel Jack Leslie and Sir Eric Miéville, Chairman and ex-

Chairman respectively of White's asked me whether I would like to be put up for membership and of course with them to sponsor me, my election was a foregone conclusion. It is uniquely carefree and jaunty. In consequence it is very popular, and it now takes anything up to fifteen to twenty years to get in, so long is the waiting list. The Club occupies a comparatively small but beautiful house at the top, east side of St James's Street. I know no more stimulating, yet levelling place. One finds gaiety and camaraderie there. The atmosphere is amusing, lighthearted, yet murderously critical of pomposity and any form of side. It is a thoroughly civilized place. I suppose my only claim to fame as a member is that I introduced Coca-Cola to the bar. Wheeler, the head barman, ought to have been a banker: I have rarely come across a man with such capacity for judgment of men. His assessments are startlingly accurate.

Many years ago I also joined The City of London Club where I lunch occasionally and never fail to have an interesting conversation with somebody. The weight of City celebrities congregated there between 12.30 and 2.30 p.m. is almost overwhelming. This Club has the unusual custom of what is called a 'members' election'; in other words, members vote personally for new candidates on an appointed day. Sadly, this gives vindictive and spiteful members the opportunity of the secret ballot box to express their personal dislike of budding entrants.

I belong too to the Travellers' Club in Paris. Formerly a Club with predominantly British members and invariably an English Chairman, its membership now consists more of Americans, doubtless because of Exchange regulations. There are only a comparatively few French members, for, notoriously, Frenchmen are not at home in clubs – no women. It is a pleasant rendezvous on a visit to Paris, situated as it is in the Champs Elysées, in a house of historic grandeur. The standard of bridge is high, and so are the stakes.

As time has passed, I have also joined numerous dining societies which are so popular amongst Englishmen. I speak for instance of the Ends of the Earth Club, the Chatham Dining Club, the Pilgrims', The Society of Merchants Trading to the Continent, The Parlour and the Tuesday Club. All these are serious affairs where one can associate at dinner with one's fellow members and frequently listen to guest speakers of political or economic eminence, invited to discuss important current events. Most of these dining clubs meet three or four times a year, and the quality or the speeches is apt to be higher than the food and the wine.

I still regard Hurlingham with its lawns and beautiful trees, affectionately, as one of the most dignified old-world spots I know. How foreigners love to be taken there!

I have lately joined The Portland, because so many of my friends are members, *not* in order to play bridge! The game to me is simply a relaxation, and I only like it in small doses. Although I had my first lesson in 1915 in the desert outside Cairo in those far-off First War days, I am a deplorably uninspired player. But I enjoy the fun and the banter, which are often to be had in clubs and homes where the stakes are reasonably low. They say that the more skilful the player, the more pleasant he is as a partner. Certainly I need encouragement from my partner; criticism is only self-defeating!

I almost forgot the old Union Club at Brighton, on the front, near the Bedford Hotel, of which I was a member for many years. In the days of Queen Victoria and King Edward VII when Brighton was frequented by the rich and the royal, the Union was very fashionable. In my day it was a decaying, dirty, ill-kept sort of place, with mostly old and decrepit members. It came to its inevitable end, and some little time after I resigned, I am told it sold its valuable premises for a huge sum, distributing the spoils amongst its rapidly declining membership.

I might as well take this opportunity to mention my golf clubs. I have remained an execrable golfer. I took up the game after the First War when my left leg had been injured, fully conscious of my own defects as an athlete or games player. I have never bothered to take the game seriously, but probably that is just my excuse. Verulam at St Albans was my first club, but in 1930 I joined New Zealand Golf Club, West Byfleet. At that time new members were hand-picked by Mure Fergusson, the tyrant Chairman, end-all and be-all of the Club. There was no Committee – he was the Committee – and because it was very difficult to get in, all the snobs in town and elsewhere clamoured to join! Membership was excluded for those living in the neighbourhood. I was pushed in by Max Bonn, who was 'a *propriétaire*', because I was an unknown, but I have enjoyed my membership more than I can say. Mure Fergusson was succeeded as Chairman by Colonel Leroy Burnham, one of the great golf stylists, who was a popular and effective Chairman. Now Dick Twining is in charge – a renowned games player. In a busy life New Zealand has been a haven of rest and peace. There is no 'pro', no shouting 'fore', no rush, no pressing, hardly any competitions – none of the things which, for me, a poor player, make life on a golf course so intolerable. Instead there is quietude and there is joy. Long may it survive!

My wife and I take great pleasure in our games there. We always play together. I give her six strokes and as often as not, she just beats me. I say I am never tested. She says I like playing with her because she is the only person who will leave London on a Saturday before 9 a.m. to be on the first tee twenty-five miles away at 9.50 a.m., play eighteen holes, have lunch and be back in London in time for a matinée. I think she is right!

It is one of those strange coincidences in life that although I am such a moderate performer at the game, I have achieved the thrill of doing a hole-in-one on three occasions and have once holed a five bogey in two with a drive and a three iron. I don't take any pride in, or boast about these events, for they contain such a large element of luck but, for such as me, it is an unusual record nonetheless.

For perfection in a golf course, I select Muirfield, near Gullane in Scotland, the 'Honourable Company of Edinburgh Golfers'. I became a member some years ago when as a family we used to go to North Berwick regularly for our holidays. It is golf at its best.

I have wondered sometimes what it is that appeals to me in Club life. I think it is the anonymity and at the same time the companionship one finds, and between the Garrick, White's, and the St James' there is wide variety. If you do not want to talk, there is no need to; if seeking a brief, jolly, doleful, or superficial little chat with a friend, it is mostly available, and if feeling profound, there is usually another bore who is willing to join in.

In the nature of things London clubs will have their difficulties in the future and there may be some amalgamations. Although they have been essentially man's domain up to the present, some clubs now enjoy popularity because they permit ladies as guests for meals in a limited way, or have instituted ladies' annexes. These are signs of the times which may point the way to the pattern of the future, even though resistance in certain quarters will be most obdurate.

Making Speeches

It is inevitable that at a certain level one has to be prepared to be asked to 'say a few words': perhaps to propose a toast, perhaps to give an opinion on the current economic situation, or perhaps to address an Annual General Meeting and answer shareholders' questions – anything. One may be forewarned, but it is not possible to dodge speech-making. It is an inherent part of public or semi-public life. These horrors have to be faced and an appearance on television is quite terrifying – at least so I found my debut on the B.B.C. Brains Trust. A natural, practised orator can derive much pleasure from addressing audiences. Hitler knew he had a magnetic appeal and he consciously used it to hypnotize the Germans, although most of us here thought he sounded fanatically wild. But I can see what a drug speaking can be, especially to a particularly gifted orator. This is a rare phenomenon, but if any reader has it, I beg him to resist it! It is deadly.

Except perhaps in Australia, public speaking, particularly after dinner, is more prevalent in England than in any other country I know, although in the North American Continent, the epidemic has a pretty strong hold too. When I think what an ordeal speaking can be, it is astounding how many people are reasonably proficient in the art, for an art it certainly is. Like most other things, it is a question of getting used to it. I once asked a famous politician what the secret was. 'Doing it, and doing it again and again,' he said. 'It is a combination of technique and self-confidence. I could get up on my feet at any moment and talk, or at least make a show, on almost any given subject.' That is a rarity. I find most of my friends are tormented at the thought of making a speech and very few seem to grow out of their fear and worry. I have been through various phases – not that I have ever been called upon to make a speech of major importance. My audiences have mostly been captive – those who have no alternative but to listen – but all the same the effort called for seems no less an effort because of that. Entertainment or interest must be provided, or preferably a combination of both – unless one is to be just a bore, put on to pass the time. One always knows whether one has gone over. The amount of comment afterwards is the indicator.

I have written elsewhere about my period of service on the Chelsea Borough Council. It was in the Council Chamber and Committee Rooms where I broke my personal ice as a speaker in my capacity as Chairman of the Finance Committee. The representatives of the minority party, though few, were vociferous, and they prided themselves on asking awkward questions. These required incisive and clear replies, or as likely as not, they were countered by even more pointed shafts. Ill at ease and lacking experience, I often found my task confusing and arduous. But being thrown into deep water then proved of useful assistance to me later on. My state of near panic at that time has melted after all these years into one of mere anxiety, and gratitude when the occasion is past.

My progress has been slow. Years ago I tended to write out the first word or two of all important sentences to give me my cues. This meant that I was practically reading my speeches, although I managed to avoid reeling off page after page verbatim from a script, as so many do. How I long on such occasions for the inevitable words, often so slow in coming: 'and finally, Ladies and Gentlemen . . .'! Frequently that is to me the most pleasant moment of the speech.

Later I resorted to just heads of paragraphs, and now I incline towards division of my remarks into two, three or four main categories. If I have had sufficient time for thoughtful preparation, I find this method of, so to speak, departmentalizing my subjects is the best and perhaps the least troublesome to my listeners. This subdivision of my comments also gives relief to my memory. But woe betide me if I have not considered my subject deeply enough beforehand. It is essential to think the whole speech through very carefully from beginning to end. I rehearse and rehearse. The bath is my favourite place, but walking in the park or along the street offers a suitable opportunity for preparation and revision. One can dry up very quickly and there is no more terrifying ordeal. I shall never forget a dinner given by the Garrick Club in honour of one of its most distinguished members, Mr Somerset Maugham. In responding to his toast he spoke to us about the pleasures of growing old. He had explained that although he had naturally given the subject much thought, he had decided to speak without notes, just letting his ideas unfold as he went along, and I think he added that this was his first attempt at speaking in this way. All went well for a few minutes and we were enthralled by his story, spoken in characteristically perfect English, when suddenly Mr Maugham stopped. At first we thought he was just hesitating before proceeding to his next theme, but it was soon apparent that he had lost his way, and for what seemed an age, he stood before us in obvious distress: nothing would come. At long last, feeling the sincerity of our sympathy and support, he smilingly resumed and gave us renewed joy. But the occasion was never to be forgotten; Mr Maugham's hesitation probably did not endure for more than sixty seconds but they were the longest sixty seconds I remember.

Brevity and sincerity are amongst the foremost factors which contribute towards a good speech. I speak of ordinary little speeches, day-to-day affairs, such as some of us have to face in the ordinary course of our duties. I do not refer to major political affairs where every word has to be weighed, although even these can be lightened or enlivened by a tone of sincerity, and with humour. The utter insensitivity of some speakers is extraordinary: they will calmly deliver diatribes of immense length, full of platitudes, completely oblivious of the depressing effect they have. They become enveloped in their own volubility and ignore, or do not observe, the restlessness of their audience. An essential feature in making a speech is to establish quick contact with one's listeners. It is always easy to sense, and if you feel unable to achieve this fairly soon, you might as well cut your remarks short and sit down for all the good you will do.

I have frequently seen advertisements guaranteeing proficiency in public speaking, and presumably they can be valuable in certain cases. But I have preferred to stumble along in my own way, fearing that simplicity may be lost and tricks and gestures might result in a stilted or professional manner. Few men are born orators. More profess to dislike speaking, but I cannot say I feel so strongly as that, and anyway it is usually something I have to do. But certainly I would avoid it whenever it is at all possible, as it is a burden every time.

The most brilliant speaker I have heard was the late Lord Birkett. His phrasing was perfect, his sense of humour delicious, and of course his tone of voice was persuasive, almost caressing. Yet I hope it is not sacrilegious to say that at times I found him too polished, too studied. I almost longed for a contemptible split infinitive to relieve the monotony of such a high standard, beyond the reach of most mortals. One never had that feeling listening to the supremely rugged oratory of Sir Winston Churchill, particularly thrilling in its unexpectedness, although I believe he has admitted on many occasions he is a writer rather than a speaker.

Lord Brabazon is in constant demand as an after-dinner speaker, and doubtless could be occupied every night in the week if he so chose. He has achieved fame in this respect because he sets out to make people laugh, and most of us want to laugh. He succeeds because he understands that human beings can, all unconsciously, present the strangest and most humorous situations. With brilliant aptness, Lord Brabazon seizes on such situations and recites them solemnly and baldly, always in a kindly way but with a word of exaggeration here, or a subtle sly dig there. You begin by giggling at such natural human absurdities, and finally give way unresistingly to laughter.

I do not remember hearing Lord Brabazon tell a dirty story in a speech. I hope I shall not be considered pompous or prudish if I deplore the growing habit amongst speechmakers of reciting lewd or profane jokes, especially after dinner, in order to gain acclamation from their audiences. I recall such an occasion which I am afraid is typical of most dinners held exclusively for men, notably reunions and regimental dinners. To begin with, there were too many speeches for my taste, five of them. Two of the speakers, both prominent persons, opened their remarks with more or less bawdy stories, and as they gathered strength, proceeded to cap these with nastier and coarser references, prefixed by the inevitable 'That reminds me . . .' There was no doubt as to their popularity, for the applause and the laughter were uproarious. It was a lighthearted event, and ponderous discourses would have been quite inappropriate. All the same, I went home depressed, mostly owing to the welcome these dirty references received, and sadly I realized it was not just polite laughter but genuine appreciation. I am told this is one of the facts of life. I cannot change it, but I can deplore it.

Happily we do not all like the same things, but those speakers who in my experience have been most effective and afforded the truest pleasure are those who strive for a less obvious but admittedly more difficult line. They give interest and get their laughs too, by gentle, topical, almost impish leg-pulling, and by palpable understatements or gross exaggerations, knowing full well that after good wine and food, men are generally excellent audiences, tending to become relaxed and benign, childlike almost, and ready to be amused by extraordinarily simple things, which need be neither vulgar nor profane. This is my taste, but I am afraid I am in the minority.

Recently I have been in contact with the famous Mr Leonard Brockington, probably Canada's outstanding authority on public speaking and a deeply inspiring war-time broadcaster who is a mine of exceptional literary knowledge. He maintains, quite correctly I think, that there are really no such things as impromptu speeches unless, of course, a man is called upon without any notice whatever. Even then anybody who speaks well on such an occasion must have a background of experience, study or training which comes to his aid. For the experienced speaker life is one continuous preparation for the next impromptu speech.

As we all know, the spoken word is meant to be heard and not to be read. Some speeches make magnificent listening but provide difficult and dull reading and vice versa. Burke, whose speeches belong to the immortal heritage of English literature, often bored the House, whereas I have been told Gladstone unfailingly roused his listeners. Nowadays old-fashioned oratory has died out. People have not the time to listen and radio and television are merciless in their cutting. Speakers mostly use simple words but there is still room in classical utterance for fine polysyllabic sentences in the grand manner, of which the following by Sir Winston Churchill is a good example: 'We see monstrous shadows moving in convulsive combinations through vistas of fathomless catastrophe.' But he alone could get away with that!

Jews and Gentiles

There are large numbers of Jews in the banking world. Naturally there are good and bad, but even in these more enlightened days, it is impossible to disguise the fact that in many minds in this country there exists a deep suspicion of, and prejudice against, Jews as a race which prevents individual cases from being judged on their merits. The under-current is strong and clamorous. There is no doubt about it. It is especially evident in clubs. We are admittedly nothing like as drastic as in the United States where for all practical purposes there is a total ban on Jews entering Gentile clubs, but feeling here often runs high when a Jew is presented for membership. His case is inevitably scrutinized and discussed more attentively than others and in greater detail, because he is a Jew. It is muttered: 'He's all right by himself, but if we let him in, won't he bring his less desirable friends with him and swamp the place?' Lively minds are thus often excluded by a small minority of fearful, prejudiced people.

From early boyhood I have knocked around with Jews and I am much indebted to them for friendship as well as support and guidance. I have never found it difficult to get on with them and I value their association. I learn from them and they stimulate me. The Head of Pitman's School was a Jew – nobody could have been more helpful or more open-hearted and wise. Three of my partners were Jews and no better men ever trod the earth. Two Jews fought beside me in the First War and there were no more gallant fellows. We may be fortunate in banking with the Jews with whom we come into contact, but never have I been hotted-up or done down by any Jew. They have been infallibly scrupulous in all their dealings.

Mostly Jews come out on top because they are clever and industrious. They have a rhythm of their own, they show application, and they want to get on quickly and as a result they often do. There are some who like to outsmart, to be flamboyant and noisy, and these traits do not make for popularity although I must say they are not exclusively Jewish. As a rule Jews are highly competitive in business, and although some are sensitive others are thick-skinned. Some live too much for material success and give undue priority to their business lives, but that characteristic is also not peculiar to them and it is their own affair if they like it that way.

In this country we have countless Jewish men and women of high distinction in the arts, in music and in the legal profession. In addition, we have enormously benefited in business, science and medicine by the accession of Central European Jews who chose to come here after the appalling cruelty and massacres of the 1930s and '40s, a good proportion of whom are well educated.

It was an inspired moment for the golfing world when Lord Cohen was appointed captain of the Royal and Ancient at St Andrews three years ago. He is the famous ex-Lord of Appeal whose services in the national interest over very many years are widely recognized and admired, nowhere more so than in The City of London, where his reputation was considerably enhanced after the Cohen Committee of June 1945 dealing with Company Law. I am convinced the decision, once taken, was not given a second thought: it afforded pleasure in all parts of the world where golf is played. It was not only a personal tribute to Lord Cohen himself, but to Jewry in general, for Lord Cohen would be the last to claim that he was in or near the front rank of golfers.

In the world of business, think of Lord Marks, head of Marks & Spencer; he has built a tremendous business which serves the public by bringing goods of high quality and design within everyone's range, and he has donated generously to education and medicine: of Sir Isaac Wolfson, who created Great Universal Stores, the greatest mail order organization in the country, an exceptional man; his Wolfson Charitable Foundation has given vast sums to charity. There is Mr Charles Clore, Mr Take-over, whom I will mention elsewhere. From nothing he has built a remarkable reputation for astuteness in business. He it was who at a certain moment taught us that assets must be put to work; he brought about revolution in many board-rooms, shook up the laggards and thereby indirectly rendered a great service to British industry. There is Mr Jack Cotton – a man of genius in the property world, with an international reputation. He has established an immense property empire by sheer farsightedness and ability. Sir Leon Bagrit of Elliott Automation, who has been a most successful pioneer in the computer and electronic business. These are public figures and they deserve the fruits of their phenomenal labours, which have been to the immense benefit of the nation as a whole. No reasonable man can deny this. We are proud of them. And I must not omit to mention the late Sir Montague Burton, who amongst other generous and constructive acts, established three professorships of International Relations in English Universities.

There is also the Jew whom one does not necessarily regard as being rich but who has in a different way made a powerful mark in the world. The following, prominent in a variety of fields, spring to my mind: Sir Solly Zuckerman, Solomon, Sir Jacob Epstein, Moiseiwitsch, Yehudi Menuhin, Myra Hess, Sir Michael Balcon, and the first Lords Reading, Burnham and Melchett.

Of those mentioned I have only actually met Epstein. I had known him slightly over many years and always admired his work as creative and courageous; in fact we bought one of his busts of a favourite model, Pola, before the Second War and derive considerable enjoyment from it. Finding myself with some mornings available about ten years ago, I went to see Epstein and asked him to do a head and shoulders of me. I felt it might be a more desirable work as a present for my wife than one of those stilted, photographic portraits painted so frequently nowadays by so-called fashionable artists, paid for by the yard and utterly dead-pan. After some humming and hawing, Epstein decided he could make something of me and we went ahead. It took twenty hours to complete, two hours a morning for ten blessed and interesting days: blessed and interesting because he was such a thoughtful and intelligent character. I was glad to have him to myself for so long; it was fun and it was lively, all the while. The bust turned out to resemble me – indeed it was most recognizable. It was undoubtedly a strong piece of work, and whether it got all the contours of my face just as God had made them, does not seem to me to matter. We have it mounted on a swivel so that the back of my head can be inspected, if desired. My wife, I think, prefers that view, and indeed most of our guests share her opinion, recognizing more quickly who it is from the rear! Epstein himself would not have cared, one way or the other. A great sculptor, if perhaps really at his best as a modeller.

It fascinates, and sometimes surprises me, that when talking of Jews such as those to whom I have referred above (and of course I could add to the list such names as the Rothschilds, the Samuels and the Warburgs, who are amongst the leaders in the banking world) one so often hears it remarked that 'we hardly think of them as Jews'. This is supposed to be a compliment, yet often those of whom we are talking are themselves very proud of being Jews. Perhaps our attitude arises from the fact that they have been to public schools or have so much assimilated the British way of life, at a certain level, that it has become part of them: or in a different category they are so intelligent, cultivated and kind that their friendship is automatically appealing and welcome; or sometimes in certain cases their humility, generosity and sincerity hold our affection and respect. Of course many Jewish families have been established in this country for centuries and their habits and ways of life are consequently indistinguishable from those of any other Englishman.

What then is the problem? It is that the best Jews are unbeatable, but I am afraid that a section of the rest, though no worse than the average, as so often happens with a recently emancipated group, have not yet learnt the rules of our particular game and cloud the horizon for those who have. I do not see an immediate solution: but it worries me, because I cannot help feeling that there is still unjust discrimination against Jews. I am sure it is unreasonable and no less than a disservice to our country to discourage them and to put barriers in their way. We could all do with some of their qualities.

My hope is that time will bring still less prejudice so that this liberalization will of itself automatically assist the Jew to play a fuller and increasingly important role in our national life. At a period when Great Britain is becoming more and more the centre for people of all races and nationalities, equality of opportunity must be available for all. In a broader sense we should take care that the same conditions which have bred racial tensions in the United States should not be allowed to establish themselves here.

Chapter 22

IN THE CITY AGAIN, there was progress and expansion for the firm. The volume of business was increasing and no doubt our own expertise as well, for from 1946 until 1951 we undertook a record number of new issues, placings and underwritings, for many diverse concerns. Not all were successful such as the issue in 1947 for I. H. Lavery & Co. cake manufacturers. In February 1948 an offer for sale on behalf of Hulton Press Limited also went awry. The poor reception accorded the cake issue was due to too much goodwill in the price, and slab cake which was almost a staple food in the canteens after the war, was gradually being superseded by meat, as rationing was reduced. Although oversubscribed, the issue was killed by adverse press comment, and did not hold its price. Hulton Press met with a poor response, not because it was a bad issue, but coming at a highly sensitive moment in our economic situation, when a politician, I believe it was Sir Stafford Cripps, made a depressing speech the day before the lists opened, the public took fright and abstained. From all appearances beforehand, we were preparing to engage policemen to keep the applicants in order!

Hulton Press published *Picture Post*, our last weekly magazine devoted exclusively to news in pictures, now out of publication, and the only British competitor to *Paris Match*. The Hultons, Teddy and Nika (Sir Edward and Lady Hulton), who owned Hulton Press, have a mixture of magic and genius in them and we enjoyed an easy and pleasant negotiation together.

The difference between a huge success and a dismal failure is remarkably small. One can feel the barometer falling when there is only a sparse demand for prospectuses and when the happy clamour of public interest in the banking hall is missing; a coolness and lack of interest not unlike a first-night flop in the theatre.

1952 and 1953 saw the beginning of a new type of financial operation in The City which almost became an epidemic and caused much discussion and not a little disturbance – 'Take-over bids'. Some of these had a well conceived, constructive and useful basis and were objective. They were of the very stuff of free enterprise and progress and without them inefficient managements and the outmoded uses of assets might be allowed to continue too long.

Take-over bids saw their origin as a result of financial restrictions during and after the war, when owing to prudent management and years of husbanding of resources, the balance sheet ('break-up') value of the shares of certain companies was well above their Stock Exchange quotation. A bidder seeking to exploit this margin could afford to make a tempting offer to existing shareholders, well above the then current price. If successful, he had bought assets worth vastly more than he had paid and was thus enabled 'to reorganize', and in the process to strip and sell certain of them to his great advantage.

That was roughly the genesis of the original take-over movement and it certainly had a dynamic effect on many managements. Seeing their shares undervalued on The Stock Exchange by comparison with the asset value, they hastened to be more realistic in their dividend distributions, a change from the conservative payments during and since the war. Without a doubt many boards of directors, seeing the red light, were gingered up to be more generous, lest they themselves might be menaced.

Much water has flowed under the take-over bridge since those early days, and ample protection is now afforded and a more or less regular formula as to procedure exists, approved by Issuing Houses as well as The Stock Exchange.

Take-over bids have altered the face of British industry during recent years. They have been a phenomenon of post-war financial activity but they cannot all by any means be achieved by 'smarty' financial technique only. The claim is that by more advanced and concentrated managerial supervision, or by integration of resources and skills, much better joint results can be obtained than if the two components worked separately. There have been dozens of these merger-cum-take-over operations since the war, some big, some small; some aggressively undertaken like the

[231]

Harrods take-over in which there were many contenders for control. On the whole they have worked out as well as anticipated. They are indispensable to economic progress and as a principle there can be no logical objection to them. Suffice it to say that on the whole the tendency has been to the benefit of both industry and workers. It has in so many cases improved competitive power by reducing overheads and giving opportunities to individuals to blossom in more progressive circumstances.

Generally speaking, I am a 'take-over' protagonist, and having played a leading part in negotiating some of the more hard fought battles I will recount some of my experiences and discuss some of The City reactions and effects, as I saw them. The whole field of take-over is fully and ably described in *Bid for Power* by George Bull and Anthony Vice, which I enjoyed reading.

The sweetest for us was in the summer of 1959, but this was not really a take-over in the battling sense, rather more of a merger. On 23 June Lord Kemsley asked me to come along for a meeting at Kemsley House in Gray's Inn Road in the late afternoon. We had acted for Kemsley Newspapers as far back as March 1947 when we successfully converted their outstanding debenture stock and I had then established a close relationship with Lord Kemsley. I admired his nobility of outlook and especially his handling and development of *The Sunday Times*. His four sons who were all associated with him in the business were also our friends.

I was ushered into Lord Kemsley's room and to my surprise, found his sons were with him. I realized something fundamental was happening for me to be received by all the male members of the family. Father sat at his desk, two sons at either end and myself opposite. I think, but have never been certain, that 'the boys' had been pressing Lord Kemsley to lighten his load, and that he had seen the wisdom of so doing, even if reluctantly. Anyhow Lord Kemsley said he and the family were inclined to dispose of their 40% interest (1,000,000 shares) in Kemsley Newspapers if they could obtain a satisfactory price. Would my firm handle the negotiations for them? And what did I consider their shares were worth to an interested buyer?

To the first question I replied that I was sure nothing would afford my partners and myself greater pleasure. Before I could give an opinion on the second question, Lord Kemsley said he was hoping for £6 million, i.e. £6 per share. Did I consider this a serious possibility? Thinking rapidly I expressed grave doubts and said that if we could get £4½ million or £5 million, I thought we should be doing extremely well, particularly as the market price on The Stock Exchange was 42/- per share, equal only to £2,100,000. However, I suggested I should go away and discuss the matter fully with my partners and that we should meet again the next day at the same hour.

This time I was accompanied by my partner Charles Villiers, who was a good friend of the entire Kemsley family and who eventually guided the operation through. Lord Kemsley then said that in a conversation with Mr Roy Thomson, the latter had shown more than a passing interest in purchasing *The Sunday Times* and his other newspapers. Did we know him? What did we advise? We recommended that we should approach S. G. Warburg & Co. whom we knew to be Thomson's financial advisers, to ascertain whether the interest was real, and if so, to be allowed to work out a proposition in negotiation with them. Finding that Warburgs had already been requested by Mr Thomson to give the matter their urgent consideration, Henry Grunfeld, one of their chief partners, Charles Villiers and I set about the problem straightaway.

Secrecy is highly important in these operations, and I remember being anxious when on one of my visits to Kemsley House I was spotted by a rather 'narky' stockbroker who would be quite capable of putting two and two together. Some people need but little evidence upon which to build up a story, especially at that time when take-overs were in the air. Happily, he suspected nothing, despite the fact that I was being shown out by the Chairman and his four sons.

After a concentrated week-end, Grunfeld came forward with an ingenious proposal, which had all the elements of a satisfactory operation for all parties. It is difficult even for me to be sure I can make the story understandable to the reader without enumerating too many of the details of the operation. But in essence it involved a merger between Scottish Television, controlled by Mr Roy Thomson, and Kemsley Newspapers Limited, the merger as a matter of fact being effected by the acquisition by Kemsley Newspapers of Scottish Television. The bulk of

[233]

the consideration for Scottish Television was to be shares in Kemsley Newspapers which would go to Mr Thomson and his associates.

The scheme also covered an arrangement with the Kemsley family who were to sell their holdings of one million shares to Mr Thomson and his associates at a price of £5 per share. These arrangements in themselves would give Mr Thomson control of Kemsley but there were a further 1½ million shares in Kemsley Newspapers held by the public. How were these to be handled so as to ensure that these 'outside' shareholders were given the opportunity of selling their shares for cash at the same price as that received by the Kemsley family? It was a *sine qua non*, agreed by all parties, that this must be done, but how, since a direct cash offer was not feasible?

Heads were put together and an underwriting arrangement was worked out under which the public shareholders were given the opportunity to sell their holdings, if they so wished, at a price of £4 10s. od. per share. The cost of these arrangements was relatively high, for it was an unusual transaction and it involved sub-underwriting and 'overriding' commissions, 2% stamp duty and legal and bank charges: in all a total of £500,000 or 6/8d. per share on the 1,500,000 shares under consideration. Such costs were generously met by the Kemsley family who put up the £500,000 necessary for the purpose, thus reducing the net price which they received for their own shares to £4 10s. od. per share, but at the same time permitting all shareholders to be treated *pari passu*, which was certainly a right principle. I think that after all expenses were paid, we retained something over 7d. per share for all our labours.

Thus Kemsley Newspapers, including *The Sunday Times*, England's premier Sunday newspaper, passed out of the hands of Lord Kemsley who had been associated with it for more than forty-four years. A sad moment for him personally in very many ways but a happy arrangement for the Kemsley shareholders who by a stroke of the pen saw the price of their holdings much more than doubled. Happy too for the redoubtable Mr Thomson, who achieved his heart's desire in obtaining control on an attractive basis of a fine, highly reputable and developing newspaper group based on London, to add to his other, ever expanding interests in this field.

Both were ideal men to negotiate with. There has never been a more

[234]

congenial operation. After the whole affair was over I could not help ruminating about these two men, Lord Kemsley and Mr Roy Thomson, so dissimilar, yet both having so successfully made their own way from humble origins, both leading figures in the newspaper world.

The operation completed, Lord Kemsley presented me with a photostat copy of the cheque for four-and-a-half million pounds which he received from Mr Thomson on behalf of his family for their shares in Kemsley Newspapers. The balance of one million was paid in the form of a ten-year Note.

ERRATUM
For 'four-and-a-half million pounds'
read 'three-and-a-half million pounds'

Chapter 23

Perhaps the fiercest, most momentous and most far-reaching take-over bid of recent years was the battle for the control of British Aluminium, which was fought out at the end of 1958 and beginning of 1959.

It was fierce because it produced intense heat and it set friend against friend in such an alarming way that at times one doubted whether the situation could ever be resolved or how the bitterness in City relationships could ever be eradicated. It was momentous because it was a tussle involving many leading banking houses. There were, however, certain notable exceptions namely Barings, Rothschilds and Philip Hill who were believed to view with more than a degree of regret the schisms being created in City banking circles. Apart from these three houses, it was Warburgs, Schroders and Helbert Wagg versus The Rest, captained by Lazards. It was far-reaching because undoubtedly fundamental changes sprang from it in merchant banking which as it happened, worked out in the end for the great benefit of The City, industry, and even for the nation as a whole.

In an operation in which as Chairman of my firm I took a prominent part, I would not wish to say anything which might seem to revive unpleasant memories. I am too devoted to my friends for that and much too anxious for the maintenance of City prestige and harmony. But the affair is an important piece of City history and I do not see how I can refrain from a fairly detailed reference to it. Although the banking world gained much from the experience, outside interests watched with surprise and even wonderment the rare event of an open battle being waged so hotly between such unexpected contestants on an unusual stage, The City of London. Be all this as it may, we must not forget that basically, the British Aluminium contest was merely a business proposition on which there was a fundamental disagreement. And whilst the atmosphere was decidedly unhappy at the time, none of the unpleasantness, as far as I know, still rankles. We differed, but we carry on and are still learning from what took place. That is the past and we build upon it. We must keep things in proportion.

All the same, there is no disguising the fact that the operation while it lasted was one of the most harassing and emotionally worrying periods in my fifty years in The City. It rent asunder well-established and ancient associations and induced gossip, mixed with harsh comments from hitherto friendly quarters. Apart from the controversy amongst opposing City groups which was bad enough, there was discussion on the question of an important part of British industry passing to American control. There was also the loud cry, invariable in a forced take-over, from those who are rigidly against the capitalist regime and regard take-overs as deplorable and based only on speculation, showing no sympathy with the human factor.

The battle monopolized many of my waking hours and those of my partners who took leading parts in the affair, particularly David Murison. Not only were there endless meetings of varying duration, called at any time – that was normal – but we were living in a state of constant anxiety. The usual sense of elation and excitement one enjoys in such operations, as moves in the game emerge, was missing in this case, and was replaced by feelings of apprehension about their after-effects on City relationships as a whole, so powerful were the reactions.

I may be giving the impression that this British Aluminium affair was simply a battle of wits between two sets of banking houses. Naturally it was the aspect which immediately touched us, but it was very much of a combined operation. The T.I. team itself was obviously extremely active in leading the thinking throughout, supported magnificently by American friends in Reynolds, to say nothing of the valuable counsel being offered by solicitors, accountants, and other experts who were constantly at hand.

Without going into all the details, it will be remembered that the row started at the beginning of November 1958, when Tube Investments

[237]

and the Reynolds Metal Company of Virginia, who had established a close relationship in the aluminium field and who had been acquiring shares in the British Aluminium Company, desired to have an association with that Company for future development. These original passes were repulsed by British Aluminium, whereupon T.I. and Reynolds made their wishes more categorical by expressing to the B.A. Board a few days later their willingness to purchase all the British Aluminium shares on an attractive basis from the holders. This scared the British Aluminium Board, some of whom apparently hastened off to the United States for talks with their old friends Alcoa, or Aluminum Company of America.

Meanwhile T.I. and Reynolds, fearing that something detrimental to their interests was being arranged, announced towards the end of November 1958 that, subject to there being no material change in British Aluminium's capital structure, they would bid the equivalent of 78/- per share (half cash and half in shares) for all the British Aluminium shares not already held by them: the shares to be vested in a U.K. Company with a 51% British interest thus ensuring British control for all time.

The suspicions of T.I. and Reynolds were well founded, for a notice was released to the Press on 28 November 1958 by British Aluminium that they had signed an agreement whereby Alcoa would subscribe all the authorized but unissued shares of British Aluminium, amounting to 4,500,000 shares. No price was disclosed.

That was the line-up, and the gloves were off.

Many queries flooded into the minds of interested parties. Wouldn't the Alcoa arrangement in effect give control to the Americans, inasmuch as they would have a one-third stake with the balance distributed amongst 14,000 other shareholders with varying holdings? Wasn't the T.I.-Reynolds offer likely to be more attractive financially? Why had the Board of British Aluminium not sought the authority of their shareholders before negotiating an agreement of the nature contemplated with an American concern? Even if there were no question of foreign control, ought not the shareholders to have been consulted beforehand?

In fairness to the British Aluminium Board I ought to state that they appeared genuinely to be convinced – I think erroneously – that the T.I.-Reynolds arrangement would in fact give effective control to the

Americans because of their greater experience in the aluminium industry, despite the fact that 51% of the capital of the new holding company was to be British.

At last the B.A. Board was forced to state the price of issue to Alcoa, and when it was found to be 60/- per share (a price based on the pre-take-over period), there was a howl of protest from financial commentators. The fat was really in the fire for the B.A. Board, and almost the entire press opposed them. All sorts of questions of financial principle were involved. The subsequent moves in the fight prominently occupied the newspaper headlines and it became the most widely discussed matter, crowding out other contesting material.

Meanwhile the B.A. Board countered the T.I.-Reynolds bid by promising to jack up their dividend from $12\frac{1}{2}$% to $17\frac{1}{2}$% per annum, which the financial editors considered only served to underline the unattractiveness of their arrangement to let Alcoa have 4,500,000 at 60/- per share. But this was only a 'warding-off' move in the game. It had little effect and fell flat.

Soon, what I can only describe as a David and Goliath situation came to light. On New Year's Day 1959 it was announced that a Consortium of fourteen concerns, a mixed bag of bankers and others, had been formed and would offer 82/- cash (4/- more than T.I.-Reynolds) for about 1,700,000 B.A. shares, on condition that those who sold would undertake not to dispose of a further 1,700,000 shares for three months. The Consortium claimed that they already had the support of holders of 2,000,000 B.A. shares, so that this holding plus the 3,400,000 mentioned above, making a total of 5,400,000, i.e. more than half the capital, would be sufficient to prevent T.I.-Reynolds from gaining control of B.A. and achieving their plans.

At the time, I likened this to Alice in Wonderland, for I could not comprehend how there could be any justification for letting Alcoa in for a one-third interest at 60/- per share, which with the balance distributed amongst over 14,000 different shareholders, would mean in effect tantamount American control, whilst at the same time recommending shareholders not to sell to T.I.-Reynolds at a vastly higher price when British control would be guaranteed. It was claimed to be in the national interest, but we could not see it, and as a matter of fact, many members of the Consortium have since admitted to me how much they regretted participating in this unreal proposition.

It was a David and Goliath affair because Warburgs, who were the Reynolds advisers, Schroders and my firm, Helbert Wagg, who jointly advised T.I., found the might and magnificence of many of their friends and competitors ranged against them. This was a highly unwelcome situation for The City, publicly carrying on an internecine fight. It was brain against brain, skill against skill, conviction against conviction, each move being carefully considered before being put into action. Both sides profoundly believed they were doing the right thing, in the best interests of all concerned, including the national interest.

Certainly the alliance of bankers and friends had no success and as everybody knows, T.I.-Reynolds obtained control of B.A. not only by an active purchasing campaign on The Stock Exchange, but by raising their bid price. Very big figures were involved and in one week alone 1,300,000 shares were bought at over £4 per share. At the end of the first week in January it was all over – David had defeated Goliath and British Aluminium was saved for Great Britain.

In retrospect I often wonder who gained most. At this moment the answer must certainly be the B.A. shareholders who sold their shares. Sales of aluminium and new uses of it have been miserably disappointing ever since, and have fallen far short of the expectations set at the time of the take-over. T.I.-Reynolds must look to the future for the fulfilment of their hopes, but I would estimate that the aluminium industry was an attractive one in which to be interested, despite its present state of doldrums. This operation was long-term, and the pluses will surely outweigh the minuses before too long.

But did this ferocious contest leave its mark on The City? Did it affect its prestige? There can be but one answer to both questions: in the affirmative; although in the second case, I consider only temporarily. I believe that the British Aluminium affair provoked a remarkable transformation in The City. Old citadels tumbled, traditional strongholds were invaded, new thought was devoted to City problems, there was a freshness and alertness unknown before, dramatic to watch. And this transformation has been achieved whilst old relationships have been resumed, differences have been forgotten and new alliances have been made. Everything has long since been tranquil and harmonious, nevertheless it is different. The merchant bankers are more on their toes; they vie with one another to give a better service to industry and their clients, some even advertise the facilities they can offer; there has been a girding of loins, resulting in more enterprise and competitiveness and less reliance on the 'old boy' idea. Of course these advances might have taken place anyhow, but I do not believe I am exaggerating when I say that most of them date from the British Aluminium episode, and the effects have spread beyond just banking, and have included the whole City. So let us be grateful to British Aluminium and leave it at that, without more dissection or detailed analysis.

I believe that there is some similarity in the recent period, when new names are rising in banking, and deservedly building sound reputations, to the early 1920s when Helbert Wagg, almost unknown but with a new power, were successful in creating a firm base for themselves in The City. We were breaking through the barrier and establishing ourselves and we achieved satisfactory results by determination, efficiency and a marked concentration on the business in hand. That is why I rejoice when I see the upsurge of worthy newcomers, and wish them luck and success, having only a fellow feeling, and not one iota of jealousy or resentment at their encroachment, knowing that it is those who render the best service who get the best results.

Chapter 24

IT IS ALWAYS PLEASING to a man's vanity for his services to be sought by opposing interests at the same time. This is what happened in the case of the Mirror-Odhams contest, for on 24 January 1961 I received an urgent telephone message from Mr Roy Thomson requesting me to attend a meeting at 11 a.m. that day at the offices of Simmons & Simmons, solicitors in Threadneedle Street, on 'a very important matter'. So, putting all else on one side, I kept the appointment, accompanied by my partner Charles Villiers.

We were shown into a small room and, being the last to arrive, we were quickly able to guess at the reason for our summons when we saw before us not only Mr Roy Thomson himself but also Sir Christopher Chancellor, Mr Shard and Mr Gibson of Odhams and Mr Bucks of Rothschilds. I knew we should not stay long if my surmise was correct, and so it proved. When Mr Thomson asked us to act for him in some negotiations he said he was engaged upon with Odhams, I stopped him short before he could say too much. After expressing the great pleasure his invitation afforded us, I told him we were precluded from taking part on his behalf as we were the financial advisers of Albert E. Reed & Co. in which the *Daily Mirror* was substantially interested, thus putting us in the opposite camp. This unforeseen intimation caused some amusement and some rueful smiles. I said we were of course flattered, but Mr Thomson would appreciate that in the circumstances we had no alternative but to retire from the meeting.

In some ways I was sorry, for with my partner Robert Hollond I had had a very happy negotiation with Mr Shard and Mr Gibson in April 1959 when Odhams bought Hulton Press, on what seemed to us a highly attractive basis. It certainly was, both for Odhams and also for the Hulton Press shareholders who had suffered a marked depreciation in the price of their holdings, and who by this take-over were enabled to recover a substantial part of the discrepancy. It was difficult to see how else the resurgence would have come about, at any rate for some time.

Later, it transpired that Thomson Newspapers called upon the services of the ebullient and alert Kenneth Keith of Philip Hill, Higginson & Erlangers, since Warburgs, his regular financial advisers, were also unavailable as they had for some time been in the *Daily Mirror* camp.

The whole affair started as a result of a suggestion from the *Daily Mirror* side towards the end of January 1961 that a merger on certain terms with Odhams would be advantageous for both companies, mainly to avoid further cut-throat competition in the field of women's magazines. This proposal was not apparently to the liking of the Odhams Board who turned quickly to Mr Roy Thomson whom they appeared to regard as a more suitable partner. Rapid discussions ensued, with the result that twenty-four hours after the meeting to which I had been invited, an announcement was made giving full terms of a merger between Thomson Newspapers and Odhams Press. It was to be a real merger on a 50/50 basis, neither side having the control – not an easy arrangement to put into harmonious effect.

Obviously this projected 'wedding in the vestry' caused the deepest stirrings amongst the *Mirror* Board and its advisers. They were convinced that the interests of all parties would best be served by *Mirror*'s merging with Odhams, which would far outweigh any possible advantages of the latter's proposed link with Thomson Newspapers, but they had been repulsed in their approaches. And here, with the publication of the details of the Odhams-Thomson merger, was proof positive that no progress was to be made by further talks. Action, strong and definite, was essential on the *Mirror*'s part, and obviously it must follow the line of a bid for Odhams, lock, stock and barrel. There was no alternative but to take the grand step and buy them – make a 'take-over' bid. It could all have been so happily arranged if Odhams had been willing for discussions but they weren't. They preferred Thomson to King and his friends.

27 January saw frenzied activity in *Mirror* circles, deciding the terms

[243]

of the take-over, and at night, with the full approval of Warburgs and my firm Helbert Wagg, the press were informed that a take-over was proposed. This was the day when I first came into contact with Mr Cecil King, the Chairman of the *Daily Mirror* Group. It was the first occasion on which I had seen him in action. I was impressed. This huge tall hulk of a man struck me as having leadership in him. He was speedy of decision and cut right into the heart of a problem, using the minimum of words. He has the reputation of an *enfant terrible* in the press world, but this is only because he never minds sticking his neck out and finds it utterly impossible to understate his arguments, or to disguise his true opinions. I knew at once that if we were to be involved in a tussle, he would be staunch and correct in all his dealings. The tussle indeed proved a severe one, involving incessant meetings and discussions at all hours of the day and night. Indeed, at times the complications and difficulties seemed insuperable, but Cecil King never faltered. Always calm, never petty, I saw in him a man with a majestic outlook. *Daily Mirror* shareholders owe him much. He reigns over the *Mirror* Empire and as such must be one of the most powerful men in the country. I expect he enjoys his power, but he never abuses it. Perhaps he is disdainful and cynical at times, even intolerant, and perhaps he believes too much in giving his readers what they want rather than what may be good for them. He always says: 'Who am I to withhold enjoyment from my readers? They know what pleases them. I am not a nurse.' Yet surely he shapes and co-ordinates public opinion and is fearless and uncompromising: for instance he advocates our entering the Common Market – I hope not only because his deadly enemy Lord Beaverbrook takes the opposite view! They say the *Daily Mirror* is read by fifteen million people each day. Terrific power, isn't it? I am one of those readers. I find it lively and direct and I like its appeal to youth – that's what gives it its huge circulation. I even contributed an article myself to the *Daily Mirror* on 24 November 1961: 'Where are the great voices?' in which I pleaded that in these revolutionary days in which we were living voices should be raised, telling the people and proclaiming our determination to face facts and to discard outdated concepts of former grandeur for a new realism. Our words no longer rock the globe, I admitted, but all the same we still speak with authority and our influence still weighs in international council chambers. The Editor of the *Daily Mirror* vouchsafed to me that at least three million people would have read my article from beginning to end, but my exhortations brought no apparent result.

Cecil King had some stalwart associates to support him in his fight for Odhams. The leading one, until he went off on an overseas visit, was Hugh Cudlipp, a splendid, flamboyant swashbuckler, gifted with a delicious flow of words which he sprays around with the utmost *bonhomie* and forthrightness. He wrote a pungent description of this takeover bid, in the fullest detail, in his book *At your Peril*, where the reader can catch all the nuances, as the game proceeded. I recommend it. In one or two references to me, Cudlipp, using some of his more controlled adjectives, called me 'durable, tall, straight-backed and commanding'. I am not certain if I'm flattered.

There were also at that time James Cooke, now retired, and Ellis Birk; the former with as astute a financial mind as you can meet. Ellis Birk, a lawyer with a rapier-like mind, was a tremendous force in the policy discussions – the sort of man I should not welcome in opposition to me, yet most correct in his directness. In the intervals between amending the drafts of the circulars he did his best to convert me to his Left Wing thinking; he was unsuccessful, but I noticed that when I wrote my article for the *Daily Mirror*, I was led to describe myself as 'an off-beat Tory'. I am not sure what I intended thereby, although I meant it as evidence that I am not by a very long chalk a full-blooded Right-winger.

In these financial contests, and I have participated in a great number of them in one way or another, there are many aspects. For me, the human factor has always been the dominant one and the part I have most enjoyed, and been most interested in – not the financial side although this obviously has its place. One sees men metaphorically stripped naked, and in the dazzling and blinding limelight in which such negotiations almost inevitably take place, a man's worth and the strength of his character are quickly assessable: whether he is self-centred and vain, or whether, regardless of his own personal position, he is willing to judge an operation purely and simply on its merits. The tests are severe but intensely interesting, and those who emerge unscathed are much more numerous than most detractors or observers would imagine. In my opinion the *Mirror* Board excelled in this direction, if I may say so without being suspected of being patronizing. I enjoyed the negotiation because of that, even though it was so exacting and demanding in its call for concentrated attention.

We were fortunate to be working in co-operation with S. G. Warburg & Co. Ltd, as joint financial advisers of the *Mirror* Group. I admire Siegmund Warburg, not only for his courage in starting a new life in this country and making an unqualified success of it, but for an almost monastic indifference to passing pleasures which seems to endow him with an unusual appreciation of the intangible, yet very real, things of life. I rate him high in the international banking fraternity. He delegated the leadership in the *Daily Mirror* negotiations to Henry Grunfeld, on whom fell, as a matter of fact, most of the burden; nobody assumed it with greater willingness, or with more good humour and satisfaction. We were of course ably supported by teams from both our Houses, led by George Warburg for Warburgs and Robert Hollond for my firm. But Henry Grunfeld slaved ceaselessly. He and I made one determined effort to prevail upon the Odhams Directors to call off the contest before it got too hot, but without avail. Thus the fight was on and soon blood was spilt, financial blood, newspaper blood, and labour blood. Financially there were the various counterblasts from either side, the *Mirror* upping its price in the face of the promise of increased dividends by Odhams as they struggled hopelessly to shake off their aggressors: newspaper blood because the T.U.C. and the Labour Party were anxious lest the *Daily Herald*, a considerable money-loser, might be sacrificed if the *Mirror* got control of Odhams: and labour blood because in the inevitable integration of magazines which would follow, it was questioned how the employees would stand. Would some lose their livelihoods?

All these obstacles were overcome; Odhams lost the battle as everybody knows, the arrangements with Mr Roy Thomson having of course fallen by the wayside. The *Mirror* have long since set about the task of co-ordinating Odhams into their Group, under the Chairmanship of Hugh Cudlipp, who is also manfully trying to make the *Daily Herald* a paying proposition. This may be one of his hardest tasks, but he will assuredly persist. For the rest, I ought in honesty to say that the stubborn resistance on the part of the old Odhams Board had the result of securing for their shareholders a better bargain than looked possible originally. The final offer was five *Mirror* shares, plus 5/- in cash for every share in Odhams, compared with four and a half *Mirror* shares for each Odhams share. The value this put on Odhams shares was about 63/6 compared with 40/- when the talks first started.

Thus ended one of the most monumental take-overs of recent history. Apart from the immediate participants, it was a challenge to the Conservative Party as well as to the Opposition. Was it proper for such a transfer of newspaper power to take place as a result of a financial transaction? This and many other questions recur for our consideration. My partners and I never doubted the rightness of the operation. We shall see over the years whether the vesting of so much power in one quarter was wise or whether again we shall witness the corruption which Lord Acton in his famous dictum said follows inevitably in such cases. Somehow I do not expect to be disappointed, but a gigantic burden falls on Mr Cecil King's shoulders, and his successors whoever they may be.

Chapter 25

ONE OF THE REALLY DRAMATIC MOVES in the take-over world was the announcement on 26 May 1959 by Mr Charles Clore that he intended to make a bid for what amounted to 75% of the share capital of Watneys at 60/- per share. It was probably one of the most far-sighted acts of his remarkable career for he had the genius to realize the vast potentialities of the brewery industry before the investing public had appreciated them fully.

Mr Clore became the talk of the town. His bid excited the special interest of the working man, who rejoices in his pub, 'the English pub' – sacred to so many. But ironically it was the shareholder, not the working man, who would take the ultimate decision, if the bid were persisted in, whether the control of Watneys should change. It was daring and original thinking on Mr Clore's part.

But apart from this question, was Mr Clore well advised to tilt his lance at Watneys, the centrepiece of the brewery industry, with all their interlocking arrangements with other breweries, and thus arouse instinctive and powerful opposition? Could he break into this closed shop – the old brewing families of Great Britain – with any chance of success? Could he overcome the resistance of those formidable battalions? Mr Clore promised a revolution – a transformation of these clubs of the British people. Ought Mr Clore not to have started on a less grand scale, little by little becoming established and known as a brewer, as Mr E. P. Taylor has since done? But was there not ample justification for Watney's claim that as the leaders in this particular field, they had already done much to improve their public houses? Were not Watney's plans for further development, especially of their properties, already formulated? Could they not, in due time, thus give proof of this to their shareholders, and so defeat the onslaught of Mr Clore?

These and many other questions came into my mind and surely into the minds of all interested observers. I therefore determined to take a hand in the situation, to use such influence as I might have, on an entirely personal basis, with both the parties concerned, to see whether I could be of any assistance. Both Mr Clore and Mr Combe, the Chairman of Watneys, were friends of mine, and it distressed me to see them in combat. I could visualize no true satisfaction for either, if this battle were played out to its bitter end. Apart from his opinion of the future of the brewery industry in general, Mr Clore undoubtedly had his eye on the development of the valuable Stag Brewery site in Victoria, London, and other properties. I believe he had been somewhat incensed at what he thought was the dilatory approach of the Board of Watneys in this direction, for he was reported to have a sizeable holding of Watney Ordinary shares himself. Mr Combe, on the other hand, had been laying his plans for the further development of the Company, especially the properties, carefully and without undue haste, when the bomb burst and he found himself threatened by a take-over bid, without any previous notice.

The price of Watneys shares had been rising from about 40/- before the bid, and stood at 51/6, compared with the equivalent of 60/- per share offered by Mr Clore. Mr Combe's first reaction was to announce that the bid was entirely unacceptable in view of the prospects of the Company. He promised a statement as soon as the valuation of the properties which, he announced, had already been put in hand, was completed. Meanwhile there was an impasse, a curious lull. Mr Clore had let it be known that he was not prepared to pay a price which discounted the future too much and had not sufficient regard for the time and effort which would be needed before the ultimate benefits would accrue. Yet the price on The Stock Exchange had risen to over 70/-, or more than 10/- above Mr Clore's bid. Clearly something must happen: either Mr Clore should be prepared to pay at least 80/- per share if he were to be successful, or the negotiations must be dropped. It was an absurd state of affairs.

It was at this moment, about the middle of June 1959, that I was impelled to do something, I felt I could make a useful contribution by offering to act as an independent *homme de confiance* in an endeavour to bring the opposing parties together. I knew Mr Combe was anxious to

[249]

meet Mr Clore, so I sought an appointment with the latter, telling him on the telephone that I had a most pressing matter to discuss with him. It so happened that I had an important golf match the next day which was due to start at 10 a.m. Could I possibly be received at 8.30 a.m.? Mr Clore at once agreed and I duly arrived at his office in Park Street at that hour. He was there with his colleague, Mr Leonard Sainer, looking for all the world as if he had been at his desk for hours. They were studying papers assiduously. I explained the part I wished to play, an entirely independent one. I ventured to give Mr Clore my dispassionate opinion of the Watney affair, saying that things had reached such a state that unless he was prepared to raise his bid to what looked like a mighty high level, his chances of success seemed to me remote. I made other points of a general nature, and begged him to agree to meet Mr Combe for a talk that afternoon, and meanwhile to turn over in his mind the desirability of achieving a mutual agreement to call off the bid.

I suggested Crewe House as a rendezvous, feeling fairly confident that even the keen press-hounds would not be able to track down the parties there. So at 3.30 p.m. that afternoon Mr Clore and Mr Leonard Sainer joined Mr Combe and his colleague, Mr John Haslewood under my neutral chairmanship. After a short discussion it was clear that Mr Clore was unwilling to be goaded by Stock Exchange projections into capping his previous bid. Somewhat to my surprise, the meeting was not reproachful on either side and it was decided to issue forthwith the following notice:

WATNEY MANN LIMITED

The Chairman of Sears Holdings Limited and of Watney Mann Limited have met. Friendly discussions have taken place and Sears Holdings Limited have now decided not to proceed with their proposed offer to the Watney Mann stockholders.

(signed) Charles Clore
Simon Combe

19.6.59

The original of this historic 'armistice agreement' was given to me for retention. I have it framed at home. I prize it highly, because I feel it is evidence of a wise and fair decision in which I was able to play a helpful role, willingly, informally, unofficially. Both Mr Clore and Mr Combe know that I am publishing these details of my hand in the matter, hitherto a complete secret, as far as I am aware. It goes without saying that Mr Combe was in the closest consultation on every step with his own financial advisers, Baring Brothers, and I know how much he owed to them.

But I feel I would be wrong if I did not add that Mr Clore's intervention could not have failed to point the way for subsequent activity and mergers in the brewery field. He showed he was alive to the possibilities and without doubt he set the ball rolling for others.

Mr Clore is in himself a study, a phenomenon of this age. He is a master of finance and presumably an extremely rich man. His name is bandied about all over the place. He is so famous that he is the frequent subject of music hall jokes. He now shoots, farms and owns racehorses. How has he done all this? I am blessed if I know, but I suspect Mr Clore is a genius. In fact he must be. He is staccato in expression, unassuming in appearance, ungracious in manner sometimes, uncommunicative, quiet, and certainly a realist, yet with vision; a man of decision and courage.

The wise Mr Combe had already been on his toes also, and quietly and astutely had put in motion a complete revaluation of the Watney properties, with all the resultant possibilities. It would have been tragic, for him and his colleagues, if at that very moment of development he had been prevented, under a new master, from carrying his plans into effect. No doubt the projects would in any case have proceeded, even if modified or extended, but the whole thing would not have been the same.

These are the reasons why I said the decision to agree to disagree was a wise and fair one in all the circumstances.

Chapter 26

IT IS OFTEN FASCINATING to contemplate how business comes along, and how accidental, and indeed incidental, the circumstances sometimes are.

One such extraordinary coincidence was my introduction to the International Business Machines business. The history of this situation started in New York with a friendship which I developed in the early 1950s with Walter Rosen, senior partner of Ladenburg Thalmann, the well-known bankers. Mrs Rosen, a sister of Colonel John Dodge – that happy and lovable man who created the popular Ends of the Earth Club to further Anglo-American friendship and co-operation – was an adept performer on a queer instrument called a theramin. It was in June 1951 that Rosen arranged a concert for his wife at the Wigmore Hall. This was preceded, a day or two earlier, by a cocktail party at Claridge's for the press, to which my wife and I were invited.

Although not appreciating particularly the wailing notes produced by Mrs Rosen's musical apparatus, I loyally agreed to be present. Amongst the large number of people at the party I happened to be introduced to a charming young lady. She proved to be Mrs Christobel Norrie, whose husband was an American named Lanfear Norrie (although shortly thereafter this marriage was dissolved and she became the wife of Neville Berry, son of Lord Kemsley). In our talk together Mrs Norrie displayed a surprisingly acute interest in City and business affairs, and she plied me with many pertinent questions regarding my work, disclosing an impressive and unusually intelligent knowledge of such matters, especially for a woman. The proceedings over, we bade one another adieu and I thought that was the end of a pleasant little interlude.

But no! the next morning Mrs Norrie telephoned me in the office.

We expressed mutual pleasure at our talk, whereupon she said it had led her to think I might be interested to meet Mr Thomas J. Watson, the President of International Business Machines, who she happened to know was in London; under the guidance of Mr Ormonde Lawson-Johnston, he was seeking an association with a banking house in The City with a view to the establishment of a British subsidiary. Why should it not be my firm, Helbert Wagg? Would I care to go at once to Claridge's to meet Mr Lawson-Johnston if she could get him along? I murmured doubts and excuses. It all seemed so vague and unpropitious. But I underestimated the lady's intuition: she pressed me and I reluctantly agreed to be at Claridge's at 4.30 p.m. that afternoon, still certain I would be on an absurd wild-goose chase.

At Claridge's, there was Mrs Norrie accompanied by Mr Lawson-Johnston. We were introduced and she left us together 'to discuss business'. There *was* no business. It was obvious that Lawson-Johnston was as reluctant to meet me as I had been to meet him. Moreover, he mentioned something which made me prick up my ears, and convinced me more than ever that I was wasting my time. He had taken Mr Watson to see Morgan Grenfell that morning, and Mr Watson had invited them to co-operate with him. Morgans were considering the matter and would give their reply the next day. I confess I wondered why they had not immediately accepted, so when Lawson-Johnston, as a sort of consolation prize, and because he was the delightful man we later found him to be, suggested that I might like to attend a dinner he was arranging at Claridge's that evening in honour of Mr Watson and some of his colleagues, I accepted, but with a certain embarrassment and many misgivings. I was, however, naturally anxious to meet such an illustrious and famous American industrial giant as Mr Watson.

When I appeared again at Claridge's, my host, who shall be nameless, invited me to my astonishment to sit on his right, and conducted me there arm in arm, asking me what sort of a sea passage I had had. It was clear he was a little vague about his principal guest and had mistaken me for Mr Watson. Disconcerted, I gently and tactfully pointed out his error, and hastily changed seats with Mr Watson, who was on my other side.

During dinner I monopolized Mr Watson's attention. I was quick to see in him a man of outstanding character and sincerity, and I did not want to miss this unique opportunity to hear his views, so wide ranging, enthusiastic and wise. He left me in no doubt of his admiration of our Queen and of the Commonwealth, nor of his own profound belief in the United Nations.

As the meal progressed Mr Watson also outlined his talks with Morgans and was good enough to say how sorry he was to be precluded from using my firm. I at once assured him that that was out of the question, now that he had initiated talks with Morgans, who were intimate and respected friends of Helbert Wagg. He would be in excellent hands. For me it would be regrettable, but that was too bad. Mr Watson appeared highly appreciative of this attitude. It seemed natural and proper to me, but there is less finesse about business in New York. He then disclosed that Morgans had some hesitation about assisting him, since, as advisers to a competitive concern in this country, they might have a conflict of interests. If they felt they must decline, could he approach me the next day? Joyful news, but I again reiterated that not until he had broken off with Morgans could we pursue active negotiations with him.

About noon the following day Mr Watson telephoned to say the decks were clear. Morgans had, with much regret, turned him down, and he was free to negotiate with us. Would I come along that afternoon to have a cup of tea and talk things over? With my partner, Alan Russell, I duly waited on Mr Watson, and before the discussion had ended, it was mutually agreed that we should do his business. Mr Watson was most anxious to have British participation in the capital of his new enterprise and in due course, I.B.M. United Kingdom Limited was established. The original capital was £1 million in ordinary shares and in November 1951 my firm placed 40% of it amongst its clientele, i.e. 400,000 shares, at a premium of no less than 100% or 40/- per share, making it clear at the same time that no dividend could be anticipated for at least five years. Could there be a finer tribute to the standing and reputation of I.B.M. that such an operation was possible without any difficulty? And what insight into business possibilities was exhibited by Mrs Berry, as she now is. As a direct result of a chance meeting at a cocktail party, Helbert Wagg formed an association with the world's leading organization in

[254]

the computer field. That is the romance and the delightful unexpectedness of business, and indeed of life.

Not only was this the inauguration of a most agreeable business contact for my partners and myself, but it was to develop for me into a vital friendship with Mr and Mrs Watson, as well as with their younger son, Dick Watson. He is now President of I.B.M. World Trade Corporation which undertakes the operations of I.B.M. in overseas territories – a mighty and ever growing organization.

Two or three years after our original placing of the I.B.M. shares, mainly with institutions and professional investors, I thought it right for their representatives to meet Mr Watson and his son, in an informal way, so as to hear at first hand how their interests were progressing. Accordingly, some of my partners and I arranged a lunch in a private room at the Savoy and invited fifteen or twenty shareholders to be our guests. After lunch, I opened up with a few introductory remarks which Dick Watson amplified a little. I then called upon Mr Tom Watson himself. I shall never forget the occasion. He was a lean, handsome man, healthy and strong, a life-long non-smoker and teetotaller, with a delightful quiet voice, yet with an authority and sincerity which commanded immediate respect. I expected him to outline the progress of I.B.M., giving his hearers confidence and assurances about the future, supported by statistical evidence. Not at all! He said not one word in this vein. After stating his pleasure at meeting them and how happy and proud he was to have them as shareholders, he went on to tell of his admiration for the Queen, what a great ideal the Crown was, what the conception of the Commonwealth meant to him, and how firm was his belief in the United Nations. His integrity was so manifest and he made such an impression as a man, that it was probably the most successful lunch I have ever participated in. His hearers were captivated by him and to a man expressed their assurance that their investment was safe in Mr Watson's hands. All his life Mr Watson was a salesman, but unconsciously at that lunch he performed a masterpiece of salesmanship which has been an example to me ever since. It is, however, City philosophy to invest in a man and his management, rather than in a set of statistics, and perhaps to that extent it was not so surprising that Mr Watson's talk should have compelled confidence in his Company.

It was Mr Watson who adopted the slogan THINK for the I.B.M. organization. This word is inscribed in every possible position on walls, buildings, calendars, magazines, of the I.B.M. organization. Mr Watson would never agree to amplify the word, and felt, rightly, that it would set in motion in the reader's mind the sort of things he, Mr Watson, had in his own mind when he thought of the slogan.

Mr Watson was a pioneer in the sphere of automation. He had the vision, and he left no legitimate stone unturned in his drive to establish I.B.M.'s pre-eminence in the world in this new and rapidly developing industry. He knew that a business could only be successful if it were animated by the right spirit – he appreciated that his most valuable assets were men. He never lost sight of the human side of business. He was a deeply religious man. I was honoured by the friendship he showed me. When he died in June 1956 he left with us memories of his sayings and actions which we shall always retain to our inestimable advantage.

I do not believe he would have been surprised at the strides forward taken by I.B.M. since his death, for he laid the plans for them. He would have rejoiced at the success of the British Company and at the very substantial profit made by the British shareholders when in December 1959 they disposed of their shareholdings in I.B.M. United Kingdom Limited to its parent Company, I.B.M. World Trade Corporation, in order to facilitate the integration of the British Company with I.B.M. European companies in whose share capital there was no minority interest. It has throughout been one of the happiest of associations and we are grateful to Mrs Neville Berry and of course to Mr Ormonde Lawson-Johnston who, like Mr Tom Watson, died some years ago, but who became an esteemed associate of us all.

Chapter 27

I HAD INFINITE PLEASURE ONE DAY when out of the blue, the Prime Minister's Secretary, David Stephens, wrote to ask me whether I would be prepared, if invited by the Prime Minister, to become a Trustee of the Tate Gallery. I replied that I was sure I would enjoy it immensely, and on 2 September 1958 I was duly appointed. There are ten Trustees, of whom five are full-time painters or sculptors, and the rest just people interested in art, such as myself. Our term of office is seven years.

Although for many years my wife's and my own interest in pictures had been growing, I think our appetite was really whetted before the war when on visits to Paris we had the unusual advantage of accompanying our great American friends, Ruth and Gordon Washburn, to many of the galleries there. Gordon Washburn was prowling around in search of suitable purchases for the Albright Gallery in Buffalo, of which he was then the Director. Dealers hid nothing from him. Sharing these visits we were able to feast ourselves on examples of the works of some masters of modern painting, such as Renoir, Rouault, Soutine, Klee, Cézanne, and Picasso. It was a delightful experience and my wife and I gained much in knowledge and discernment. Our eyes became attuned to these revolutionary exponents of the art of our day and we began to acquire a warm appreciation of them.

Sadly, there was very little money in our purses at the time, for by comparison with today's prices, these pictures were absurdly cheap. But we did go a splash as we thought, on one occasion, and came home with a Rouault gouache for what has turned out to be a trivial sum. This picture formed the basis of our little collection and inspired us to go on, so that now we have the satisfaction of a variety of pictures on our walls. Indeed,

I know little that is more satisfying. We own no works of special value but a lively small group, on which we build as our tastes develop and expand. I have never valued possessions as such, but I confess I derive incomparable pleasure in the adventure of acquiring works of art, even on our somewhat limited scale.

I am always stunned when I go to New York, for instance, to see the incredible collections in private homes there – they make our modest holding look insignificant by comparison and I think what a pity it is that so few wealthy people in this country are interested enough to form collections of modern paintings. The cry always is that the tax reliefs on gifts and bequests in the United States form the incentive given to American citizens, which we lack here. That is true, but it is only half the story – it is the enthusiasm which is missing in this country, or is it the appreciation, or are we perhaps too unwilling to break away from accepted traditions?

Among our contemporary works the majority seem to be abstract, for I feel that it is particularly in the field of abstraction that modern artists are enabled to give expression to the strong, vital thought and feelings of today. It invigorates me to be surrounded by paintings which are exciting, alive, and challenging in their contents. Many find it easy to ridicule abstract art, but I like it because it concerns itself with ideas and with the imaginative, rather than the transposition on to the canvas of material objects. And I would go further and say that if it is genuine and sincere, it can be more difficult to achieve than representational painting because it is more the essence of an individual's creative thinking and subjective experience, and not the interpretation of any particular object.

This said, I obviously do not wish to give the impression for one moment that I am so enamoured of contemporary art as to have ceased to be enraptured by the works of the great masters of representational painting, and others. Of course I take a profound delight in them as anybody with any sense of aesthetic values must do. I am merely saying that my personal taste runs towards the more recent and abstract.

I enjoy the monthly meetings of the Tate Trustees and try never to miss them if I can help it. They take me into a different world. We are completely responsible for the affairs of the greatest modern art museum in the country, advised by the Director, Sir John Rothenstein, and the Keeper, Mr Norman Reid. Within the limits of a microscopic annual grant from the Treasury, the Trustees must work with the utmost care and discretion in their purchases and in the selection of paintings and sculptures offered to them. Though very serious, the meetings of the Trustees are also great fun, and there is much wit and sparkle round the table under the expert Chairmanship of Sir Colin Anderson. Just as no two economists or investment advisers easily agree, so I find that in the selection of pictures for the gallery, widely diversified opinions are expressed by the experts, which helps my ego. But views were unanimous when once we were invited to accept a work by a chimpanzee.

Chapter 28

I FEEL INCLINED TO SKIM OVER MY MEMORIES of the last year or two, as such recent events are still fresh in everyone's mind. My own life has proceeded on its extremely active way, always broadening and developing. The national keel, however, has hardly ever been even, and many situations, political and economic, have caused me anxiety. The Suez Canal disaster at the end of October 1956 stirred me deeply, as indeed it did most other British subjects one way or the other. At the time, I was in favour of the invasion, although miserably distressed by its execution. Looking back, Suez seems distinctly *vieux jeu*. Probably, it was the last attempt we shall ever make to impose our will on a foreign nation by force.

But it was the lowering of our morale following Suez which was so hard to bear. Our prestige suffered a crushing blow, and it was generally proclaimed that British influence in the world had fallen to zero; those who sought to belittle us asserted confidently that we were finished.

That did not matter so much, but it was most dismaying to observe the increasing tendency of too many in our own country to concur with this low assessment as justified, accepting that we were in fact a second-rate nation. It was being said on all sides with a shrug of the shoulders: 'Why worry? We are an exhausted people, our burdens are too heavy. We cannot be expected any longer to take a leading part in world affairs.' It was palpable that we were losing our old buoyancy and were becoming hang-dog. I felt it was essential to resist this mesmerism, and with all the appeal I could muster, I wrote a letter to *The Times* on 28 December 1956. I reviewed our achievements and our past contribution to world affairs, showing, I felt, an entitlement to first-class ranking. I pointed out that it is the moral worth of a nation which matters more than anything else, and that our sense of fair play and integrity of character still formed the true foundation of our entire social and economic systems. These were not sustained by mere wealth either, but were based on trust, mutual confidence and the power of good judgment and sound common sense. Knowing, as we all did, that the tasks ahead were tremendously difficult, I begged that we should not sink into a bog of self-depreciation and accept for *ourselves* an unjust and unfair evaluation. Otherwise, we should be in grave danger of losing our resolution, and with it the vision and creative ideas the hour required from us. I was gratified by the reception this letter received. It appeared to have a startling effect on public thinking, and I received numerous appreciative letters from all over the world.

In face of this depressed outlook, it was becoming more and more apparent to me that there was something radically wrong in the country. It was a fundamental and deep-rooted malady which was holding us back. Inflation was in the forefront, and countless cures were advocated. But wasn't inflation merely a symptom of our troubles? Wasn't the real cause a basic attitude which could be described as 'wanting something for nothing', a reluctance to give honest measure for value received?

I was very conscious of this, and my feeling was that the attitude must be exchanged for that of 'something for something', the more to be given, the more to be received. The thinking of each individual citizen determines the prosperity of our economy; it is the horizons of the many – workers, employers and their respective leaders – which have to expand before their values improve. The actions of one man alone can have disastrous effects upon a whole industry and upon an entire country – which points to the necessity of gaining a broader sense of responsibility and brotherhood. The need is to give more, more energy, thought, work, time and enthusiasm.

It was not until the end of 1958 that it was possible to sense a period of national recuperation. British leadership, having been dormant, and only upheld from within by a fundamental conviction which many times in the past has transformed similar situations from depression to expression, from despair to hope, was reasserting itself. Our detractors had told us we were in the doldrums, but our normal optimism and confidence gradually came to the top. The British people responded splendidly to the leadership of the new Prime Minister, Mr Harold Macmillan, who swept away many restrictions and engendered a sense of freedom, culminating in a strong pound sterling and the new found right to borrow on our own credit from the banks. So a recovery took place, as is well known, but it had its ups and downs. At times, expansion was encouraged and at others dampers were imposed. It was very confusing and long-term planning in industry was almost impossible in consequence.

Early in January 1961, I again wrote to *The Times* – this time to plead for the establishment of a Five Year Plan, and more long-term thinking and action on the part of the Government. We had witnessed the withdrawal of restrictions, only to see their re-imposition a few months later when the situation was a little less rosy; this had resulted in the familiar economic see-saw movement, the post-war 'stop-go' disease, frustrating for industry and The City alike. I did not consider it was beyond the power of Her Majesty's Government to establish a more long-term approach. My letter appeared to express current public opinion and I was even able to discuss 'planning' with Mr Macmillan. I believe that on this occasion I was ahead of Whitehall in my suggestions, and although I repeated my original plea six months later in a further letter to *The Times*, it took almost a year before 'Neddy' (the National Economic Development Council) was formed. Those in the know told me that it was the publicity given to my letters that started the ball slowly rolling amongst the Civil Service hierarchy. So they said, but it does not matter much whence a good idea emanates as long as it is put into effect.

Some of the old brigade, however, took me severely to task for recommending, of all things, planning. Planning, they said, was for the Communists and Socialists, not for freedom-loving Conservatives. One old friend greeted me at luncheon with, 'I hear you are joining the Communists!' But I was not advocating planning for planning's sake which is never of any avail. If the country could have a planned target and be shown the way, I thought many of the recent frustrations and disappointments would evaporate.

We all know the good work 'Neddy' is doing, fully supported by the T.U.C., and what great hopes are centred on its further deliberations.

[262]

As I write, the Common Market negotiations have broken down. We have been shut out by General de Gaulle, admiration for whom I have expressed earlier. But that does not prevent my saying that this latest act of his is in my opinion both stupid and retrogressive, particularly from France's angle. I was enthusiastic about our entry, as I believed our centuries of experience equipped us for active participation in Europe. However, General de Gaulle (contrary to the desires of most of my French friends) has decreed otherwise – mainly for political reasons. Somehow I am convinced that in the long run these difficulties will be overcome, but meanwhile what to do? I was keen on our entry because I felt it would give this country new zest and would have introduced that element of competition from without which would bring the best out of our people. It seemed to me we needed at this stage something outside our own control to inspire us, even compel us, to shake off lethargy and complacency.

If I am right in this, and if non-entry is not to be a severe setback, it is imperative that we so brace ourselves as to make sure – without the spur of the Common Market – that we can compete on price and efficiency with the Six. We are on our own now – once again – and unless we are to face extreme trouble, it is essential that we make supreme efforts. I have infinite faith in the ultimate commonsense of the British working man – he is the salt of the earth – but just at the moment it seems that once more 'welfare-state thinking' is gaining preponderance. Perhaps things have been too easy and too many expect the country to give them a living instead of the reverse. It appears difficult to find common ground between management and labour for progress.

Until this situation is righted, I am afraid we shall remain perched in a precarious position. Chancellors of the Exchequer can prime the pump to their heart's desires; that will help but it will only go so far towards solving the problem. It is leadership and inspiration which are needed to enable us to combat and overcome this new situation and to avoid an even worse state of affairs than that which faced us in 1956. The country needs again to be rallied, but how? Being given a target, as I said earlier? Perhaps – but I fancy there will be no permanent solution until we try better to see the other man's point of view. It is easier said than done, I know, but surely that is the direction towards which we must go. A sense of adventure and a touch of the pioneering spirit of the Elizabethan and Victorian periods might do the trick.

★   ★   ★   ★   ★

Over several years Helbert Wagg had been wooed by many other banking houses with a view to a merger. They told us our team was the envy of The City. Although some of these approaches were attractive, and all flattering, and on one occasion persisted embarrassingly, none seemed quite suitable. But one day in March 1960, I came finally to the conclusion that our business was too concentrated on investment banking and that, to reach fuller fruition, we also needed to offer our clients facilities in commercial banking. But how could we achieve this as we ourselves did not have the expertise to venture into these untrodden paths? At that moment I thought of J. Henry Schroder & Co., intimate friends with whom we had co-operated in the past most happily. I believed a union with them would be ideal and completely complementary as we could bring mutual benefits to one another and together be able to supply our respective clients with a more efficient and comprehensive service. Both of us would be more adequately equipped to meet the demands of the future and the increasing competition. So, finding my partners in full agreement, I proposed marriage to J. Henry Schroder & Co. and during the pleasant negotiation which followed, there was ample proof that the merger had all the makings of a successful association.

It was, however, the end of a saga. Helbert Wagg was a very special conception which was overtaken by the march of progress, and we had of our own free will chosen to lose our identity, in order to join in a new partnership. In the agreed designation, J. Henry Schroder Wagg & Co., Limited, poor Helbert was perforce eliminated, but the name of Wagg, with all its tradition and reputation, is preserved.

So these two old Houses, both established for well over one hundred and fifty years, became one, with ramifications all round the world: true merchant bankers, adjusted to modern conditions, poised and ready to expand their business at home and abroad. Theirs is a professional and skilled function, whether it be granting a commercial credit, advising on investments, raising capital, buying or selling foreign exchange, arranging the details of mergers or take-overs, or numerous other matters which are life and blood to the merchant banker.

Having seen the merger well and truly launched, I relinquished my partnership on 31 January 1963. As I told my partners when I announced my decision, I felt my job with them was done and that somewhere there were fresh tasks yet to fulfil and much work to do. Obviously, it was a wrench to uproot myself from something which had been the basis of my existence for so long and had provided me with such a wonderful working life. I was thinking especially of my extremely happy relationships with my partners and the staff, but friendships such as these do not fade. I have always been active and busy, and since those far-off days when at the age of twenty-five I was given charge of the Foreign Exchange Department, I have been saying 'yes' or 'no' many times a day. Fortunately, taking decisions has never presented me with any difficulty, and has been made easier by knowing that I need never look over my shoulder at anybody nor doubt the veracity of any of our contacts. The basis of banking is judgment of people and situations. But to succeed, good judgment is essential and imagination too, as well as the ability to make up your mind without undue delay in assessing the worthiness of propositions.

*   *   *   *   *

As I end this book, I am tempted briefly to retrace my steps. It is a long way back to St Mary Abbots School, Kensington, and to my dear old schoolmaster Ben Jones, who, by his earnest coaching, ensured me a fair education: to my slogging years at Pitman's and to the friendly bus driver: to that exciting but anxious day when I was given my first job with Max Bonn: the 1914 War, and the misery and discomfort of the trenches in that first winter of mud and battle, attack and defence: Room 40 in the Admiralty, pitching me into the very heart of unknown things and people: the frenzy of the 1920s and my foreign exchange days: the slump: then my marriage: the children: becoming a partner: the Treasury during the Second War: the Chelsea Borough Council: my first directorship: then Tillings, Tube Investments and Babcocks; finally my Chairmanship of Helbert Wagg and the extraordinary development of this banking house.

[265]

These are some of the bare events, but behind me, in full support, there have been the guiding hands of my mother in the first half of my life and of my wife for the past thirty-two years. My family life has always been a sure shield for me and something to cherish and work for: without this, so many careers seem empty and fruitless.

Each day in my life has been an unfoldment, and I have counted my blessings and have been grateful for them as they have come along in plenty. It is the diversity of interests and the stimulating companionship of my friends which have contributed to make life for me so constructive and so exhilarating. Every day something different, some new problem to tackle, something unexpected to be handled.

★   ★   ★   ★   ★

I do not doubt that The City of London will rise to any occasion. I have the utmost confidence in its future and in its sense of service. But The City must keep alert, be willing to accept modern thinking, never be resistant to, or jealous of, the infusion of new blood, and ready to learn from its mistakes.

I know The City of London is in the forefront of progress, and that it is the mainspring of our industry and commerce. It is the financial and business nerve centre of our nation and of the Commonwealth, perhaps even of the world. I have enjoyed my years there more than I can say. Part of my heart will always be in The City where I have found so much satisfaction and pleasure and witnessed such vast changes and progress.

Banking has been my main function, and it is of course only one part of City life, though indeed a vital one. I have endeavoured to show that banking, and especially merchant banking, leads into so many varied and even unusual fields, and that it is the reverse of dull or impersonal, as many believe.

There was a story going the rounds during the war about Sir Winston Churchill and Mr Roosevelt which, even if untrue, is apt. The former was staying at the White House and one morning he heard a knock on the bedroom door. He said, 'Come in,' and was dismayed to find his visitor was the President himself in his invalid chair. Sir Winston had expected one of his assistants and was in his birthday suit. But nothing abashed, he laughed, 'You remember, I told you we should hide nothing.' Like Sir Winston, The City has nothing to hide, and it also has a big job to do.

It is because I appreciate The City so much and because I am certain it will forge ahead in the years to come, that I unhesitatingly recommend a career there. It beckons alert, intelligent men and women and although the early dog-days may seem arduous, The City offers outlets for enterprising and useful work. It will bring with it associations with many people, some lively, some astute, some generous, some tough; all progressing in an area becoming more skilled and more professional all the time, and in which there is less and less chance of true success without hard study and concentrated work. Some appear to find the road easy, but mushroom success is rarely lasting.

I have tried to paint a true and faithful picture of The City. I hope my story will find a sympathetic reception in quarters where the 'Square Mile' has not been properly understood. If I have managed to throw light on some of its mysteries and demonstrated that those who work there are normal, decent citizens, willing at all times to offer their best endeavours towards a solution of the complexities of modern business conditions, I shall be happy that I have succeeded in my task. And if I have also helped my readers to detect the humanity which is to be found in abundance in City circles, the warmth, the kindliness, as opposed to the accepted picture of hard, unrelenting people working solely for their own enrichment and aggrandisement, I shall be even more content.

Index

Eton, 177–9

Falconer, Alec, 168
Falk, O. T., 125–6
Faudel-Phillips, Sir Benjamin, 57, 59–60, 63
Financial press, the, 201–2
Fergusson, Mure, 219–20
Fishmongers, Worshipful Company of, 81
Flangham, H. F., 175–6
Foreign Office, 145
Franco, General, 193–5
Fraser, Alice Mary (*née* Barnard), mother, 1–6, 10, 12, 15, 16, 20, 21, 23, 25, 28–9, 31, 36, 81, 104, 105, 265
Fraser, Cynthia (*née* Walter), wife, 81, 103, 105–9, 114, 115, 149, 199, 220, 257, 265
Fraser, Douglas, brother, 2
Fraser, Edith, sister, 2, 17, 24, 65, 104
Fraser, Harold, brother, 2, 24, 26, 93–4
Fraser, Harry, father, 1–9 *passim*, 21, 24
Fraser, Janet Mary, daughter, 109, 116, 177–8, 212–13
Fraser, Nicholas Andrew, son, 108, 115, 177, 213
Fraser, Robert Hugh, son, 108, 115, 177, 213
Fraser, W. Lionel: wins Campden Scholarship, 16; joins Bonn & Co., 30; rejoins, 64; and London Scottish regiment, 41; 1914–18 War: active service, 42–51; Naval Intelligence, 52–62; joins Helbert Wagg & Co., 65; Director, 109; Chairman, 180; first visit to New York, 73–5; elected to Fishmongers Company, 81; Chairman,

Broadstone Investment Trust, 96; first close contact with Stock Exchange, 102; marriage, 105; Second World War, at Treasury, 117–39; awarded C.M.G., 139; as British Censor, Banque d'Etat du Maroc, 145; Director, Spicers Ltd, 157; Director, Thomas Tilling, 160; member of Chelsea Borough Council, 173–5; Chairman of Issuing Houses Association, 181; Director of Atlas Assurance Company, 190; Director of Tube Investments Ltd, 191; Chairman of Babcock & Wilcox Ltd, 191–2; Trustee of Tate Gallery, 257
Frazer, Jack, 95
Freeman, Air Chief Marshal Sir Wilfrid, 191–2
Freemasonry, 82
Fry, Richard, 202

Galbraith, J. K., *The Great Crash*, 100
Gamper, Fritz, 39, 65
Garrick Club, 85, 215–17
Gas Light and Coke Co., 97
Gaulle, General de, 134–5, 263
Gaumont British 4½% Mortgage Stock, 109
General Strike 1926, 96
Gillies, Sir Harold, 216
Golf, 219–20, 227
Green, Edmund, 59
Greenly, Sir John, 192
Grunfeld, Henry, 233, 246
Guindey, Guillaume, 133, 136
Gunson, Gordon, 180
Gutt, Camille, 132

Haggard, Marjorie (later Mrs Charlton), 59
Hague, Sir Kenneth, 191, 192, 195

[273]